W9-BFD-913

Silver·Burdett Making Music

## Coordinating Authors

Hunter C. March        Will Schmid        Sandra L. Stauffer

## Program Authors

Jane Beethoven
Susan Brumfield
Patricia Shehan Campbell
David N. Connors
Robert A. Duke

Judith A. Jellison
Rita Klinger
Rochelle Mann
Nan L. McDonald
Marvelene C. Moore
Mary Palmer

Konnie Saliba
Carol Scott-Kassner
Mary E. Shamrock
Judith Thomas
Jill Trinka

PEARSON
Scott Foresman

**Editorial Offices:** Glenview, Illinois • Parsippany, New Jersey • New York, New York
**Sales Offices:** Needham, Massachusetts • Duluth, Georgia • Glenview, Illinois
Coppell, Texas • Sacramento, California • Mesa, Arizona

ISBN: 0-382-36575-5
2008 Edition

Copyright © 2005, Pearson Education, Inc.

All Rights Reserved. Printed in the United States of America. This publication is protected by Copyright, and permission should be obtained from the publisher prior to any prohibited reproduction, storage in a retrieval system, or transmission in any form by any means, electronic, mechanical, photocopying, recording, or likewise. For information regarding permission(s), write to: Permissions Department, Scott Foresman, 1900 East Lake Avenue, Glenview, Illinois 60025.

11  V082  09

## Contributing Authors

| | |
|---|---|
| Audrey A. Berger | Mary Ellen Junda |
| Roslyn Burrough | Donald Kalbach |
| J. Bryan Burton | Shirley Lacroix |
| Jeffrey E. Bush | Henry Leck |
| John M. Cooksey | Sanna Longden |
| Shelly C. Cooper | Glenn A. Richter |
| Alice-Ann Darrow | Carlos Xavier Rodriguez |
| Scott Emmons | Kathleen Donahue Sanz |
| Debra Erck | Julie K. Scott |
| Anne M. Fennell | Gwen Spell |
| Doug Fisher | Barb Stevanson |
| Carroll Gonzo | Kimberly C. Walls |
| Larry Harms | Jackie Wiggins |
| Martha F. Hilley | Maribeth Yoder-White |
| Debbie Burgoon Hines | |

## Listening Map Contributing Authors

| | |
|---|---|
| Patricia Shehan Campbell | Kay Greenhaw |
| Jackie Chooi-Theng Lew | David Hebert |
| Ann Clements | Hunter C. March |
| Kay Edwards | Carol Scott-Kassner |
| Scott Emmons | Mary E. Shamrock |
| Sheila Feay-Shaw | Sandra L. Stauffer |

## Movement Contributing Authors

| | |
|---|---|
| Judy Lasko | Wendy Taucher |
| Marvelene C. Moore | Susan Thomasson |
| Dixie Piver | Judith Thompson-Barthwell |

## Recording Producers

Buryl Red, Executive Producer

| | |
|---|---|
| Rick Baitz | Michael Rafter |
| Rick Bassett | Mick Rossi |
| Bill and Charlene James | Buddy Skipper |
| Joseph Joubert | Robert Spivak |
| Bryan Louiselle | Jeanine Tesori |
| Tom Moore | Linda Twine |
| J. Douglas Pummill | |

# CONTENTS

# HELP WANTED: Careers in Music

**Careers in the Music Industry**

# American Music Mix

## America's Popular Styles and Performers

# Music Then and NOW

## Historical Contexts and Styles

# The Beat Goes On

## Playing in Percussion Ensembles

# A HANDFUL OF KEYS

## Playing Keyboard Chords and Progressions

# Guitars Unplugged

### Playing Guitar Chords, Progressions, and Strums

# Lift UP Your VOICE

**Singing in Unison and Parts**

# Musical Tool Kit

## Music Theory and Fundamentals

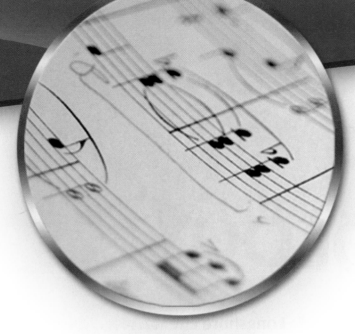

# PERFORMANCE ANTHOLOGY

# HELP WANTED:
# Careers in Music

**Careers in the Music Industry**

MTV MUSIC TELEVISION®

"With recording, the music of the world becomes available at any moment—just like an encyclopedia."

— *Marshall McLuhan (1911–1980)*

▲ Orchestrator Doug Besterman

◄ Tori Amos

# Make a Music Career

When you think of a career in music, you probably think of a rock star or other performer. There are many different kinds of careers that require musical knowledge but do not involve performing. These careers range from teacher to technology expert. Explore the possibilities of a life in music!

## In the Techno Loop

Did you ever want to be a deejay (DJ)or mixmaster? Dance and "techno" (short for *technology*) music are composed by stacking layers of music. These layers are often used in a **loop** format. They can include

- percussion parts
- bass lines
- keyboard or synthesizer "pads" (background chords)
- lead guitar
- vocal samples

DJs have choices when they perform. They can simply play other musicians' recordings or songs. More often, they improvise their own music or record **samples.** They mix these samples together to create rhythmic or melodic interest. Sometimes DJs even sample environmental sounds, such as street noise or speech.

**Listen** to these techno pieces. **Identify** the layers heard in each song. What is the role of repetition in each mix?

 ### Believer
**written and mixed by BT**
1-1  BT (Brian Transeau) originally composed *Believer* as part of his first film score.

 ### El condor pasa
**written by Daniel Alomias Robles, Jorge Milchberg,**
1-2  **and Paul Simon**
**mixed by DJ Sammy**
This track features Native American instrumental sounds and vocal samples.

 ### Suzuki
**written and mixed by Burnt Friedman**
1-3  Various guitar timbres and repeated spoken parts are included in this mix.

**Victor Calderone** ▶

**loop** A recorded melodic or rhythmic pattern that repeats continuously.

**samples** Short excerpts of sound from a previously existing source.

## Looping with MIDI

Now **create** your own mix. Practice each of the tracks on a MIDI keyboard. Your teacher will help you learn each of the patterns. Use the looping function found with MIDI sequencing software to record and loop each of the parts separately.

After recording, **improvise** and record other tracks.

### Careers
# TECHNO DJ
# Victor Calderone

**Victor Calderone** (born 1967) is known as a world-class DJ among **house music** enthusiasts. He was introduced to dance music at the age of 15 by his older brother, Cesar. His passion for dance music quickly developed into the foundation of his career. Calderone is best known for his dance-friendly remixes of the music of Sting, Madonna, Destiny's Child, and Bette Midler. When remixing the music of well-known artists, Calderone works to preserve the integrity of the songs while enhancing elements that will make the music stronger for dancing. Calderone's remix of Sting's song *Desert Rose* enjoyed an impressive nine consecutive weeks on top of the Billboard dance chart.

## Hear His Work

**Listen** to *Blow Your Horn Dub Mix*.

### Blow Your Horn Dub Mix
1-4

**by Beyoncé Knowles**
**as mixed by Victor Calderone**
This dance mix is an example of Calderone's unique approach to remixing.

**house music** A type of disco music with samples of other music and various sounds mixed in.

# I Write the Songs

*"Music is the most personally satisfying [of all the] things I do...."*

—*Joan Baez*

There are lots of ways to write a song. Some songwriters start with lyrics. Some songwriters begin with a **chord progression.** Still others start with a **lick.** Some write the words and the melody at the same time.

Joan Baez, Will Smith, and Tori Amos are three very different music makers with successful careers. **Describe** their different writing and performing styles.

---

**chord progression** The order in which chords are played in a piece of music.

**lick** A short melodic or rhythmic pattern; a motive.

## Melody and Lyrics Together

**Listen** to Joan Baez's hit song *Diamonds and Rust.* **Describe** the relationship between melody and lyrics in the song.

### Diamonds and Rust

**written and performed by Joan Baez**
**1-5** This song tells a story from Baez's own life.

## Music MAKERS

# Joan Baez

**Joan Baez** (born 1941), nominated for six Grammy Awards and winner of eight Gold Albums, was born in Staten Island, New York. Baez made her performing debut at age 14, singing and playing ukulele at a high school talent show. She became nationally famous with her 1959 Newport Folk Festival debut and first album, *Joan Baez,* in 1960. In the mid-1960s, Baez championed the work of songwriter Bob Dylan and began to focus on using her music as a vehicle to promote nonviolence, an effort that continues today. As one of the most accomplished folk singers of the 1960s, Baez has influenced nearly every aspect of popular music in her career. She continues to write and perform.

## Rap in Black

**Listen** to *Black Suits Comin' (Nod Ya Head)*. **Identify** ways that the background music supports the lyrics of the rap.

### Black Suits Comin' (Nod Ya Head)

**1-6** by Will Smith, Mark Sparks, Ron Feemaster, Lenny Bennett, Lance Bennett, and LeMar Bennett as performed by Will Smith

This song was featured in the successful box office hit *Men in Black II.*

## A Song Takes Shape

**Listen** to *A Sorta Fairytale* made famous by Tori Amos. **Identify** the instrument timbres and form in this selection. Where do you hear background vocals being performed?

### A Sorta Fairytale

**1-7** written and performed by Tori Amos

This song is from her 2002 album, *Scarlet's Walk,* which was written about a road trip she made to all fifty states.

# Tori Amos

Born Myra Ellen Amos, singer/songwriter **Tori Amos** (born 1963) was a child prodigy. She began playing piano by age two-and-a-half, was singing and performing in the church choir by age four, and was studying classical piano at the Peabody Conservatory in Baltimore by age five. In her early teens, Amos began writing her own songs and performing at clubs. It was these performances that led to a recording contract that sparked her career as a successful writer and performer. She released her first solo album, *Little Earthquakes,* in 1992, which was an international success. Since that time, Amos has gained a dedicated following through her intense and heartfelt performances.

# Will Smith

**Will Smith** (born 1968) began his Grammy Award winning music career as a hip-hop pioneer in the late 1980s with the duo DJ Jazzy Jeff & the Fresh Prince. This was followed by even greater success as an actor, starring first in the television show *Fresh Prince of Bel Air,* then in the movies *Men in Black, Men in Black II, Six Degrees of Separation,* and *Ali.*

## Write a Song

One of the biggest hurdles in songwriting is getting started. One simple tool you can use is to brainstorm about events in your daily life and write down several potential song titles. Try some humorous titles such as "Lunchroom Blues," or "My Dog Ate My Math While I Took a Bath." Choose your favorite. You can also work with an existing poem, such as the one below.

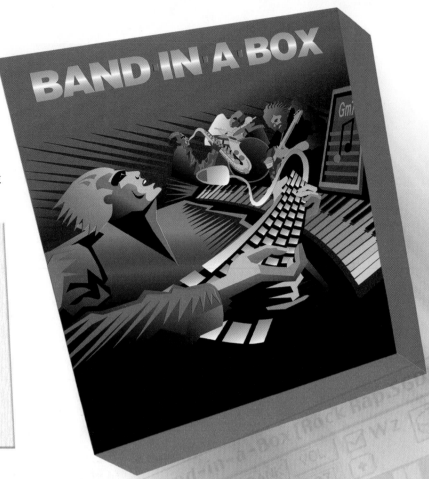

### THINK POSITIVE

Every single person has a different style.
To get to know them may take a while.
Love your neighbor,
Put your fears on the shelf.
If you want a better world,
Why not start with yourself?
—James McBride

## Song Writing with Technology

Technology can help your songwriting career. Music software programs make writing and playing back melodies, chord progressions, and rhythm patterns simple.

**CD-ROM** You can use *Band-In-A-Box* to help compose a song. Select a style from the style menu (Blues, Heavy Rock, Pop Ballad, and so on). Test some chord progressions by entering chords, and play it back until you are satisfied with the sound. Create a rap with the style you have selected.

Look at the chord progression below. With the help of your teacher, use a keyboard and the chords below to **create** a short composition. Enter the chords into the program. Play back the progression using different music styles programmed into the keyboard. Speak the words of your song in rhythm as you listen to the progression in your selected style. You can also experiment with changing the chord progression.

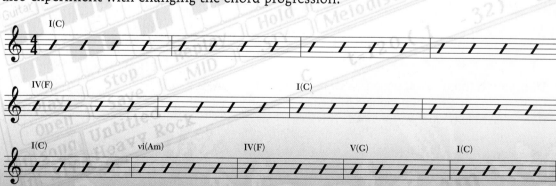

## Put It Together

Add melody to your words to **create** a **refrain.** The refrain of a song is usually brief and repeats several times. For example, in *A Sorta Fairytale*, the refrain begins with the words "And I'm so sad. . . ."
You may need to adjust the rhythm of your melody as you work on the refrain.

Take the challenge! **Create** a **verse** with a classmate. You can explain your song title in the verse, or use a stanza of the poem you selected. Experiment with melody and lyrics. When you finalize your verse, perform the verse and refrain together. Make a video or audio recording to preserve your work.

## Go a Step Further

Another way of preserving your song is to **create** a **lead sheet.** Notation software can be used to write out and print your work.

With your teacher's help, create a lead sheet using notation software.

- Play your melody notes into the program.
- Use the chord tool to enter any chord changes.
- Use the lyric tools to enter the lyrics below the staff.
- Add titles, composer credits, and a copyright notice.
- Save and print your work.

**ON YOUR OWN**

Notation software makes writing out a melody easier. Use the "Record Melody" feature in *Band-In-A-Box* to create notation for your melody.

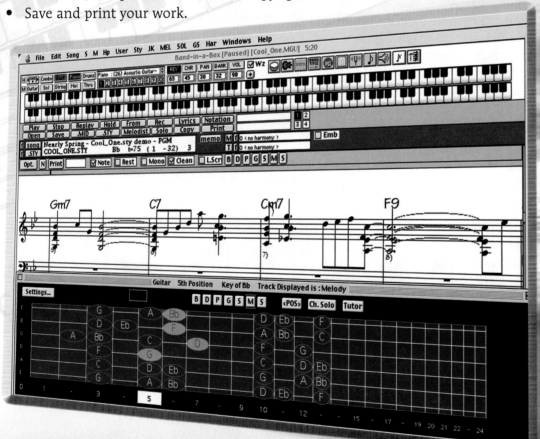

---

**refrain** The section of a song that repeats, using the same melody and words.

**verse** A section of a song where the melody stays the same when it repeats, but the lyrics change.

**lead sheet** A shorthand score or part, which can provide melody, chord symbols, accompaniment figures, or lyrics.

# WHO OWNS A SONG?

**What** are five important items you own? How do you protect them? How would you feel if someone used them without your permission?

Songwriters own the songs they compose. They protect their songs by requesting a **copyright** for them. Copyright laws are based on two basic rules: the owners have exclusive rights to their songs, and these rights have a time limit. After that time period, the song becomes **public domain.**

## Exclusive Rights

In 1976 Congress added guidelines to the copyright law so that the owner of a song controls five elements.

- Making copies of the sheet music or recording
- Selling the copies and recordings
- Performing the song
- Making an arrangement of the song
- Displaying the song

A singer who wants to make a first recording of a song must ask for permission. The owner sells the singer a license to record the song. A royalty is paid on each copy of the recording that is sold. This is one way a songwriter can earn money from a song.

## Registering Your Property

If you wanted to copyright an original song you would register it with the United States Copyright Office. The Copyright Office will register a song for a fee of $30.00 if it is original and available in print or a recording. Contact the Copyright Office to learn about the official registration process.

You can also create a "poor man's copyright." Put a copy of your song in a stamped, sealed envelope with your name and address on the outside, then mail it to yourself. The post office stamps the date and time that the envelope was handled. When you receive it back, put it *unopened* in a safe place. Some courts will recognize the date on the *unopened* envelope as proof of copyright.

## PRO TIPS

Performers whose songs have been recorded but not notated or published are also protected by copyright laws.

---

**copyright** A legal right granted for exclusive publication, sale, or distribution of a literary, musical, dramatic, or artistic work.

**public domain** Belonging to the general public.

## Let Me See Your License

There are many different kinds of licenses regarding the use of a song. Every license sold is a paycheck to a songwriter! Here is an outline of the process.

### Songwriter

Songwriter creates a song and claims. . .

### Copyright

Copyright is licensed to. . .

### Publisher

Publisher resells licenses.

**Note This**

Each musical birthday card that plays "Happy Birthday" pays the publisher and songwriter a mechanical license.

**Mechanical License:** Permission and notification to record, including CDs, cassettes, computer chips, video clips, and so on. An audio sample also requires a license.

$ →

← permission

permission →

← $

**Commercial License:** Music used for advertising on radio and television.

$ ↕ permission

permission ↕

$ ↕ permission

**Broadcast License:** Radio and television stations buy licenses to broadcast music. ASCAP, BMI, and SESAC collect the money for these licenses and pay the artists.

**Performance License:** Concert halls and clubs pay for the acts that sing or play copyrighted music in their space.

**Synchronization (Sync) License:** Music used for a video, television show, or movie. A songwriter's best friend!

# Front and Center

The success of the composer's song often depends on how well it is performed. Vocal performers and entertainers present songs to the public in concerts, films, videos, musicals, and recordings. A singer's vocal style and image help sell the song.

### Music MAKERS

Baritone **Josh Groban** (born 1981) discovered his love for singing by accident. In junior high, he joined the school vocal group because "everyone else was doing it." In high school, he attended the Interlochen Arts Program in Michigan and discovered not only that he had significant talent, but also that he loved to sing.

In his short career, Groban has already sung with Celine Dion, the Corrs, and with Charlotte Church at the Closing Ceremony of the 2002 Winter Olympics.

**Listen** to a duet between Josh Groban and soprano Charlotte Church.

### The Prayer

**by David Foster and Carole Bayer Sager**
1-8    **as performed by Josh Groban and Charlotte Church**
This song is popular as a wedding duet.

*Josh Groban*

## Sing a Song!

Select a song from Performance Anthology, which begins on page I-1. Decide how you will perform it and show your personal style. What dynamics will you sing? What tempo will you choose? How will you use movements and facial expressions to demonstrate the meaning of the song?

## Checkpoint

Discover the following information about the song you chose to perform.

- Who composed the song?
- When was the song copyrighted?
- Who owns the copyright?
- Who performed the song on the recording?
- Who produced the recording?

You will need to look at several different pages in your textbook to find the answers to the above questions. The composer of the song will be listed on the same page as the song. The copyright date and the copyright holder will be found in the credits at the end of this book. Information about the recording can be located in the booklet that accompanies the CD package.

**MIDI/Sequencing Software** Choose a MIDI file and experiment with new tempos. Sing your song choice several times with various tempos. How does altering the tempo affect your performance?

# A Different Type of Coach

All successful performers owe part of their success to a coach. Singers often study with a vocal coach to improve their overall performance. A coach usually has an area of expertise, such as expression, diction, or language.

**Diction** is important in all styles of music. A vocal coach might give a singer exercises to improve diction so that their words are clearer, or they might demonstrate ways to pronounce specific words.

A vocal coach also suggests facial expressions and body gestures that convey the message of a song. The coach and student work together to try different **dynamics, tempo, articulation,** and phrasing to match the mood and style of each song. Every performer interprets a song in an individual way, and the vocal coach's job is to help the performer develop a unique performance.

## A Song to Coach

**Sing** this song, or choose another from this book and learn to sing it.

Leontyne Price ▶

CD 1-9

## Alleluia, Amen

*Traditional Round*

Al - le - lu - ia    al - le - lu - ia,    A - men,    a - men.

**ON YOUR OWN**
Find out the rates for vocal coaches or private teachers of music in your area. Consider contacting local college or high school teachers.

**diction** Clarity and distinctness in pronouncing words.

**dynamics** The degrees of loudness and softness of sound.

**tempo** The speed of the beat.

**articulation** The manner in which notes are joined in succession. For example, *staccato* and *legato* are types of articulation.

## Game Time

Practice being a coach. Listen to one or more classmates perform a song they know. Look for the good points of the performance and encourage the performers. Identify ways to improve the performance, such as dynamic changes, diction, tempo, and movements. Then switch roles.

## A Dynamic Duo

Once the coaching is complete, it's time for rehearsal. A solo singer can work with a band or with an accompanist.

The accompanist is an accomplished musician who chooses to work with another artist. Critical to a successful performance, the accompanist plays for the singer at the coaching sessions and sometimes at the performance.

A good accompanist listens to the singer and follows any variations in tempo, dynamics, and phrasing. The accompanist may give advice about a particular song to the performer, such as correcting pitches or rhythms or other problems. Accompanists can transpose a song so that it is in a more comfortable range for the singer.

## Careers
# VOCAL COACH
## David Garvey

**David Garvey** (1922–1995) was born in Pennsylvania. He was an accomplished pianist who also coached and accompanied operatic singers, violinists, and ensembles around the world. Beginning in 1955, Garvey became accompanist and coach of the distinguished soprano, Leontyne Price. Their long-standing musical collaboration was well known throughout the United States and Europe. They performed in hundreds of venues, including the White House for each President from Lyndon Johnson to Bill Clinton. They also performed for the King and Queen of Spain, and for Prince Charles and Princess Diana—a televised recital that won an Emmy award. Garvey was a professor at the University of Texas where he coached performers and taught coaching and accompanying. For many years he coached young musicians at the Meadowmount summer music camp.

**Digital Audio/Analog Recording** Perform the song you composed, or another song, and record it. Use digital audio or an analog recorder, such as a tape recorder. Play back your recording and decide what changes you could make to improve your performance.

When you hear your favorite musicians in a recording, the sound is carefully balanced and perfected in a studio. When we go to a live performance, we expect that the sound will be similar to the recording, even though a performance venue, such as a stadium or large concert hall, is completely different from the tiny studio space.

The live sound engineer is responsible for making the music at a concert as balanced and as close to our expectations as possible. A good sound engineer is experienced in the use of different types of sound equipment, has knowledge of acoustics, and knows how to run sound equipment to create the best live sound possible.

You can find sound engineers in other venues as well, including theater productions, churches and temples, and political rallies.

## TODD TILLEMANS

### Careers SOUND ENGINEER

**Todd Tillemans** (born 1960) has served as the sound engineer for many popular music acts including Garth Brooks, Guns 'N' Roses, and Amy Grant. When Tillemans is not on the road touring, he is involved in designing and installing sound reinforcement systems for churches, theaters, and schools.

Although many sound engineers are trained in university programs, Tillemans entered the music field as a bass player in popular music groups. He became an assistant engineer and **rigger** and worked up to head sound engineer. Tillemans is constantly reading about and trying new equipment. One of the challenges of his job, he says, is keeping up with changes in technology. Tillemans lives in Nashville, Tennessee.

---

**rigger** One who hangs speakers and lights for a performance.

## Sound Setup

Choose a soloist and small group to sing "I'm on My Way." How might you set up microphones for your singers to perform this song?

**I'M ON MY WAY**

CD 1-11

*African American Spiritual*

1. I'm on my way (I'm on my way) to the free-dom land, (to the free-dom land,) I'm on my way (I'm on my way) to the free-dom land, (to the free-dom land,) I'm on my way (I'm on my way) to the free-dom land, (to the free-dom land,) I'm on my way, ___ thank God, I'm on my way. ___

2. I asked my friends . . . to go with me, . . . *(3 times)*
   I'm on my way, thank God, I'm on my way.

3. If they won't come . . . then I'll go alone, . . . *(3 times)*
   I'm on my way, thank God, I'm on my way.

4. I'm on my way . . . and I won't turn back, . . . *(3 times)*
   I'm on my way, thank God, I'm on my way.

# Tools of the Trade

The sound engineer must know about a lot of equipment to do a good job. An engineer must also work very closely with technicians and riggers to make sure the equipment works together and is placed in the best position.

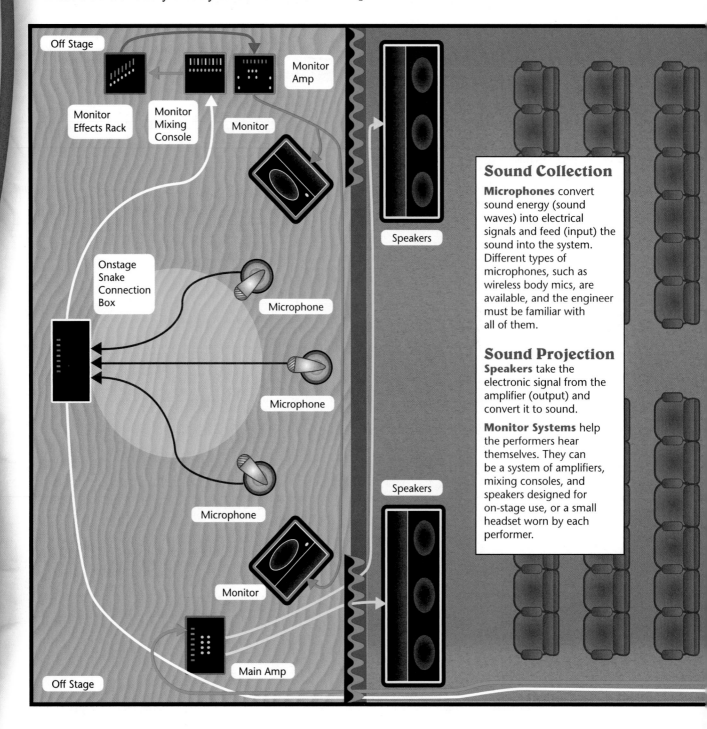

Off Stage

Monitor Effects Rack

Monitor Mixing Console

Monitor Amp

Monitor

Speakers

Onstage Snake Connection Box

Microphone

Microphone

Microphone

Monitor

Speakers

Main Amp

Off Stage

## Sound Collection

**Microphones** convert sound energy (sound waves) into electrical signals and feed (input) the sound into the system. Different types of microphones, such as wireless body mics, are available, and the engineer must be familiar with all of them.

## Sound Projection

**Speakers** take the electronic signal from the amplifier (output) and convert it to sound.

**Monitor Systems** help the performers hear themselves. They can be a system of amplifiers, mixing consoles, and speakers designed for on-stage use, or a small headset worn by each performer.

# Setting Up

This is one way a stage can be set up for an amplified music production. Some of the connections shown in this illustration you may never see—they can be built into the walls or underneath the floor of the hall. Some hall setups are almost entirely wireless.

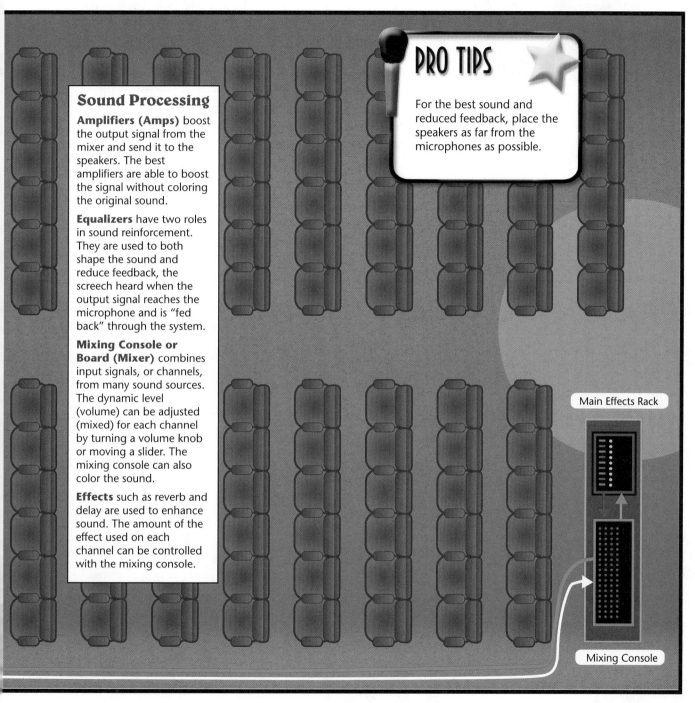

### Sound Processing

**Amplifiers (Amps)** boost the output signal from the mixer and send it to the speakers. The best amplifiers are able to boost the signal without coloring the original sound.

**Equalizers** have two roles in sound reinforcement. They are used to both shape the sound and reduce feedback, the screech heard when the output signal reaches the microphone and is "fed back" through the system.

**Mixing Console or Board (Mixer)** combines input signals, or channels, from many sound sources. The dynamic level (volume) can be adjusted (mixed) for each channel by turning a volume knob or moving a slider. The mixing console can also color the sound.

**Effects** such as reverb and delay are used to enhance sound. The amount of the effect used on each channel can be controlled with the mixing console.

### PRO TIPS

For the best sound and reduced feedback, place the speakers as far from the microphones as possible.

Main Effects Rack

Mixing Console

# Using Sound Reinforcement

To perform "I'm on My Way" at your school auditorium, what equipment would you need and how would you set it up? How would you engineer the sound differently to perform it in a smaller space? **Discuss** the requirements for each venue to create the best possible sound.

## WHERE IT ALL BEGAN

The history of music recording shows us how technology changed the way that business is done, as well as increased people's interest in music. When radio broadcasts began to play free music on the air, it worried the phonograph dealers who depended on customers to buy their players. Sound in movies upset Broadway artists who feared that people would go to movies rather than musical productions. Television took attention and advertising away from radio because customers preferred to see and hear their favorite artists. Person-to-person file exchange programs threatened CD sales because people downloaded recordings for free. What caused the problem? The answer is simple: money.

# Important Moments in History

| 1880 | 1890 | 1900 | 1910 | 1920 | 1930 |

**1877** Thomas Edison invents the cylinder phonograph.

**1880s** The gramophone, which plays a flat disc, is patented. The first commercial disc recording appears in the U.S. in 1894.

**1900s** The jukebox is invented.

**1910s** Jazz recording releases stir sales of phonograph players.

**1920s** Radio is available to play musical recordings. *The Jazz Singer*, the first movie with sound, shocks the audience.

**1925** The first all-electric phonograph is built.

**1930s** The first albums appear by 1935. Single recordings make stars of Frank Sinatra and Doris Day.

◀ Edison cylinder phonograph

EDISON STANDARD PHONOGRAPH

A–18

▲ Horn gramophone

▲ Atwater Keat radio

# Count It Up!

Make a list of all of the technology in your home that can play music. Remember to count all of the radios, televisions, video games, CD players, and so on. Do you have a greeting card that plays a tune? Estimate the cost of each piece of equipment and recording. Your family can help you with these estimates. Add them all together. You will discover why the music business is a multi-billion-dollar industry!

## Note This

Many of the manufacturers of today's equipment, including blank tapes, pay a fee called a surcharge just for selling the equipment. The money goes to a fund that is paid to the artists and songwriters.

## On Your Own

Music is a form of entertainment. Find out how people in America entertained themselves in 1880. Were there movies? Radio? Television? How did people travel? Compare the 1880 activities with the entertainment choices that you have today.

---

| 1940 | 1950 | 1960 | 1970 | 1980 | 1990 |

**1940s** Columbia releases the first 33 1/3 vinyl LP (long playing record).

**1950s** Television grabs attention from the radio. The public can see their favorite performers. Stereo sound is introduced.

**1960s** 8-track tapes and players are installed in cars. The Beatles create a sensation.

**1970s** Cassette players gain popularity. Digital recording techniques are introduced.

**1980s** MTV shows music videos, and fans can hear and see their favorite artists on TV. CDs (compact discs) and the Sony Walkman™ are introduced. Samplers add to creativity and copyright problems of record producers. The Sony Walkman™ starts a fad.

**1990s** New recording technologies like DAT (digital audiotape) and improved home recording techniques raise interest in recordings. The Net, the Web, and MP3s show that electronic delivery of music is possible.

Portable cassette player ▶

▲ Vinyl record

▲ 1950s portable television

Portable CD player ▲

# 8

# Make a Recording Happen!

The easiest place to record a song is in a professional recording studio. The studio staff is expert at recording each instrument and voice, adjusting a weak or out-of-balance performance, and creating a clear and accurate recording. The studio produces the **master** that is sent to a record company or duplicating service.

## Recording

All recorded sounds are routed into a mixing console. The sound engineer monitors the sound through speakers, headphones, and/or a computer screen. Each of the inputs is assigned to an output channel. Each output channel is recorded on a separate track of a recorder. The engineer must match inputs to outputs and keep track of them. This matching is called *bussing*.

## Mixdown

When recording is complete, the multitrack recording is played back. The engineer balances the outputs of all the tracks according to the overall sound desired. For example, the engineer may send more volume to the right or left to make the mix sound as if the instruments are in different locations, or the vocals may be adjusted so the dynamics are less exaggerated.

## Equalization

EQ (equalization) adjusts the timbre or tonal balance of each track. In this way, each instrument can be clearly heard within its frequency range, but noise outside its range is reduced. The balance changes after equalization is applied. The engineer keeps notes about all settings. A computer may be used to automatically save the settings.

## Effects (FX)

Effects (FX) such as reverb are added at different levels to the tracks. Finally, the master levels are monitored and adjusted so that the master output is not distorted. The final mix is recorded to tape, disk, or burned directly to CD.

---

**master** The original recording used to manufacture copies.

# Who's Who in the Studio

The studio staff fills several roles. Here's a breakdown.

|  | Producer (Music director) | Recording Engineer (Ears) | Asst. Engineer (Helper) |
|---|---|---|---|
| Pre-production | • Schedules workflow<br>• Hires studio musicians<br>• Approves arrangements<br>• Distributes parts to each performer | • Selects microphones and placements<br>• Sets up, calibrates and connects all equipment<br>• Sequences order of recording session<br>• Prepares recording media | • Helps set up the studio and equipment |
| Recording | • Makes final decisions about which "takes" are keepers (evaluates musical performance) | • Operates mixing console: watches levels, listens for audio problems<br>• Documents studio setup and mixer settings<br>• Announces takes<br>• Records rhythm tracks; overdubs (layers and corrects) instruments and voices<br>• Plays rough mix for performers and producer | • Runs recording equipment<br>• Documents takes, keepers, and outtakes<br>• Assists engineer in general |
| Mixdown | • Suggests types of mixdowns<br>• Approves final mix | • Creates mixdown, assembles recording | • Puts away equipment |

**Sequencing Software** Select a MIDI file and explore the differences that occur as you pan from the left to right channels.

## Meet an Audio Producer

**Listen** to this interview with Buryl Red, executive producer for the recordings that accompany this book.

 *Interview with Buryl Red*

1-13

# 9

# From Song to Print!

**Arts Connection**

▲ 14th Century Italian painting of a monk transcribing music

After a song is created, it may be prepared for publishing. To get a song ready for print, a different team of musicians takes over.

## Transcriptionist

From the Middle Ages, when music notation first appeared, into the twentieth century, music was notated by hand. Songwriters wrote down their compositions, or played them for a transcriptionist to capture in score form. Although musicians today have not abandoned the handwriting method altogether, transcription is often done using a computer and notation software. Songwriters and music publishing companies hire transcriptionists to write down the music as accurately as possible.

A transcriptionist needs to be able to

- determine the **form** of a song.
- notate rhythms and melody, key and time signatures, and chord symbols.
- transcribe lyrics with accurate grammar and spelling.

## Transcription Starts Here

**Listen** to *America* and **analyze** the form of the song. Tap the beats to determine the time signature and number of measures. Prepare a layout of *America* using notation software or score paper. Include the time signature, the correct number of measures, the lyrics, and as much of the melody as you can write down. *Hint:* The first pitch is F. Compare your transcription to the song notation on page I-2.

### *America*

**Traditional; words by Samuel Francis Smith**

1-14  The melody of *America* is the same as the British national anthem.

---

**form** The overall plan of a piece of music.

# Orchestrator/Arranger

If a song is to be notated for performance by multiple instruments, it is given to an orchestrator/arranger. An arranger may add harmonies to the existing chord structure or interpret the song in a new way. An arranger usually has few restrictions on interpretation.

An orchestrator has a more specific goal: to create instrumental parts for a performance with more instruments. The orchestrator might be given a lead sheet and a list of instruments to write into the orchestration. The instrumentation may be determined independently, or some of the parts may already be included in the transcription.

After getting to know the song well, the orchestrator writes parts for each instrument.

A good orchestrator needs these skills:

- strong knowledge of music theory and composition.
- understanding of what combinations of instruments sound good together.
- knowledge of instrument transpositions and ranges.

**Listen** for the musical choices made by the orchestrator for *Down in the Valley*. **Identify** which instruments the orchestrator chose.

### Down in the Valley

1-15 **Folk Song from Kentucky**
**orchestrated and arranged by Buddy Skipper**
Mountain dulcimer and penny whistle are included in the instrumentation.

## Careers
# ORCHESTRATOR
# DOUG BESTERMAN

**Doug Besterman** (born 1965) grew up in Muncie, New York. He started piano lessons at five years old, moved on to French horn, and graduated with a degree in music history and theory. Along the way, he became interested in theater and worked in summer stock and regional theater companies. Working in summer stock gave him practical experience in orchestration, where he had to reduce the original orchestrations to fit a small ensemble.

Besterman's big break came when he was recommended for a Broadway play written by Alan Mencken (*Beauty and the Beast*). He won two Tony Awards for the orchestration of the Broadway musicals *The Producers* and *Fosse*. He also orchestrated the movie scores for *Mulan, Anastasia, Chicago,* and others. Besterman lives in North Hollywood, California.

**Listen** to one of Doug Besterman's orchestrations from *Chicago*. What instrumentation choices did he make to create an authentic 1920s sound?

### Overture/All That Jazz

1-16 **from *Chicago***
**by Danny Elfman, John Kander, and Fred Ebb**
**orchestrated by Doug Besterman**
Several themes from the musical are included in this selection.

# GET IT HEARD!

VIDEO HITS ONE™

**M**usic is heard everywhere—in your car, your home, and public places. It's not enough to write the songs. They have to be delivered to the public.

## Live or Recorded?

Most people agree that the best way to experience music is a live performance. Live performers bring power to a music selection through their facial expressions, physical movements and interaction with the audience. From the singer in the coffee shop to the orchestra soloist or rock star, "being there" is part of the fun.

Many fans, however, cannot travel to live performances. These music-hungry fans depend on recordings to hear their favorite tunes. For the songwriter and recording company, this means big money! Record sales generate money for the recording artist, and the sale of the permission to record a song brings money to the songwriter. This permission is called a **mechanical license.**

Recordings also allow fans to hear the music when and where they want. Outside of live performance, this is the fans' favorite music delivery system.

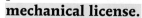

**mechanical license**
Permission to record sounds, usually for a fee.

▲ Amy Grant

## Music Is Out There!

Since the 1920s, radio stations have been a reliable music delivery system. Some radio shows play the "top 40" or "countdowns" of the top ten hits of the day, or top hundred songs of the year. Radio DJs generate interest in music by playing songs in a particular style. Web radio is available anywhere there is a computer with Internet access.

Television, like radio, has long included shows featuring popular performers. In 1981, MTV rocketed onto the scene with the introduction of music videos. New stars were created from this exposure, and the recorded music business boomed.

## Computer, the Internet, and CD Burners

The new technologies of the 1990s changed the music business scene in a big way. A music fan could go on-line, find a song, and burn the song on a blank disc.

Fans love the freedom to listen to new music and artists as well as the power to select the songs they really want to keep for their own use. As the legal questions of Internet music are resolved, more and more artists will win fans by offering new releases over the Net.

▲ Aerosmith

**ON YOUR OWN**
Review Lesson 3 on copyright in this module. Of the five exclusive rights, which ones are violated when a fan downloads and burns a CD?

▲ Bono and the Edge of the group U2

## Share What You Know

Help others understand the many roles of those involved in music. From among the professions you've been learning about, select one that seems particularly interesting to you. Prepare a presentation for a class of younger children or your peers that illustrates what you've learned about that profession. Your presentation may be placed on poster board, on overhead transparencies, or on slides made with presentation software.

Include in your presentation basic facts about the life of the professional—e.g., job title, responsibilities, daily routine—and descriptions of the person or persons that you observed working at this job. Compose a list of questions to ask after your presentation that will cover the facts you presented.

Allow time for your audience to ask questions of you as well. Talk to your teacher about how to prepare for this part of your presentation.

# American Music Mix

Muddy Waters ▶

◀ Carlos Santana

▲ Mary Chapin Carpenter

*"The blues had a baby, and they called it rock 'n' roll."*
— *Muddy Waters (1915–1983)*

# POP Goes the MUSiC

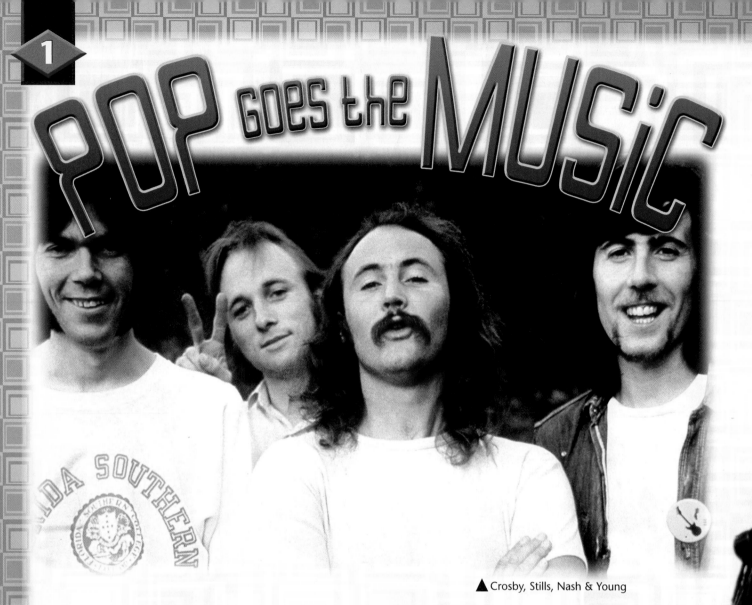

▲ Crosby, Stills, Nash & Young

American music is popular across the globe. American pop styles include jazz, country, reggae, rock, rap, and many other kinds of music. Ask several people for names of popular songs and discover how many different styles they represent.

## How Do I Listen?

People may listen for different elements when they hear a popular song. Some elements to listen for include

- instrumentation
- form
- singing style
- lyrics—storytelling, nonsense, repetition
- expression—mood and dynamic changes
- overall style—How do the elements fit together?

What do you listen for when you hear a song?

## Is This Your Style?

**Listen** to a **cover** of a song by Crosby, Stills, Nash & Young. **Describe** the music using one of the categories listed, or **create** a category of your own.

 **Carry On**

2-1

by Crosby, Stills, Nash & Young
as performed by Alana Davis

Davis's version of *Carry On* was featured in a Super Bowl™ XXXVII commercial.

---

**cover** A version of a popular song by a performer other than the original artist.

## What Do I Like?

Knowing what you like and why you like it helps you get more out of listening to music. People might like certain music for its combination of sounds, or because it reminds them of something pleasant. It may inspire them to do something they enjoy, such as dance, work on a project, or paint. They may like it simply because it sounds familiar.

Can music that you do not like be "good" music? Discuss this question with your classmates. On a note card, write the name of a group or artist that you like or don't like. Explain your choice. Use the elements from the list on page B-2 to explain your reasons. Submit the note card for class discussion.

## What's in a Name?

There are almost too many names of musical styles to remember. Musical **fusion** has created many new styles, such as Tex-Mex, Afro-Caribbean, **alternative**-rock, alternative-country, and alternative-punk. Identify a style and choose an artist or group that fits the style. You can also choose an artist or group and create a new style name for their music. Explain the style name you created by relating it to something familiar. Share your work with others.

## Name This Style

**Listen** to this selection by famous trumpeter, Arturo Sandoval. **Describe** the style in your own way. Compare your answers with those of your classmates.

### 🎧 *Manteca*

2-2
**written by Dizzy Gillespie, Walter Fuller, and Chano Pozo**
**as performed by Arturo Sandoval**

This recording was made in tribute to the composer and famous jazz trumpeter, Dizzy Gillespie.

---

**fusion** Combining contrasting styles into a new, unique style.

**alternative** Music that exemplifies an unconventional approach to a traditional style.

◀ Arturo Sandoval

# Drums, Strings, and

Pop music has a characteristic sound that is created in part by the instruments used. These instruments are changing all the time, but here are some you often hear.

## Guitars

Guitars come in two basic types:

- acoustic—the classical folk style has nylon strings. The dreadnought and 12-string styles have steel strings.
- electric—the electric guitar has steel strings, pickups to amplify the string vibrations, and controls to change the loudness and tone of the instrument.

For more information on guitars, see "Guitars Unplugged" on page F–2.

## The Bass

Two types of basses are commonly used in popular music. The acoustic double bass is played by plucking the strings. The electric bass has pickups and controls like an electric guitar. A third kind of bass, the acoustic bass guitar, looks like an acoustic guitar and plays in the bass register.

## Keyboards

Pianos and electronic keyboards are very common in pop music. An electronic keyboard uses **MIDI** so the player can control electronic sounds. The keyboard may work as a MIDI controller for external devices such as a **sampler, a sequencer,** and a **sound module**. It may also have the devices built into the keyboard itself.

## MIDI and Electronic Instruments

To make music using electronic sounds, musicians use MIDI to transmit information among controllers. Sequencers are used to record and edit MIDI data from controllers and transmit it to sound devices as entire songs. These electronic sounds may resemble acoustic instruments, voices, synthesized sounds, and environmental sounds.

---

**MIDI** An acronym for Musical Instrument Digital Interface, a communication protocol.

**sampler** Records and plays back ambient sounds, often on different pitches.

**sequencer** Automates the control of MIDI equipment.

**sound module** Hardware that contains synthesized and sampled sounds on a hard drive or memory chip.

**ON YOUR OWN**

Create a short list of songs you like that have prominent guitar and/or bass solos. Analyze which sound you prefer—acoustic, electric, or both.

▲ Electric bass guitar

# Things

## Synth Sounds

**Listen** to this recording by Will Ackerman. **Identify** which instruments you think are electronic and which are acoustic. Discuss your choices with your classmates.

### *If You Look*

**2-3**

**by Will Ackerman and Chuck Greenberg as performed by Will Ackerman, Chuck Greenberg, and Michael Manring**
This piece is one of just a few in which Ackerman uses a synthesizer.

## Rhythm Section

There are two kinds of electronic drum kits. One is a touch pad drum set. The pad sends MIDI data to the MIDI sound module. The other is a set of drum triggers that translate acoustic drums into MIDI.

## An Electronic Experience

**Evaluate** the sound of the electronic drums as you **listen** to this piece. How would you describe the timbre of the electronic drum?

### *X-Beats*

**2-4**

**written and produced by Micky Mann**
This selection features layers of several electronically produced motives.

▼ Electronic drum set

### Note This

The basic drum set is sometimes called a "trap set." Early jazz drummers grew tired of having only a bass, snare, and single cymbal, so they added "contraptions" to give them a broader range of percussive sounds.

## Latin Beat

The music of Latin America has made its way into the American pop music scene. A *salsa* percussion section may include congas, bongos, timbales, and hand percussion instruments.

## Coming to America

Many other world instruments are also finding their way into American pop music. Instruments such as the *doumbek*, originally from Turkey, *dolak* and *dhol* drums from South Asia, and *tablas*, originally from the Middle East, are used by artists such as Peter Gabriel, Cornershop, Paul Simon, and Pearl Jam.

**Listen** to *Africa* by Toto. The members of the band recreated the sounds of Africa in this recording by layering drum patterns and using synthesizers.

### *Africa*

**2-5**
written by David Paich and Jeff Porcaro
as performed by Toto
This song was a number one hit in 1983.

## Another Sound

Finger cymbals from Arabic Africa add a brilliant percussive sound to music, and are easily heard. **Listen** to *Eternal Flame*. How are finger cymbals used? When are they played in the song?

### *Eternal Flame*

**2-6**
by Susanna Hoffs, Billy Steinberg, and Tom Kelly
as performed by the Bangles
This song demonstrates the distinctive vocal harmonies of the Bangles.

## The Wind Section

Brass and reed instruments are played in many popular music groups. Trumpets are heard in *mariachi* and *norteño* music as well as in jazz. Trombones and saxophones are played in big-band music, jazz, rhythm and blues, gospel, and soul music.

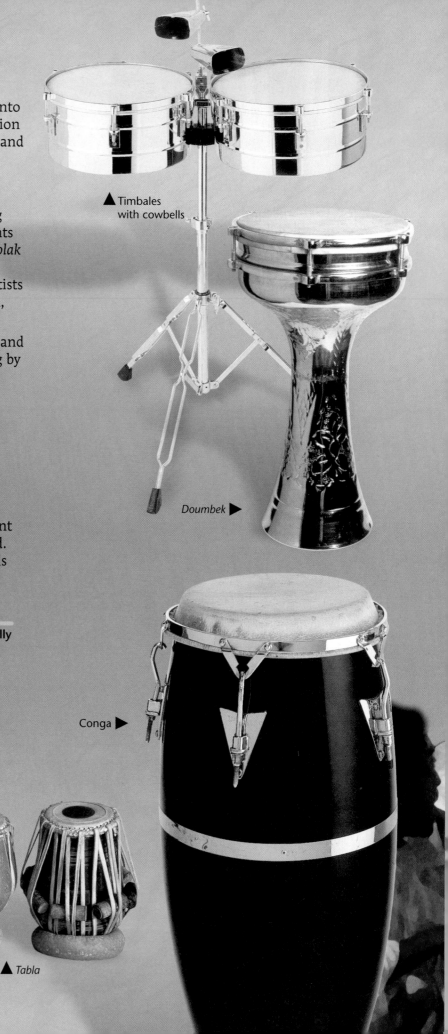

▲ Timbales with cowbells

*Doumbek* ▶

Conga ▶

▲ Tabla

## American Folk Instruments

Many folk instruments have found their way into American music. They include

- fiddle—the same instrument as a violin.
- banjo—a string instrument heard in Appalachian mountain and bluegrass music.
- harmonica—also called a *blues harp*. It is heard in everything from cowboy music to blues.
- accordion—often heard in Tex-Mex, Cajun, *zydeco*, and polka bands.

**Listen** to *You Are My Sunshine*. **Identify** the folk instruments you hear.

### You Are My Sunshine

**by Jimmy Davis and Charlie Mitchell**
**2-7    as performed by Norman Blake**
*You Are My Sunshine,* written in 1940, sold more than a million copies in the United States. This performance is from the movie *O Brother, Where Art Thou?*

## Crossing Over

Changing the instruments in a song can change the style of the music. Performing a song from one style to a new or different style is called *crossing over*. **Listen** to *Good Morning, Aztlán* by Los Lobos, a band famous for its blending of Latin folk, rock 'n' roll, punk, and rhythm and blues music. **Describe** how the choice of instruments affects their sound.

### Good Morning, Aztlán

**by David Hidalgo and Louie Pérez**
**2-8    as performed by Los Lobos**
This selection reflects Los Lobos's rock 'n' roll beginnings.

Singer Ricky Martin jamming with fellow musicians ▶

# 3

# Singin' the Blues

**B**lues is one of the roots of twentieth-century American popular music. Many popular singers and instrumentalists learn the blues as part of their basic training. Blues lyrics often include "love gone wrong" and other complaints, sometimes in a humorous or sarcastic way.

The blues were created by African Americans in the Mississippi Delta near New Orleans in the early 1900s. The style has gone through various phases, beginning with country blues, progressing to classic blues, and finally developing into urban blues.

▲ Mamie Smith and Her Jazz Hounds

## Country Blues

Early country blues singers such as Robert Johnson, Eddie James, "Son" House, Charley Patton, Blind Lemon Jefferson, and Leadbelly came from the Mississippi Delta and Texas. Contemporary blues singer Keb' Mo' (Kevin Moore) still performs in the country blues style. **Listen** to *Every Morning*. What is his blues complaint?

### Every Morning

**written and performed by Keb' Mo'**

2-9   This recording features Keb' Mo' playing an acoustic steel-string guitar with a slide or bottle neck.

## Classic Blues

Classic blues flourished in the 1920s and 1930s in cities such as Memphis, Kansas City, Chicago, and New York. A classic blues ensemble featured a female vocalist with a small jazz band. Some classic blues singers were Bessie Smith, Ma Rainey, Mamie Smith, and Ethel Waters. Backup bands often featured stars such as trumpeter Louis Armstrong.

**Listen** to Mamie Smith sing *Crazy Blues*. Her band included cornet, clarinet, violin, and trombone players, and the famous Harlem **stride piano** sensation, Willie "The Lion" Smith.

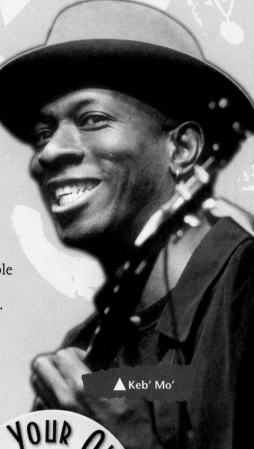

▲ Keb' Mo'

### Crazy Blues

**by Perry Bradford**

2-10   **as performed by Mamie Smith and Her Jazz Hounds**
This 1920 recording was the first commercial vocal recording by an African American female artist. It was an overnight success.

**stride piano** A style of piano playing in which the left hand moves on each beat, "striding" between low notes on strong beats and higher-pitched chords on weak beats.

**ON YOUR OWN**

See E-32 in A Handful of Keys, and page F-14 in Guitars Unplugged, for blues songs you can play yourself.

# Music MAKERS

# Muddy Waters

Muddy Waters (1915–1983) was born McKinley Morganfield in Rolling Fork, Mississippi. He got his nickname, "Muddy Waters," because one of his favorite childhood pastimes was playing in a muddy creek. While he worked on a farm as a teenager, he learned to play the harmonica and the guitar. Waters was playing local music jobs in 1941 when he was discovered by folk song collector Alan Lomax. In 1943, Waters moved to Chicago, where he became a leading urban blues singer and guitarist. Under Waters' leadership, Chicago became known for a unique blues style, which included electric guitars.

## Big City Blues

Urban blues, also known as rhythm and blues, developed in the 1940s and 1950s with the advent of electric guitars. A typical blues band also included harmonica, piano, bass, drums, saxophone, and trumpet. Among the urban blues legends were Muddy Waters, Howlin' Wolf, and Willie Dixon. The urban blues style laid the groundwork for rock 'n' roll.

**Listen** to Muddy Waters sing and play *Hard Day Blues*. **Analyze** the chord changes to discover whether *Hard Day Blues* is an example of 12-bar blues.

### Hard Day Blues

2-11
**by Muddy Waters (McKinley Morganfield)**
**as performed by Muddy Waters and James Clark**
Instrumentation in this song includes piano, guitar, and drums.

## The Birth of Rock 'n' Roll

Rock 'n' roll is jam-packed with blues ideas. Singers copy blues styles, players insert blues piano and guitar licks into their songs, and lots of rock 'n' roll tunes are written in the 12-bar blues form. For more information on the blues, see Guitars Unplugged on page F-14.

**Listen** to Stevie Ray Vaughan and Double Trouble perform *Pride and Joy*. Notice the electric guitar sound. **Compare** the electric guitar to the electric and acoustic guitar sounds in other songs from this lesson.

### Pride and Joy

2-12
**by Stevie Ray Vaughan**
**as performed by Stevie Ray Vaughan and Double Trouble**
Blues and rock are combined in both the vocal and guitar parts.

▲ Muddy Waters

# 4

# LET'S DANCE!

Popular dances are usually paired with popular songs. Here are a few famous dances.

## The Charleston

The Charleston was a popular dance in the 1920s. Many songs were played for this dance, all having the same rhythm pattern. Women who danced the Charleston were called *flappers* because the dance movements included flapping their hands on either side of their bodies.

## The Bunny Hop

This dance was created in a San Francisco high school in 1953. The lyrics to this song tell you how and when to do the dance motions. The movements are simple. Point your right foot to the right twice, point your left foot to the left twice, hop forward, hop back, and then hop forward three times.

## The Twist

This song was a huge hit for Chubby Checker both in 1960 and 1962. Dancers turn their arms and hips in opposite directions. The Twist became a regular part of a television dance show called American Bandstand. Listen to *The Twist*. Then move as the dance directions suggest.

### *The Twist*
2-13  **by Henry Ballard**
**as performed by Chubby Checker**
This song was a number-one hit in both 1960 and 1962.

## Disco

The disco dance craze began in the mid 1970s. This expanded dance style included both singles and couples dancing.

Listen to this hit from one of the stars of disco.

### *I Will Survive*
2-14  **by Dino Fekaris and Freddie Perren**
**as performed by Gloria Gaynor**
*I Will Survive* sold 14 million copies and was recorded in twenty languages.

## ON YOUR OWN

Ask your teachers, parents, dance instructors, siblings, and friends for examples of other dances that have their roots in popular music and culture. Look for recordings of the music and instructions on the dance steps. How well does the song go with the dance?

◀ **Dancer doing the Charleston**

# Break Dancing

This type of dance began during the late 1970s in the housing projects of New York. Young people would gather in a local park for a block party. Led by the music of a DJ (disc jockey), people would try to out-dance each other with floor-based flips and spins during the instrumental breaks in a song. Break dancers, known as b-boys and b-girls, became so enthusiastic that DJs had to set up two turntables and play a song back to back to extend the break length.

# Electric Boogie

The Electric Boogie is not a single dance, but a series of moves to be performed to funk, soul, techno, disco, and many other upbeat styles. Moves include the robot, glide, and moonwalk. Michael Jackson, sometimes called the king of pop, perfected this dance style. Try out some moves as you **listen** to Herbie Hancock's *Rock It*.

◀ Kevin Bacon in *Footloose*

## Rock It

2-15

**by Herbie Hancock, Bill Laswell, and Michael Beinhorn as performed by Herbie Hancock**

This 1983 MTV hit was a change in musical style for Hancock, a jazz musician.

# Is Dancing Allowed?

Teenagers have always loved to dance. *Footloose*, the movie and Broadway musical, is about teenagers in a small town who show that dancing is good for the body and soul.

**Listen** to the title track from the movie. How would you dance to this song?

## Footloose

2-16

**by Kenny Loggins and Dean Pitchford as performed by Kenny Loggins**

*Footloose* was a surprise movie hit in 1984.

## On Your Own

Create a dance to accompany your own or a classmate's original composition. Create a name for the dance. Record a music video of your performance and teach your dance to others.

## Checkpoint

Work with a partner to write a short definition for each of these terms.

1. cover
2. sampler
3. country blues
4. DJ
5. fusion
6. blues harp
7. stride piano

Match a listening selection to each of the terms above.

**Compare** the selections, using musical terms.

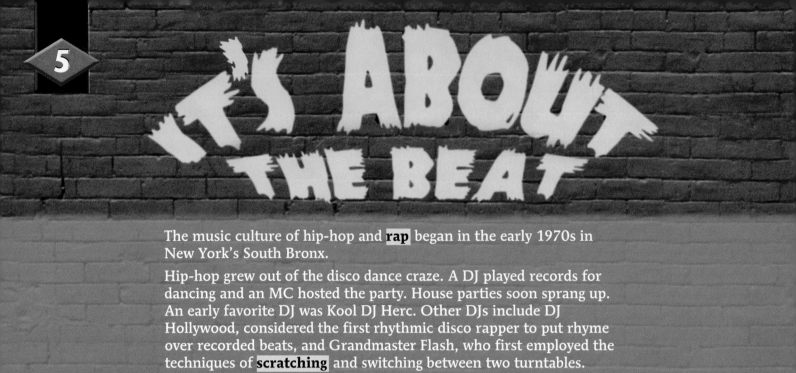

# IT'S ABOUT THE BEAT

The music culture of hip-hop and **rap** began in the early 1970s in New York's South Bronx.

Hip-hop grew out of the disco dance craze. A DJ played records for dancing and an MC hosted the party. House parties soon sprang up. An early favorite DJ was Kool DJ Herc. Other DJs include DJ Hollywood, considered the first rhythmic disco rapper to put rhyme over recorded beats, and Grandmaster Flash, who first employed the techniques of **scratching** and switching between two turntables.

**Listen** to *The Breaks*. Notice the use of repetition and rhyme.

### The Breaks

**2-17**

written by J.B. Moore, Robert Ford, Kurtis Blow, Russell Simmons, and Larry Smith
as performed by Kurtis Blow

*The Breaks* was the first rap single to be certified gold (1980).

**rap** Speaking in rhyme over a beat.

**scratching** Manually moving a record back and forth against the record needle to create a specific sound effect.

### Note This

Kurtis Blow was the first rap artist to sign with a major record company. He paved the way for other rap artists such as Run-D.M.C. and Grandmaster Flash.

## Be an MC!

Now it is your chance to make your own **def jam** and be the MC. Rather than starting off in **free style,** follow these suggestions for writing some of your own words. You may also work with a classmate or two to combine your ideas.

- Begin by thinking of a subject you would like to rap about.
- Write down key words about that subject. Avoid writing phrases or complete sentences.
- Look through your page of key words and pick some of the strongest ones.
- Make a list of rhyming words to go with them.
- Listen to the DJ track below and form some rhythmic phrases using the rhymes.

After you have written out the phrases, **perform** them with this DJ track.

### DJ Beat
**2-18**  written and performed
by Rick Bassett

## Mix It Up

**Listen** to a rap piece by Will Smith. What instrument sounds are imitated in the instrumental track?

### Block Party
**2-19**  by Will Smith, Richard Iverson, Nora Payne, Leshan Lewis, Herb Middleton, Sylvester Stewart, and Robert Ginyard, Jr.
as performed by Will Smith
This song celebrates a neighborhood gathering.

**def jam** Slang for a great song.
**free style** A style created when an MC improvises lyrics.

► Kurtis Blow

# 15

# Make Mine INDIE

In recent years, popular music artists have fought to maintain control over their compositions and recordings. Many have created their own independent (indie) recording companies rather than signing contracts with major labels. Artists have also resisted the pressure to be categorized in any one style.

### Note This
*Indie* has become a popular word in the film industry as well. The Sundance Film Festival and others like it have sprung up all over the world to celebrate the work of independent film makers.

## Music MAKERS

### Michelle Shocked

Cutting-edge indie singer and songwriter, **Michelle Shocked** (born 1962) was born in Dallas, Texas. She spent much of her early childhood traveling throughout the world because her stepfather was in the Army. Eventually she settled in East Texas near the Louisiana border, home to many famous musicians such as Willie Nelson, Leadbelly, Lightnin' Hopkins, Blind Lemon Jefferson, Lefty Frizzell, and others. In 1986, Shocked was recorded singing around a campfire at the Kerrville Folk Festival. The recordings became a hit in England under the title *The Texas Campfire Tapes*. After recording successful albums with Mercury Records, Shocked eventually formed her own recording company, Mighty Sound.

**Listen** to Michelle Shocked interpret the same song two ways. Describe the similarities and differences in the recordings.

### Joy
5-6 written and performed by Michelle Shocked
Shocked sings here in gospel style.

### Can't Take My Joy
5-7 written and performed by Michelle Shocked
This rendition features the influence of reggae style.

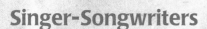

## Singer-Songwriters

Singer-songwriters are musicians who write and perform their own songs. For the first half of the twentieth century, most songwriters were not active performers of their own music.

Before 1950, popular songwriters such as Rodgers and Hammerstein, Cole Porter, Irving Berlin, or George Gershwin wrote songs to be performed by others. When rock 'n' roll appeared on the scene in the mid-1950s, the singer-songwriter came into being.

### Music MAKERS
### Jimmy Webb

**Jimmy Webb** (born 1946) is a singer-songwriter and pianist whose music has been performed by a who's who of artists. They include Frank Sinatra, Kenny Rogers, Tony Bennett, Ray Charles, R.E.M, Shawn Colvin, and Linda Ronstadt. Born in Oklahoma, Webb played the organ in his father's Baptist church and later formed his own rock 'n' roll band. After Webb moved to California, five of his songs became Top Ten hits within a twenty month period. His best-known songs include *By the Time I Get to Phoenix, MacArthur Park, Galveston, Wichita Lineman, If These Walls Could Speak,* and *Up, Up, and Away.* Webb has written a book about songwriting titled *Tunesmith: Inside the Art of Songwriting.*

### A Webb Song

**Listen** to Shawn Colvin sing a Jimmy Webb song, *If These Walls Could Speak.* **Analyze** how Colvin interprets the lyrics of Webb's song.

 *If These Walls Could Speak*

5-9  by Jimmy Webb
as performed by Shawn Colvin
Colvin plays acoustic guitar to accompany her singing.

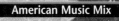

# 16

# BEYOND

## Music MAKERS

# CHICK COREA

**Armando Anthony (Chick) Corea** (born 1941) was born into a music-loving family in Massachusetts. He was playing the piano by age four, and was surrounded by classical and jazz musicians throughout his childhood.

In the 1960s, Corea worked with the great Miles Davis's band, then moved out on his own. The 1970s were spent creating his own brand of jazz fusion with musicians such as Herbie Hancock and Gary Burton. He has since written many jazz tunes and a classical piano concerto, and he continues to perform in as many genres as his imagination can hold.

**S**ome performers have made a significant contribution to popular music and culture, but do not fit into a single style category. One characteristic these performers share is individuality—the courage to be different.

**Listen** to this selection by Chick Corea. **Analyze** the musical style reflected in the music. What instruments do you hear? What other characteristics of the music do you hear?

*Fingerprints*

by Chick Corea
**5-10** as performed by Chick Corea, Avishai Cohen, and Jeff Ballard

*Fingerprints* is in 12-bar blues form.

# CATEGORIES

## Music MAKERS
## DEEP FOREST

The music of the group **Deep Forest** (Eric Mouquet and Michel Sanchez) has been described with terms such as *ambient, new age,* and *world music.* They describe themselves as *sound reporters . . . a voiceless musical duo that draws on voices from every corner of the world.* Each song has its own unique and distinct sound, which makes it difficult to classify their music under one genre or style. Mouquet believes that this is the very thing that people enjoy about it.

Deep Forest's albums, *World Mix* (1994), *Boheme* (1996), *Comparsa* (1998), *Made in Japan* (1999), and *Music Detected* (2002) use music samples and guest artists from Africa, Europe, the Caribbean, Madagascar, the Middle East, Central and South America, and Asia mixed with a heavy dose of synthesizers and advanced technology. *Boheme* won a Grammy for Best World Music Album. Their music has also been featured in advertisements.

Both Sanchez and Mouquet have backgrounds as keyboard players, and are proficient at the accordion, organ, piano, and synthesizer. They have used the Roland RSS 30, Fairlight synthesizer, Akai S1000, Korg Workstation, and Moog synthesizer in their work. In addition to being remixed by other artists, Deep Forest has also created remixes of their own songs for inclusion on their albums. The hit track "Sweet Lullaby" was remixed on their *World Mix* album as "Sweet Lullaby *Ambient Mix*," "Sweet Lullaby *Round the World Mix*" and "Sweet Lullaby *Apollo Mix*."

**Listen** to *Cafe Europa* by Deep Forest. **Describe** why it might be considered part of the pop genre. How many different styles do you hear?

### Cafe Europa

**5-12**  written by **Eric Mouquet and Michel Sanchez** as performed by **Deep Forest**

This track uses samples of Native American music.

▲ Bobby McFerrin

# 17

# Got Music?

◀ The Beatles

Muddy Waters ▶

Music has been recorded and sold on vinyl albums. Albums were replaced by tapes and then CDs. Now music of all kinds, including popular music, can be created and recorded in digital formats.

## The Digital Revolution

Recorded music stored in digital form consists of a series of zeros and ones—the binary language of computers. Digital files have been stored and transported in many ways, including CDs, DVDs, MP3s, satellite radio, and as files on the Internet. The digital revolution in music made it easy for almost any artist to share music with the world, something that once required a record company and a recording contract. Now anyone anywhere who has a computer hooked up to the Internet can listen to a song if it is posted on a Web site. Many Web sites exist just for this purpose. People can hear new songs that they would never have heard otherwise. This widespread access has influenced American popular music to include new sounds.

Shakira ▶

▼ Little Richard

▲ Aretha Franklin

## Works on the Web

Composers and performers create Web sites to showcase their latest projects. You can listen to audio samples on Web sites to see if you might like to buy the recording. Some composers also create compositions that use the Web as an interactive musical instrument. Percussionist and jazz artist Steve Houghton recorded some songs written by George Gershwin and arranged by film composer John Williams. The result was the album *The Manne We Love.* Steve Houghton's Web site was set up to play audio examples of the album as soon as the Web site opened.

**Listen** to an instrumental version of a song from this album. Notice the interplay between the quintet and the larger jazz band.

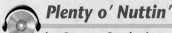

### *Plenty o' Nuttin'*

5-13  **by George Gershwin
as performed by the Steve Houghton Quintet, with the University of North Texas Two O'Clock Lab Band, directed by Jim Riggs**
This instrumental version of a Gershwin tune features percussion.

## The Future of Listening

Here are some predictions about how you might listen to music in the future. Do you think these predictions are possible? What else might be coming?

- You will attend live concerts, where the price of your ticket will include a live recording, streamed to you during the concert on your personal audio receptor or waiting for you when you get home. Live concerts become more important than studio recordings.

- Recordings will be visual as well as auditory. As you lie on your bed and listen, you will watch a piece of music displayed on your ceiling or wall, or through a virtual experience helmet.

- Making and sharing your own music will become easier. Any piece of music you play or sing will instantly be available in a notation/audio/video file that can be shared over any network. Bands will be able to easily practice or perform with individuals participating from different places or cities.

# American Music Mix

## Review and Assess

### Summary

In American Music Mix you've listened to popular music from all over the United States. You've learned about

- music from different cultures
- various music styles that constitute American music
- typical instrument choices
- various performance styles
- the cultural significance of the American music experience

You can better understand what you've learned by formulating descriptions of the music you've heard. Consider how the following musical elements are used.

- **timbre**—tone color (sound) of an instrument or voice

- **melody, rhythm, harmony, and tempo**—compositional elements
- **form**—structural element
- **dynamics**—the degree of loudness and softness of a sound
- **expression**—emotional effect on the listener
- **cultural function**—when and where is it used

One of the best ways to develop your understanding of music (or any subject, for that matter) is to explain your ideas verbally and in writing. Here are five projects that will help to show what you've learned in this module.

### Review What You Learned

Review several listening selections in this module. In small groups, discuss what elements in each selection make it distinctly part of the American music mix. Refer to the corresponding lessons for more information and reinforcement.

5-14

## What Do You Hear

Listen to the following excerpts. Each one demonstrates a different style of American music. Make five observations about each of the selections to help you determine the style.

- instrumentation
- rhythm
- harmony
- cultural influence
- emotion conveyed

Which of these elements helped you decide the style of the excerpts?

## Show What You Know

With your classmates, choose three very different pieces from the module. Write down the title and performance media. Listen to each one again. As you listen, write down a sentence or two that describes each of the following.

- musical texture
- instruments and voices used
- form—how the music is organized
- rhythm choices
- expression—dynamics, mood, tempo and how they affect the music
- where this music would likely be performed or heard

Repeat for the second and third pieces.

In small groups, discuss each others' ideas and why different members of the group came to different conclusions. Everyone need not agree at the end of the discussion, but everyone should be able to explain his or her own point of view.

## What to Listen For

Most music is intended to tell a story or to express some kind of idea: an emotion or a visual image, for example. The sound of music can make you feel energetic or sad. It can lead you to think of an experience in your past, or paint a picture in your imagination. Perhaps what's most interesting is that all of these emotions and images are conveyed through sound alone. How does music do this?

Listen to the following excerpts of music from the module. After hearing each one, explain what you think the composer intended to convey, and then explain how the composer went about communicating his or her ideas. What sounds were used?

How was the music organized? Explain the relationships between the sounds themselves and your interpretations of the sounds. For example, if a piece is intended for dancing, what does the music sound like? If there is a message, how is it conveyed?

*Pride and Joy*

*Footloose*

*Carry On Wayward Son*

*Blue Eyes Crying In the Rain*

*Rainbow in the Sky*

*Africa*

*Manteca*

## Share What You Know

Select one piece from the module that is your personal favorite. Prepare a presentation for a class or another person that will help them understand the music itself and why you like the music. You should include in your presentation basic facts about the piece including title, composer, and the approximate date of its composition.

Explain how you think the elements convey the composer's intentions—the mood, the emotion, the picture, or the idea. Include the elements of music listed on the first assessment page in your

description.

Your presentation may be placed on poster board, on overhead transparencies, or on slides created with presentation software. Play excerpts from the piece to illustrate your points.

Create a list of questions that might direct the listener's understanding of music. For example, you could ask if anyone knows the definition of *footloose* ("free to do as one pleases"). Point out that this is a perfect name for a dance piece.

# Music Then and NOW

## Historical Contexts and Styles

"When I hear music, I fear no danger. I am invulnerable. I see no foe. I am related to the earliest times, and to the latest."

–Henry David Thoreau (1817-1862)

▲ Baroque trumpet

▼ Detail from *Court Ball at the Palais du Louvre* (1852), Flemish School

◄ Members of Canadian Brass

# Hear the Music; Meet the People

Imagine you are traveling back in time to hear the music of people who lived in different centuries and countries. Whatever year and country you choose, the music there will sound unique because the people of that time and place created it.

The history of music spans all times and places. This expedition will take you through art music in Europe and the United States, with a few detours along the way.

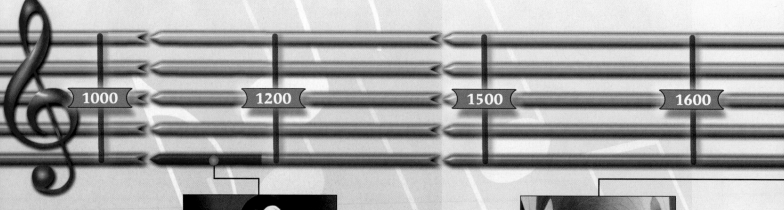

| 1000 | 1200 | 1500 | 1600 |

Hildegard von Bingen
(1098–1179)

Johann Sebastian Bach
(1685–1750)

## Medieval
(1100–1450)

## Renaissance
(1450–1600)

To begin the journey, **listen** to these excerpts. Try to match each excerpt to the person who created it or to a point on the time line. What qualities of the music give you clues about the answers?

**Montage of Historical Styles**

5-18 **as composed and performed by different people from many times and places**
This listening montage includes eight excerpts, each from a different time.

Franz Liszt
(1811–1886)

Gustav Holst
(1874–1934)

Bright Sheng
(born 1955)

1700        1800        1900        2000

Ludwig van Beethoven
(1770–1827)

Giuseppe Verdi
(1813–1901)

William Dawson
(1899–1990)

*Baroque*
(1600–1750)

CLASSICAL
(1750–1830)

Romantic
(1830–1900)

M O D E R N
(1900–Present)

# CHANT
## A WORLDWIDE TRADITION

The music we make with our voices can vary from a "plainsong" to a decorative melody that flows across an octave or more. Plainsong is also called **chant.**

In the days of the Roman Empire, monks developed a highly artistic style of chant that was heard not only in Rome but from Syria and North Africa through Europe to the British Isles and Ireland.

**Listen** to this chant. **Describe** the melody and the quality of the voices in this recording.

### O ignis spiritus Paracliti (O Holy Fire that Soothes the Spirit)

**by Hildegard von Bingen**

5-26    **as performed by the Choir of Trinity College, Cambridge, England**
Hildegard is one of the few Medieval composers whose music still survives.

---

**chant** A type of singing, with a simple, unaccompanied melody line and free rhythm.

**Music MAKERS**

## Hildegard von Bingen

**Hildegard von Bingen** (1098–1179) was a German abbess who was known for her work in literature, science, medicine, and music. She spent most of her life in an abbey, (a religious institution) where she wrote poems and set them to music. Some of her chants are very simple, but she also composed highly decorative melodies.

# Medieval Pop

The heyday of chant in Europe spanned the eighth through the fifteenth centuries. Can you imagine a song style today that will last for 800 years? Chanting voices were heard in churches, monasteries, and processions through village streets. Sometimes chant melodies were combined and harmonies were produced, as in this **motet** below.

**Sing** this chant melody from *Alle psallite cum luya.* Then follow the melody as you **listen** to this Medieval *motet* from France.

*Thirteenth-Century French Motet*

Al - le  psal - li - te  cum  lu - y - a,

## Alle psallite cum luya (Alle, Praise with, luia)

**Anonymous**
5-27    **as performed by Revels, conducted by John Langstaff**
This *motet* was found in a manuscript collection called the Montpellier Codex.

# Everybody Chants

Chant knows no boundaries. People from many cultures use chant as a way to perform poetry, express religious beliefs, or honor ancestors.

**Listen** to three examples of chant. Make a list and **evaluate** them for their chant-like characteristics. How many—or how few—pitches do you hear in these chants?

## Chant Montage

5-28    These selections from Algeria and Japan show how people from different parts of the world perform chants.

Chants have also been performed in North America for many hundreds of years. **Listen** to this Native American chant. Compare it to the chants you have already heard.

## Bear Dance

5-30    **from the Southern Ute people of Colorado as performed by the American Indian Dance Theater**
This chant celebrates the time of year when bears awaken from their winter's sleep.

---

**motet** Medieval or Renaissance unaccompanied vocal music with two or more simultaneous melody lines. The music serves the words: *mot* is the French word for "word."

▲ Ute bear dancers

# A Time for Fresh Arts

*"I always loved music; whoso has the skill in this art is of a good temperament, fitted for all things. We must teach music in schools; a schoolmaster ought to have skill in music ..."*

—Martin Luther (1483–1546)

The European Renaissance (1300–1600; for music, 1450–1600) was a time when fine arts flourished. Visual artists such as Leonardo da Vinci, Michelangelo, Raphael, and Titian created some of the greatest works of all time.

The music of the Renaissance was more complex than the music of the Medieval Era. Instead of two or three voice parts written as melodies, composers began writing four or more parts, paying attention to harmony for the first time.

## Renaissance Pop

Just like today, popular songs of the Renaissance were often love songs. Renaissance "bands" are called consorts. A consort is often a group made up of one instrument family—the same instrument in different sizes, such as five different sizes of recorders playing together. Consorts played arrangements of the most popular songs, just as many of today's bands play the top hits. People often danced to Renaissance "pop."

**Listen** to a consort of viols. **Describe** how the style of dancing to this music might be different from today's dance styles.

### Saltarello detto Trivella

**by Orazio Vecchi (1550–1605)**

**5-31**  **as performed by The King's Noyse**

*Saltarello detto Trivella* was played for a style of dancing involving small leaps.

### Arts Connection

◀ Detail from *Court Ball at the Palais du Louvre* (1582) Flemish School

## ON YOUR OWN

Use the resources of your school library or those of your local public library to locate photographs of Renaissance paintings. Share these photographs with your class.

## Plucked Strings from Persia

Another popular string instrument of this time was the lute. It is a plucked string instrument that came to Italy from Persia. Often an instrumentalist would play a tune and then improvise on that tune to make it more elaborate. Jazz musicians still do this today.

**Listen** to this lute solo. **Analyze** what the player does to make the music more elaborate.

### Danza (Dance)

**Anonymous**
**5-32** **as performed by The King's Noyse**
This piece was written circa 1590.

## A Royal Band

Royalty throughout Europe hired court musicians to play in consorts for their festivities and dancing. These consorts sometimes used a mixture of string and wind instruments. Some Renaissance instruments, such as the shawm, cornetto, crumhorn, and sackbut are loud when compared to the quieter sounds of the harpsichord, lute, viol, and recorder.

**Listen** to this music by Tylman Susato. Decide whether it would be likely to be played indoors or outside. How many different instruments do you hear? **Describe** the sounds they make.

▶ Lute

### Ronde

**by Tylman Susato (1500–1564)**
**5-33** **as performed by Convivium Musicum Gothenburgense**
This dance tune is part of a collection of dances from 1551. It uses shawms, dulcians, sackbuts, and percussion.

**Take It to the Net** For more information on Renaissance music and musical instruments, go to *www.sfsuccessnet.com*.

### *Arts* Connection

◀ A Renaissance band in action: the instruments from left to right are dulcian, shawm, cornetto, two shawms, and a sackbut in a detail from *Procession of Notre Dame de Salon* by Denys van Alsloot (1570-1628).

# 10

# DANCE THROUGH HISTORY

Where there is music, dance is not far away. Alone or in many different combinations—in lines, circles, or squares—people throughout history have been inspired to dance to music. Like music, dance meets the needs of people to celebrate, mourn, flirt, and to interpret their world in artistic ways.

## Old English Village Dances

From Medieval times onward, social dances were shared among the common people of Europe. More sophisticated dances were performed by members of the nobility. The movements of a dance were a reflection of the characteristics of the music.

**Listen** to this folk dance played on recorder. Imagine six men dancing while holding the horns of reindeer on their shoulders.

### Abbots Bromley Horn Dance

**English folk dance**
7-5 **as performed by The Revels**
People processed through the English village of Abbots Bromley to this music in the year 1400—and they still do.

**Play** the opening of the melody of the *Abbots Bromley Horn Dance* on recorder or another melody instrument.

In another Medieval-style dance called Morris dancing, men wear bells tied to their legs. They hold sticks that they strike together as they leap toward dancers across from them or to the sides. **Listen** for the bells, sticks, and the occasional foot-stepping to this fiddler's tune.

### Constant Billy

**from *The Beggar's Opera***
7-6 **by John Gay**
**as performed by The Revels**
This music accompanies Morris dancing, an English Medieval dance style in double line formation.

# French Moves from the Renaissance

By the early Renaissance, dance was evolving in Italy, France, Spain, and Germany from a loosely organized entertainment into an artistic endeavor. Dancing masters taught sophisticated dance maneuvers. Dances such as the French *branle* [BRAHN-uhl] were enjoyed by working class people and nobility alike. Dance music was performed on viols, recorders, shawms, sackbuts, and hand drums.

**Listen** to *Branle Double, Branle Simple.* Feel the calm quality of the dance. **Move** to show the steady beat and even rhythm within meter in 2. **Analyze** the music to find the form.

### Branle Double, Branle Simple

**7-7**

from *Danses Populaires Françaises*
by Thoinot Arbeau
as performed by The Broadside Band

This *branle* alternates between major and minor. Thoinot Arbeau (1519–1595) published a book in 1588 that taught people how to dance most of the popular dances from his time.

Now **move** to *Branle Double, Branle Simple* using these steps. Stand in a small circle, facing in and holding hands.

- Step-close four times to the right, moving counterclockwise.
- Step-close four times to the left, moving clockwise.
- Step-close forward four times into the circle starting with the right foot.
- Step-close backward four times out of the circle.

**Play** the melody of the *branle* on violins, guitars, recorders, and other available instruments. **Improvise** ornaments by adding notes to the melody, such as **passing tones** or **neighboring tones.**

▲ Seventeenth century dancers performing a *branle*

---

**passing tone**   A non-harmonic melody note that provides motion between two distinct chord tones.

**neighboring tone**   A non-harmonic melody note that provides motion between two identical chord tones.

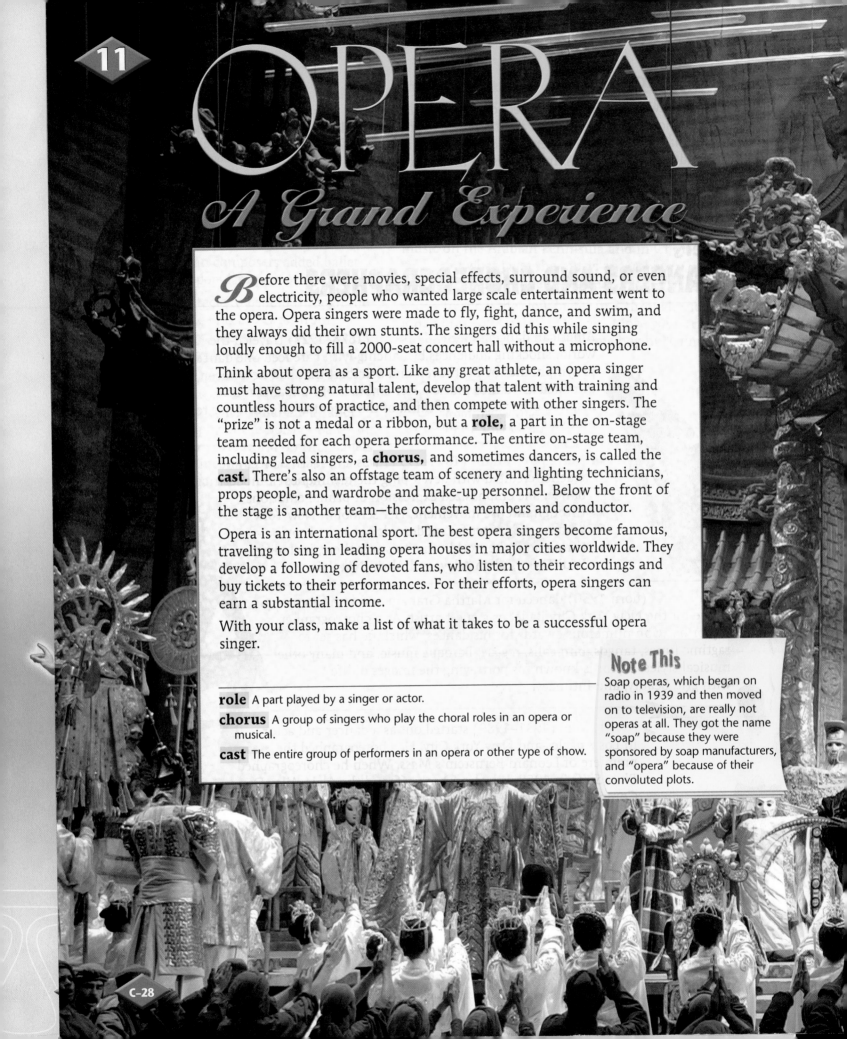

# 11

# Opera
## A Grand Experience

*B*efore there were movies, special effects, surround sound, or even electricity, people who wanted large scale entertainment went to the opera. Opera singers were made to fly, fight, dance, and swim, and they always did their own stunts. The singers did this while singing loudly enough to fill a 2000-seat concert hall without a microphone.

Think about opera as a sport. Like any great athlete, an opera singer must have strong natural talent, develop that talent with training and countless hours of practice, and then compete with other singers. The "prize" is not a medal or a ribbon, but a **role,** a part in the on-stage team needed for each opera performance. The entire on-stage team, including lead singers, a **chorus,** and sometimes dancers, is called the **cast.** There's also an offstage team of scenery and lighting technicians, props people, and wardrobe and make-up personnel. Below the front of the stage is another team—the orchestra members and conductor.

Opera is an international sport. The best opera singers become famous, traveling to sing in leading opera houses in major cities worldwide. They develop a following of devoted fans, who listen to their recordings and buy tickets to their performances. For their efforts, opera singers can earn a substantial income.

With your class, make a list of what it takes to be a successful opera singer.

**role** A part played by a singer or actor.

**chorus** A group of singers who play the choral roles in an opera or musical.

**cast** The entire group of performers in an opera or other type of show.

## Note This
Soap operas, which began on radio in 1939 and then moved on to television, are really not operas at all. They got the name "soap" because they were sponsored by soap manufacturers, and "opera" because of their convoluted plots.

# Setting the Stage

More operas have been written in Italy than in any other country. The best-known Italian opera composers are Gioacchino Rossini (1792–1868), Giuseppe Verdi (1813–1901), and Giacomo Puccini (1858–1924).

The quartet from Verdi's opera *Rigoletto* demonstrates an amazing feature of opera—several people can express very different thoughts or ideas at the same time! Each singer has an individual melody with its own lyrics. The composer makes the melodies fit together musically. Here's what the singers in this quartet are talking about:

- The Duke (**tenor,** begins the quartet): The Duke is famous for his "love 'em and leave 'em" behavior. Earlier in the opera, he claimed to love Gilda, but now he wants Maddalena to be his girlfriend.
- Maddalena (**mezzo-soprano,** sings next): She knows the Duke's reputation and is far too wise to get involved with him.
- Gilda (**soprano,** sings a high melody after Maddalena): She fell hard for the Duke. Now she is crushed to hear him giving Maddalena the same line she heard earlier.
- Rigoletto (**baritone** last to sing): This is Gilda's father. She is the light of his life. He knows the Duke's reputation, and he is furious that the Duke has ditched his daughter. He vows revenge.

**Listen** to this quartet from Verdi's opera *Rigoletto*. Talk about an international performance! Joan Sutherland is Australian, Huguette Tourangeau is French, Luciano Pavarotti is Italian, and Sherrill Milnes is American. The quartet is sung in Italian.

### 🎧 *Bella figlia dell'amore (Beautiful Daughter of Love)*

7-10
from *Rigoletto*
by Giuseppe Verdi
as performed by Joan Sutherland (Gilda), Huguette Tourangeau (Maddalena), Luciano Pavarotti (the Duke), and Sherrill Milnes (Rigoletto)
This selection is an example of an operatic ensemble, a piece for seven singers.

---

**tenor** A high-pitched male voice.

**soprano** A high female voice.

**mezzo-soprano** A medium female voice, lower than a soprano voice.

**baritone** A low male voice between a tenor and a bass

## A "Guy Duet" from France

France also produced important opera composers. Perhaps you have heard of the opera *Carmen*. It was written by the French composer Georges Bizet.

**Listen** to this duet from Bizet's opera *The Pearl Fishers*. Duets allow two singers to have a dialogue or to express a unified thought. In this scene, some fishermen are preparing for a festival. One fisherman, Zurga, is surprised when an old friend named Nadir arrives. Zurga and Nadir once had a close friendship that ended when they both fell in love with the same woman. But that is now long past, and in this duet they declare their friendship forever.

### Au fond du temple saint (In the Depths of the Temple)

**7-11** from *The Pearl Fishers*
by Georges Bizet
as performed by Plácido Domingo and Sherrill Milnes

Sherrill Milnes is singing a baritone role in this opera. This duet is sung in French.

## Brava, Diva!

The word **diva** [DEE-vah] has been used throughout opera history to identify outstanding and famous female opera stars. The crowd shouts **"Brava!"** [BRAH-vah] when they like how a *diva* sings. A *diva* usually has many enthusiastic fans and can demand large fees for singing. Of all singers, sopranos are probably most frequently called *divas*. Oddly, there is no masculine form of *diva* used in this way.

Leontyne Price, an American born in 1927 in Laurel, Mississippi, is an outstanding example of a *diva*. Her voice type is called lyric soprano. It is especially beautiful in smooth, flowing melody lines.

**diva** The term for a world-class female opera singer.

**brava** What audience members shout in praise of a female singer. For men, they shout *"bravo"* [BRAH-voh] and for a group, *"bravi"* [BRAH-vee].

▲ Jeffrey Kneelbone as Zurga and Joan Gibbons as Leila in *The Pearl Fisher*

**Listen** to Leontyne Price sing an **aria** from the opera *Tosca*. The character Tosca, the soprano role in the opera, is herself a *diva*. She is strong-willed and quick-tempered, but beautiful and charming. She is in love with Cavaradossi, who is now in prison and being tortured for information. The evil official Scarpia suggests to Tosca that he will release Cavaradossi if she will love Scarpia instead. Tosca expresses her anguish over this situation in this *aria*.

### Vissi d'arte (I Lived for Art)
**from *Tosca***
**7-12** **by Giacomo Puccini**
**as performed by Leontyne Price**
This moving aria uses dynamic contrast to convey emotion.

Sumi Jo (born 1962) is from Seoul, South Korea. She studied voice there and in Rome, and today she is a world-class *diva*.

**Listen** to Sumi Jo sing the "Queen of the Night" *aria* (also known as the "Revenge Aria") from Mozart's opera *The Magic Flute*. In the opera, the Queen of the Night has been deposed by Sarastro. The Queen commands her daughter Pamina to murder Sarastro so that the Queen may return to power.

▲ Leontyne Price in the role of Floria Tosca

### Queen of the Night Aria
**from *The Magic Flute***
**7-13** **by Wolfgang Amadeus Mozart**
**as performed by Sumi Jo (soprano)**
This *aria,* sung in German, requires great control over the higher register of the voice.

◀ Sumi Jo

# Checkpoint

Make a chart listing the similarities of each opera in this lesson. Share your findings in a report to the class.

**aria** A song for solo voice and accompaniment, which often includes a solo instrument.

# 12

# Music About a Nation

A t the end of the nineteenth century, Western art music was dominated by Germany and Italy. Although composers from other countries respected German and Italian music, they wanted to bring their own national identities into the musical spotlight. To do this, they included folk melodies and dance rhythms of their own countries in their music. They also chose subjects for **program music** and operas that specifically related to their countries. **Nationalism** in music was especially strong in England, France, Russia, the United States, and the countries of eastern Europe.

Bedřich Smetana [SMET-a-na] (1824–1884), a Czech composer, composed a set of six **symphonic poems** entitled *Ma Vlast* ("My Fatherland"), which draw on Czech history, geography, and legend. The second of these, *"Vltava"* ("The Moldau") refers to a river in the eastern Czech Republic that begins in the forest and flows north to merge with the Elbe River north of Prague [PRAHG], the capital city. Unlike most other composers, Smetana was very specific in explaining what each section of his music depicted.

---

**program music** Music that suggests or describes a nonmusical idea, story, or event.

**nationalism** A style in the nineteenth century in which folk materials (including songs, dances, or stories) of a particular country or region were incorporated into a musical composition.

**symphonic poem** An orchestral work that is based on a story or a poem, which is sometimes read before the audience hears the piece performed.

**Bridges over the Moldau River** ▶

**Listen** to Smetana's musical description of the Moldau. Follow the map as you listen, and read the descriptions of each section.

### The Moldau

**7-14** from *Ma Vlast*
by Bedřich Smetana, as performed by the Cleveland Orchestra; George Szell, conductor
Smetana composed *Ma Vlast* between 1874 and 1882.

## The Moldau LISTENING MAP

Moldau theme

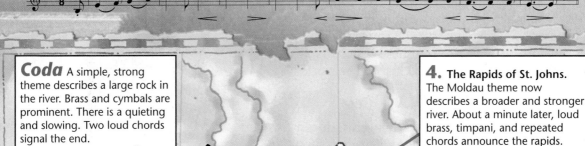

### ON YOUR OWN

Develop a plan for a piece of music that describes the state in which you live. Write a list of features of your state that you would like to depict. Describe how you will do this using music. Sketch your plan using a listening-map format. You can include music that already exists or write original music.

**Coda** A simple, strong theme describes a large rock in the river. Brass and cymbals are prominent. There is a quieting and slowing. Two loud chords signal the end.

**4.** **The Rapids of St. Johns.** The Moldau theme now describes a broader and stronger river. About a minute later, loud brass, timpani, and repeated chords announce the rapids. Cymbals and piccolo join in a *crescendo*. The final statement of the Moldau theme is in major.

**Prague**

**Elbe River**

**Bohemian Forest**

**Moldau River**

**CZECH REPUBLIC**

**3.** **Moonlight— Dance of the Water Nymphs.** A slow, lyrical upper string melody floats over the rippling water figure. After the harp is heard, an urgent *crescendo* is played with French horns prominent.

**1.** **The sources of the river.** The "rippling water" motive starts with one instrument, then two, then more. Violins introduce the main Moldau theme in minor. Hunters in the forest are announced with brass fanfares.

**2.** **A Village Wedding.** Listen for long French horn tones with a repeated note above them. A dance tune is introduced softly, then more prominently. The section ends with a low, repeated note.

# 13

# FOLK ROOTS IN ART MUSIC

What do you collect—baseball cards, seashells, dolls or comic books? How do you store or display your collection? Suppose you were a collector of songs and dances that had never been written down. How would you go about collecting them? What would you do with them once you found them?

Musicians in many times and places have collected traditional melodies, folk songs, and folk dances. They have found different ways to preserve the songs they collected. Were it not for the dedication of these collectors, a great deal of wonderful music would be lost to the world.

## New Music out of the Old

Two folk music collectors of the early twentieth century were Béla Bartók (1881–1945) and Zoltán Kodály (1882–1967). Bartók and Kodály collected the folk songs of their native country, Hungary. Working individually and together, they compiled collections of folk songs. Both published folk-song collections, and both used elements of folk music in their compositions of art music.

**Listen** for gypsy-style fiddling, melodies that sound like folk songs, and syncopation in this music by Kodály. Kodály's parents were amateur musicians. He grew up hearing music played at home.

*Arts* **Connection**

▲ A Hungarian painting of Zoltán Kodály at age 40 by an unknown artist (1922)

### Dances of Galanta

**by Zoltán Kodály**
**7-15 as performed by the Philadelphia Orchestra, conducted by Eugene Ormandy**
Galanta is a town in Hungary where Zoltán Kodály lived when he was young.

**Listen** to an excerpt from the "Intermezzo" from *Háry János Suite* by Kodály. In this composition, Kodály features a *cimbalom*, a Hungarian folk instrument that is a type of hammered dulcimer.

### Intermezzo

**from *Háry János Suite***
**7-16 by Zoltán Kodály**
**as performed by the Cleveland Orchestra, conducted by George Szell**
*Háry János* is a Hungarian folk opera by Kodály.

▲ A *cimbalom* [TZEEM-bah-lohm] is a large Hungarian hammered dulcimer.

## A Collection of Rhythms

**Play** these rhythms, which are based on Hungarian folk songs.

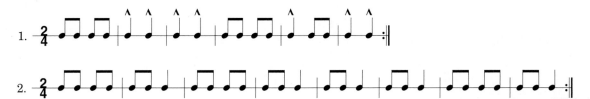

**Listen** for these rhythms in five of Bartók's *Fifteen Hungarian Peasant Songs*. **Identify** the rhythms when you hear them.

### Fifteen Hungarian Peasant Songs

**7-17**
No. 7, 9, 10, 13, and 14
by Béla Bartók
as performed by György Sándor
Bartók composed these pieces between 1914 and 1918.

Bartók was influenced by new musical styles of the twentieth century. No matter what he wrote, his music always had a distinctive sound. **Listen** to an excerpt from *Concerto for Viola and Orchestra*. What qualities of this music might make you think it was written by Bartók?

### Concerto for Viola and Orchestra

**7-22**
Movement 3
by Béla Bartók
as perfomed by Marcus Thompson and the Slovenian Radio Symphony Orchestra
Bartók moved to the United States in 1940 because of World War II. His *Concerto for Viola and Orchestra* is one of his last compositions, written in 1945.

▲ Béla Bartók was an extraordinary pianist. He composed many piano pieces.

## Careers COLLECTOR
# Maud Karpeles

**Maud Karpeles** (1885–1976) was from Great Britain. She worked with another famous collector named Cecil Sharp. She collected folk dances, notating them by writing down what the dancers were doing in specific measures of the music. Karpeles worked in England, but she and Sharp came to the United States to explore the isolated folk music of Appalachia. Karpeles summarized her experiences with folk music by saying, "Folk music is a democratic art in the true sense of the word."

# 14

# STRIKE UP THE BAND!

Bands became popular in Europe and North America in the 1800s. Many military groups started marching bands, and communities organized bands for entertainment. Factory workers played in bands for recreation and schools started bands to teach students about music. Today, many people still enjoy playing in and listening to bands. **Describe** how a band is different from an orchestra.

## British Band Music

Gustav Holst (1874–1934), a British composer, wrote two **suites** for band. Like other composers of his time, he was interested in the folk music of his country. He used folk melodies for themes in his second suite for band. **Sing** or **play** this melody; then **identify** the tune.

Now **listen** for the "Greensleeves" melody in "Fantasia on the Dargason," part of Gustav Holst's *Suite No. 2* for band. In this music, "Greensleeves" is one of two melodies played at the same time. Trace the music whenever you hear the melody of "Greensleeves."

### Fantasia on the Dargason

from *Suite No. 2 in F Major*

**7-23**   by Gustav Holst
as performed by the Eastman Wind Ensemble

Holst composed this suite for band in 1911. It became very famous and it is still played by bands today.

---

**suite** A type of musical composition with several short parts or movements of varying character. Frequently these parts are written in dance forms.

# Music MAKERS

# Percy Grainger

**Percy Grainger** (1882–1961) was born in Australia, moved to Germany as a child, lived in England as a young man, and eventually moved to the United States. Grainger also traveled to many countries, performing as a pianist in Europe, Australia, New Zealand, and South Africa. He played with great energy and sometimes even pounded on the piano with his fists. Audiences and critics thought that his playing was wild, intense, and even shocking.

Grainger loved folk songs and, like other musicians of his time, he collected folk melodies. In England, he went on "song-seeking" walks into the country. According to one of his friends, Grainger walked up to people in the countryside and asked them if they knew any songs. Evidently, many of these strangers actually sang songs for him. Grainger used the folk songs and fiddle tunes he collected in compositions for pianists, singers, orchestras, and bands.

## One Tune–Three Arrangements

One day in 1906, Percy Grainger heard three fiddlers in the English countryside playing a melody as people danced. Grainger wrote down the melody and arranged it three different ways. **Listen** to excerpts from *Shepherd's Hey*.

### Shepherd's Hey Sampler

**by Percy Grainger**
- **7-24**   as performed by Percy Grainger on piano,
- **7-25**   as performed by The English Chamber Orchestra,
- **7-26**   as performed by Cleveland Symphony Winds

Percy Grainger arranged "Shepherd's Hey" for piano, orchestra, and band.

▼Eastman Wind Ensemble

**Take It to the Net** To find out more about Gustav Holst and Percy Grainger, go to *www.sfsuccessnet.com*.

# 15

# NEW COLORS

During the Impressionist Period in France (1880–1920), visual artists and composers broke the established rules about the arts. Two of the most famous people of the time were painter Claude Monet (1840–1926) and composer Claude Debussy (1862–1918). Each made a lasting contribution to the world of the arts.

Claude Monet based his paintings on impressions, or emotions created by the play of color and light. The result was a sense of blurred detail and movement in his paintings.

**Analyze** the painting *Regatta at Argenteuil* by Claude Monet. How does it suggest impressions that the eye might see? How does it suggest the play of light? What happens to color as a result?

### Arts Connection

*Regatta at Argenteuil* (1872) by Claude Monet

## Colors in Sound

Claude Debussy created images with sounds rather than paint. He used a variety of composing techniques to create musical impressions of scenes from nature, such as the moon reflecting on water or waves dancing in a lake.

One technique Debussy used was to compose with scales that were not commonly used in Western music at the time. One is the pentatonic, or five-tone, scale. Another is the whole-tone scale, which uses only whole steps.

**Play** the following scales upward and downward on a keyboard. **Improvise** a melody using notes from each of these scales.

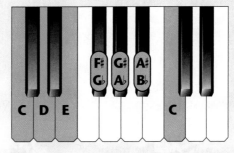

▲ C♯ pentatonic scale

▲ C whole-tone scale

## Two Images of Water

Debussy wrote several compositions in which he attempted to give listeners a sense of the movement of water or objects on water. One of these compositions is *Voiles* [VWAHL] (Sails) for piano.

**Read** the opening melody below as you **listen** to *Voiles*. This selection uses both the pentatonic and whole-tone scales. Identify the kind of scale Debussy uses first. How does this music create an impression of sailboats on water?

### Voiles (Sails)

**by Claude Debussy**
7-27    **as performed by Paul Crossley**
Debussy composed the two sets of *Preludes for Piano*, between 1910 and 1913. *Voiles* is one of those preludes.

*Jeux de vagues* (Joy of the Waves) is the second movement of Debussy's larger work for orchestra called *La mer (The Sea)*. Debussy uses instrumental timbres to create a sense of the waves dancing.

**Listen** to this section of *Jeux de vagues*. **Identify** which of the following instruments are playing. Write the name of each instrument in a list as you hear it. You may hear some instruments more than once.

- trumpet    • violins    • flute    • clarinet
- harp    • English horn    • oboe    • bells

### Jeux de vagues

**by Claude Debussy**
7-28    **as performed by The Philharmonia Orchestra, Pierre Boulez, conductor**
*La mer*, written between 1903 and 1905, is an example of program music.

### ON YOUR OWN

Using a pitched instrument, invent your own scale. It can be made up of any pattern of whole and half steps. Create a short piece using your scale that describes an impression you have of a scene or a feeling you have experienced. Play your piece for others. Evaluate how well your piece created that impression.

# 16

# MUSIC IN THE U.S.A. ROOTS TO CLASSICS

Just what is American music, anyway? The music of the American people ranges from the traditional roots of immigrants and enslaved people to Western art music, from the music of North America's first inhabitants to the latest popular music.

## Spiritual Roots

African Americans who journeyed from slavery into freedom weaved their experiences into the songs they sang. The songs became known as spirituals because the lyrics were linked to stories and scenes from the Bible. Spirituals are rooted in the cries, shouts, and hallelujahs of people striving to move beyond their shackles. They were sung in dwellings, plantation fields, and churches.

As you **sing** "Swing Low, Sweet Chariot," think about the words and how they might have given people hope that they could someday escape slavery.

> *". . . but I know something of men, and knowing them, I know that these songs are the articulate message of the slave to the world."*
>
> —W.E.B. DuBois

## Spirituals in Concert

The Florida A&M University Concert Choir has a long tradition of presenting African American art music in an academic environment. This art form has reached such an esteemed stature in academia today that many groups now regularly perform spirituals.

**Listen** to the recording of *Ev'ry Time I Feel the Spirit*. **Describe** musical elements that give this spiritual its unique sound.

### Ev'ry Time I Feel the Spirit

**8-1** African American Spiritual
**as performed by the Florida A&M University Concert Choir**
This is a performance of the spiritual as arranged by William Dawson.

**Listen** to *Study War No More*. **Compare** the vocal qualities of this performance with those of *Ev'ry Time I Feel the Spirit*.

### Study War No More

**8-2** African American Spiritual
**as performed by Sweet Honey in the Rock**
This is a performance of the spiritual as arranged by this female singing group.

**Music MAKERS**

# William Dawson

**William Dawson** (1899–1990) was an important American composer and arranger. He published a large repertoire of African American spirituals and folk songs. As a choir director and music teacher at Tuskegee Institute in Alabama, he helped shape the concert-style spiritual. Dawson became an internationally known guest conductor. His arrangements of spirituals are still performed by choirs today.

# SWING LOW, SWEET CHARIOT

*African-American Spiritual*

CD 8-3

**REFRAIN**

Guitar: capo 5

Swing low, sweet char - i - ot, _____ Com-in' for to car-ry me home;

Swing low, sweet char - i - ot, _____ Com-in' for to car-ry me home.

*Fine*

**VERSE**

1. I looked o - ver Jor - dan and what did I _____ see? _____
2. If you get _____ there _____ be - fore _____ I _____ do, _____
3. I'm some - times _____ up, I'm _____ some - times down, _____

Com - in' for to car - ry me home;
A band _____ of an - gels
Tell all _____ my friends I'm
But still _____ my soul feels

*D.C. al Fine*

com - in' af - ter me,
com - in' _____ too, _____ Com - in' for to car - ry me home.
heav'n - ly _____ bound, _____

## A Blend of Jazz and Classical Styles

Along with spirituals and gospel music, jazz is an American-grown art form. Some composers in the United States have succeeded in fusing American roots into their classical compositions. **Listen** to one of the best-known American symphonic works, *Rhapsody in Blue.* What makes it sound "American?" **Read** the opening clarinet theme; then listen for it in the music. You will hear the clarinet slide up to the first note of this melody.

### *Rhapsody in Blue*

**by George Gershwin**

**8-4** **as performed by the Columbia Symphony Orchestra**

*Gershwin* composed *Rhapsody in Blue* over the course of three weeks in 1924 .

The premiere performance of *Rhapsody in Blue* was billed as an experiment in dressing jazz up as symphonic music to make it more acceptable. Until 1924, the lively rhythms and melodic slides of jazz music could be heard in clubs and dance halls, but not in the concert

▲ One of the few women to lead a band during the 1920s and 1930s, Gertrude "Ma" Rainey helped popularize African American music.

hall. *Rhapsody in Blue* became famous, making George Gershwin the first composer to successfully blend jazz and classical music.

# George Gershwin

### Music MAKERS

George Gershwin (1898–1937) was born in New York City. Before he was 30, he was America's most famous composer of pop music. He studied piano for just a few years but was a fast learner. After a brief career playing songs on Tin Pan Alley to sell them for publishers, Gershwin became a rehearsal pianist for musical theater productions. He soon began writing songs with his brother, Ira, as lyricist. In the 1920s and 1930s the brothers wrote musical pieces for broadway shows, including *George White's Scandals* (1920–1924), *Our Nell* (1922), *Lady Be Good* (1924), *Primrose* (1924), *Tip Toes* (1925), *Song of the Flame* (1925), *135th Street* (1923), *Oh Kay!* (1926), *Strike Up the Band* (1927), *Funny Face* (1927), *Girl Crazy* (1930), *Of Thee I Sing* (1931), and *Let 'Em Eat Cake* (1933). His symphonic poem *An American in Paris* and his opera *Porgy and Bess* were high points in his career.

◀ George Gershwin

## An American Fanfare

The sound of America is embedded in the sound of brass instruments. In a trio or quintet, or as part of a town band, brass instruments are part of the American musical landscape.

**Listen** for brass instruments in *Fanfare for the Common Man* and follow the map.

### Fanfare for the Common Man

**8-5**
**by Aaron Copland**
**as performed by the London Symphony**

Aaron Copland composed *Fanfare for the Common Man* during World War II.

**ON YOUR OWN**

Interview five people of various ages and ask them to define American music. Invite them to name songs and other musical works, composers, and styles.

## FANFARE FOR THE COMMON MAN LISTENING MAP

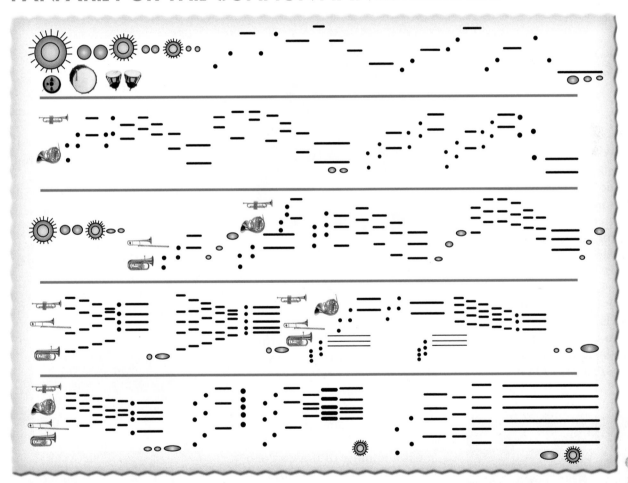

## A Favorite Composition Teacher

Nadia Boulanger ▶

Many American composers of the twentieth century studied in Europe. Aaron Copland, Elliott Carter, Roy Harris, and Leonard Bernstein went to Paris to study with the leading French teacher of composition, **Nadia Boulanger** [boo-lahn-ZHEY] (1887–1979). Boulanger taught harmony, counterpoint, and musical analysis. She was the first woman to conduct the New York Philharmonic and an entire symphony in London.

# Signature STYLE

Composers writing today find their inspiration in many different places. Some enjoy the sounds they can create using electronic technology. Others like to explore the timbres of single instruments or combinations of instruments. Some composers are driven to express emotion or paint pictures with sound, while others like playing with rhythmic or melodic ideas. The possibilities are endless.

Just as you have a unique way of signing your name, composers develop unique approaches to composition. That is their signature style.

## Music MAKERS

### John Adams

**John Adams** (born 1947) learned to play the clarinet as a child. He studied music and now works as a conductor, composer, and performer. In 1989 he won a Grammy for his opera *Nixon in China* and in 2003 he won a Pulitzer prize for his symphonic work *On the Transmigration of Souls*. Adams has been known as a **minimalist** composer, using repetition to create his music. He has also included many different musical styles in his pieces.

### Joan Tower

**Joan Tower** (born 1938) spent her childhood in South America. The rhythmic energy of South American music has always inspired her. She has won many awards for her compositions. Tower has been composer-in-residence for several orchestras and festivals. She is a founder of the Da Capo Chamber Players and enjoys playing the piano.

### Bright Sheng

**Bright Sheng** (born 1955) was born in Shanghai, China. He studied piano as a child. When he graduated from high school, he played piano and timpani in a Chinese dance company, and he studied Chinese folk music. After the Chinese Cultural Revolution, he moved to the United States with his parents. Sheng has won many awards for his compositions and served as composer-in-residence for the Seattle Symphony.

**minimalism** A compositional style that strives to reduce music down to simple sound by using repetition of all elements for long periods of time.

# Three Composers—Three Styles

John Adams, Joan Tower, and Bright Sheng have all composed solo pieces as well as compositions for small and large ensembles. Read about each of them and listen to their music to discover their signature styles.

First **play** this rhythm.

Now **listen** to *China Gates* by John Adams. **Describe** what Adams does to change the rhythm. Listen closely and **identify** the small changes in the music.

## China Gates

**by John Adams**

**8-6**  **as performed by Alan Feinberg**

This piano solo was written in 1977 with young players in mind. It shifts without warning between two modes, an event similar to a "gate" in electronics.

**Listen** to *Wings*, a work for solo clarinet. Joan Tower's inspiration for this piece was watching a falcon in flight. **Describe** the qualities of the music that suggest a flying falcon. How does Tower use the timbres and different registers of the clarinet to suggest flight?

## Wings

**by Joan Tower**

**8-7**  **as performed by Robert Spring**

Joan Tower has written several compositions for clarinet. Robert Spring teaches at Arizona State University.

**Listen** to *Guessing Song*, which is based on a folk melody. **Describe** how the music suggests the feeling of children at play. What new sounds does the cello make?

## Guessing Song

from *Seven Tunes Heard in China*

**8-8**  **by Bright Sheng**

**as performed by Yo-Yo Ma**

*Guessing Song* is from a set of seven cello solos written in 1995.

**Take It to the Net** To learn more about minimalism, visit *www.sfsuccessnet.com*.

# Music Then and NOW

## Review and Assess

In Music Then and Now you've listened to music from many different cultures, experiencing the varied richness of musical expression. You've heard many instruments and vocal sounds that may have been unfamiliar and this exposure may have led you to explore some of this music further.

This assessment is an opportunity for you to think more deeply about what you've heard by formulating descriptions of the music you've been listening to, taking into account the following aspects.

- **timbre**–tone color (sound) of an instrument or voice.
- **melody, rhythm, harmony, dynamics, and tempo**–compositional elements.
- **form**–how the piece is organized.
- **dynamics**–the degrees of loudness and softness of a sound.
- **expression**–emotional effect on the listener.
- **cultural function**–when and where is it used.

### Review What You Learned

Look at the time line on pages C-2 and C-3. This time line depicts periods in the history of Western culture–the culture of Western Europe and North and South America. The lines indicate arbitrary points in time. Historians chose these breaks in the time lines based roughly on changes in the musical styles and the culture. One thing is certain: music has changed and continues to change over time.

Choose any three listening selections from Music Then and Now. As you listen, think about where they might fall in the time line and why.

8-9

## What Do You Hear 2

Listen to the following pairs of excerpts. The two excerpts in each pair are from different periods in the history of Western music. Decide which piece was written first. Explain your answer by describing two features of each piece that place it in an earlier or later time period. Consider the following in formulating your explanations.

- Instrumentation
- Melody
- Harmony
- Rhythm

### Exercise 1

Was excerpt A written earlier or later than excerpt B?

How did you decide?

### Exercise 2

Was excerpt A written earlier or later than excerpt B?

How did you decide?

### Exercise 3

Was excerpt A written earlier or later than excerpt B?

How did you decide?

## Show What You Know

One of the best ways to develop understanding of music is to explain ideas verbally or in writing. As you listen to your selections, write down two sentences that describe each of the musical and expressive elements listed below.

- **timbre** What instruments and voices do you hear?
- **compositional elements** How fast is the tempo? How will you describe the rhythm? What does the harmony sound like?
- **dynamics** How are dynamics used?
- **form** How is the music organized? Are musical ideas repeated?

- **expression** What emotion does the music make you feel?
- **cultural function** When would you likely hear this music? Where would you expect this music to be performed? Does it have a public function, like a parade, or is it more personal?

In small groups, discuss each others' ideas and discover why different members of the same group came to different conclusions. The group need not agree, but the members should be able to explain their points of view.

## What to Listen For

Most music is intended to tell a story or to express some kind of idea: an emotion or a visual image. The sounds of music can make you feel energetic or sad, can trigger a memory, or paint a picture in your imagination. Think about how all of these emotions and images are conveyed through sound alone. How does music do this?

Listen to these selections from Music Then and Now. After hearing each one, explain what you think the composer intended to convey, and how the composer communicated ideas, using the list on p. C-46. For example, if a march sounds "triumphant," what in the music creates this sound? If a piece is intended for dancing, how do the elements change?

## Share What You Know

Select one piece from the module that is your personal favorite. Prepare a presentation for the class or another person that will help them understand the music itself and why you like the music. You should begin your presentation with basic facts about the piece including the title, composer, and composition date.

Explain how you think the elements convey the composer's intentions—mood, emotion, a picture, or an idea. Include the elements of music description listed on p. C-46.

Your presentation may be placed on poster board, on overhead transparencies, or on presentation software. Play excerpts from the piece to illustrate your points.

Create a list of questions that might direct the listener's understanding of the music. For example, a descriptive title such as "Be-Bop Bach: Prelude No. 2" might suggest a combination of musical styles from different eras.

# The Beat Goes On

*Odaiko* drummer ▼

"If your
heart is beating,
you're a drummer.
Let the drum connect
your heart to your hands.
Let your hands learn
to dance."

*Alan Dworsky and Betsy Sansby (1996)*

▲ Volta balafon player,
Ghana, Africa

George Saddleback from
the Samson Cree Nation ▶

◀ Blue Man

D–1

# APPLAUSE!

Hand clapping has accompanied song and dance from the early days of human existence. In Africa, clapping provides background rhythms for chanting, singing, and dancing. On the Polynesian islands of Samoa, men use *pati* (flat, right angle hand claps) and *pö* (hands together and cupped) to accompany dance songs. The Spanish Flamenco style has a very specific type of rhythmic clapping, called *palmas*, to support the *gitano* singing and dancing. African slaves in the United States were not allowed to use drums, so they clapped hands and slapped their torsos and thighs to accompany songs and dances. This type of body percussion is called *hambone* and is often performed in call-and-response style.

Experiment with various ways of clapping. **Listen** to the sound of your hands as you clap. Cup your hands and capture the air between them to produce a low popping sound. Create a high sound by slapping four fingers into a flat palm.

**Perform** the clapping ensemble below. Begin with the low popping sound of the first part. Then add the other parts.

◀ African clapping tradition

## Hand Clap Ensemble

*Music by Anne Fennell*

Low pop

High slap

Regular clap

Finger slap

Flamenco *palmas* ▲

## Clapping Groove

**Listen** to *Goodbye, Ev'rybody (Farewell Shout)*. Notice the rhythm of the hand claps and how the repetitive clapping supports the song. **Analyze** the form as you listen to the song again.

### Goodbye, Ev'rybody (Farewell Shout)

**African American folk song**
8-15 **as performed by Valentine Pringle**

This song is part of *The Long Road to Freedom,* an album of music with African roots produced by the actor/singer/humanitarian Harry Belafonte.

## Do the Hambone

Learn this call-and-response hambone ensemble. First **improvise** eight beats of solo clapping or hambone rhythms as a *call*. Then **perform** the eight-count *response*. Notice that the eight-count *response* is measures three and four of "Hand Clap Ensemble."

*Music by Anne Fennell*

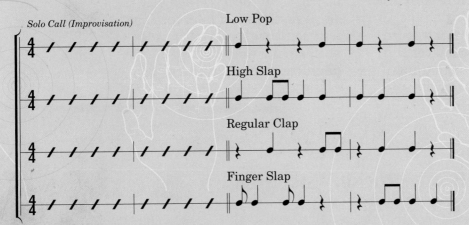

*Solo Call (Improvisation)*

Low Pop

High Slap

Regular Clap

Finger Slap

**ON YOUR OWN**

In small groups, create a layered hambone ensemble. One person begins with a repeated rhythm pattern. Each other group member creates a new rhythm pattern that complements it. Performers begin one at a time. Determine how the ensemble will end, and perform your ensemble for the class.

Now **perform** the ensemble to accompany "Hambone." Take turns improvising the call.

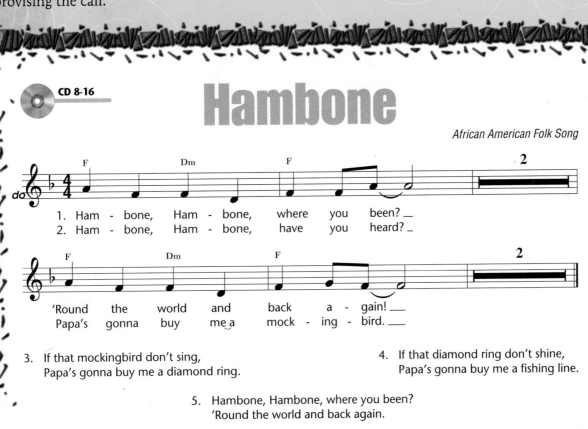

CD 8-16

# Hambone

*African American Folk Song*

F          Dm          F          2

1. Ham - bone,   Ham - bone,   where   you   been? __
2. Ham - bone,   Ham - bone,   have   you   heard? __

F          Dm          F          2

'Round   the   world   and   back   a - gain! __
Papa's   gonna   buy   me a   mock - ing - bird. __

3. If that mockingbird don't sing,
   Papa's gonna buy me a diamond ring.

4. If that diamond ring don't shine,
   Papa's gonna buy me a fishing line.

5. Hambone, Hambone, where you been?
   'Round the world and back again.

# BEAT BOX

You can drum on almost anything from tabletops to plastic bottles to car tops and fenders. Start by collecting some cardboard boxes of different sizes. Test them and choose boxes that sound good when hit like a drum. Experiment by playing on the boxes with both of your hands and with wooden sticks or dowels. The boxes might sound better if taped shut, but you may prefer a loose rattling sound. Feel free to decorate your boxes with colorful designs and patterns.

**Play** each of the parts in the "Box a-Rockin' Ensemble" separately. Practice the vocal syllables under the small box part before playing it on the box. Then play the *dig-ga* rhythms and hum the *(mm)* rests softly with your voice. Add one part at a time, and **perform** together as an ensemble.

## Box a–Rockin' Ensemble

*Music by Will Schmid*

Large Box (Low)

Pizza Box

Small Box (High)
(vocal syllables)

*(mm)   ga-dig-ga (mm ___ )   ga-dig-ga (mm ___ )   ga-dig-ga (mm ___ )   dig-ga dig-ga*

Medium Box

▲ **Large Box (Low)**
Use one slightly cupped hand to play in the middle of a large box. Try all sides to be sure that you have the best low bass sound, similar to the bass speakers on a car radio.

▲ **Pizza Box**
Find a large flat pizza box. On beats 1 and 3, play an open tone by letting your hand bounce off of the flat surface. On beats 2 and 4, slap the middle of the box and keep your hand on the box rather than bouncing off.

▲ **Small Box (High)**
Locate a small box that makes a sharp high pitch when struck. This part may project better if played with sticks, but it can also be played with the hands on the edge of the box. Wait for the large box to play before performing this part.

▲ **Medium Box**
Play the low notes in this part with one hand in the middle and play the high notes on the edge with the other hand. Accent the fourth note and the last note in each measure.

# Create Box Pieces

**Improvise** short rhythm parts for a new box ensemble. First work out each part. Then determine who will play each part. Practice the parts together as a group until everyone is satisfied with the result. Now **perform** the piece for the class.

## ON YOUR OWN

Listen to a variety of recordings and find music that works with "Box a-Rockin' Ensemble."

Share your recording with your classmates in a performance of the "Box a-Rockin' Ensemble."

## Music MAKERS

**BLUE MAN GROUP**

**Blue Man Group** is a creative multimedia performance group made up of bald and blue characters, originated by Chris Wink, Matt Goldman, and Phil Stanton. The group takes audiences through a multi-sensory experience that combines theatre, percussive music, art, video, science, and vaudeville. In the live show, a three-member back-up band also performs.

Behind their elaborate presentation is a unique musical style, characterized by instruments they created. The group uses PVC pipes as percussion instruments that are struck with foam rubber paddles. The length of the tube determines the pitch. One of the instruments, called a Drumbone, is a trombone-like percussion instrument. The large curvy tube is in two parts. While one Blue Man holds one end of the instrument and another plays the tube with mallets, the third blue man pulls the other end of the tube in and out to change the pitch. Another instrument is the Backpack Tubulum. It is used as both musical instrument

▲ Playing the drumbone

and rocket launcher! Blue Man Group also plays drums ranging in size from 6 inches to 6 feet in diameter. Every drum is tuned to a specific pitch to follow chord progressions in the compositional pieces. Blue Man Group regularly performs in New York, Boston, Chicago, and Las Vegas.

◄ Blue Man

**Listen** to this performance by Blue Man Group and **identify** the sound sources.

## Rods and Cones

**by Matt Goldman**

8-18   **as performed by Blue Man Group**

Blue Man Group recorded this piece in 1999 on their album *Audio*. Although the stage performance has only three back-up musicians, this recording has fourteen additional performers.

# 3

# Caribbean Congas

Drumming in West Africa and the Caribbean usually includes a combination of drums, bells, and rattles. Drum ensembles often sit in a circle so that the players can both see and hear each other.

Playing conga-type drums requires several hand positions. Practice the **open tone** and the **bass tone** techniques shown in the photos. Keep your hands relaxed and bounce off the drumhead as if it were a hot stove. The bass tone may feel like dribbling a basketball.

## Echo Drumming

**Play** this drum pattern by following a leader. Watch the leader's hands and **listen** to the tone of the leader's drum.

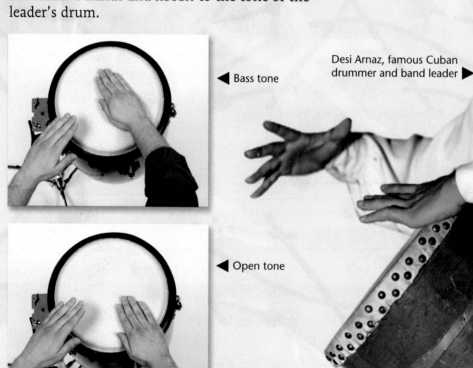

◄ Bass tone

◄ Open tone

Desi Arnaz, famous Cuban drummer and band leader ▶

Leader *(open tone)* *(bass tone)*

Class

---

**open tone** Called "high," is a high-pitched sound produced by playing with your fingers close to the rim of the drumhead.

**bass tone** Called "low," is a low-pitched sound produced by using a cupped hand in the center of the drumhead.

## Play the *Rumba*

The *rumba* is a dance that originated in Cuba in the seventeenth century. It is popular today throughout the Caribbean, and it is the foundation for contemporary *salsa* style.

Begin to learn the *rumba clave* part by saying this rhythm pattern as you tap the beat with your feet.

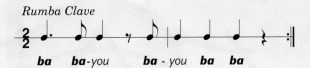

*Rumba Clave*

**ba    ba**-you    **ba** - you    **ba    ba**

Continue saying the rhythm aloud while you clap on the syllable *ba*. Transfer that rhythm to the claves, as shown in the ensemble below.

*Rumba* has two basic, easy-to-learn drum parts. Practice the low drum part, starting with three muffled bass tones. To play the muffled bass tones, relax your hands and let them fall on the drumhead. Alternate hands in the middle of the drum. Follow the three bass tones with one accented open tone.

**Play** the high drum part, beginning with two muffled bass tones. Use one hand for bass tones and the other hand for the open tones. Next add the rattle, playing a steady beat. Finally, add the stick part to complete the *rumba*.

## Cuban *Rumba* Ensemble

*Traditional*

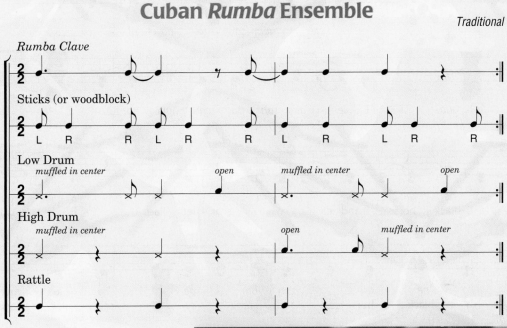

### Note This

In the 1960s Puerto Rican and other Hispanic Caribbean musicians in New York City developed a new style of music by combining elements of jazz, Cuban *son*, and Puerto Rican dance music. Fania Records, founded in 1964 by bandleader Johnny Pacheco, promoted the new style by calling it *salsa*, which means "sauce" in Spanish.

▲ Carlos "Patato" Valdez from the Conga Kings, a contemporary Cuban group.

**CD-ROM** Open *Band-in-a-Box* and find a *rumba*-style accompaniment. Set the accompaniment to play in a continuous loop and practice your percussion part with it.

## Rumba Elegua

This Cuban song is sung to Elegua, the guardian spirit of entrances, roads, and paths. It is often sung at the beginning and end of Cuban ceremonies. **Sing** *"Elegua"* and accompany the song with the *rumba* ensemble.

### Note This

The Yoruba people of Nigeria brought songs for Elegua with them to Cuba. Elements of the Yoruban language are still present in many Cuban songs.

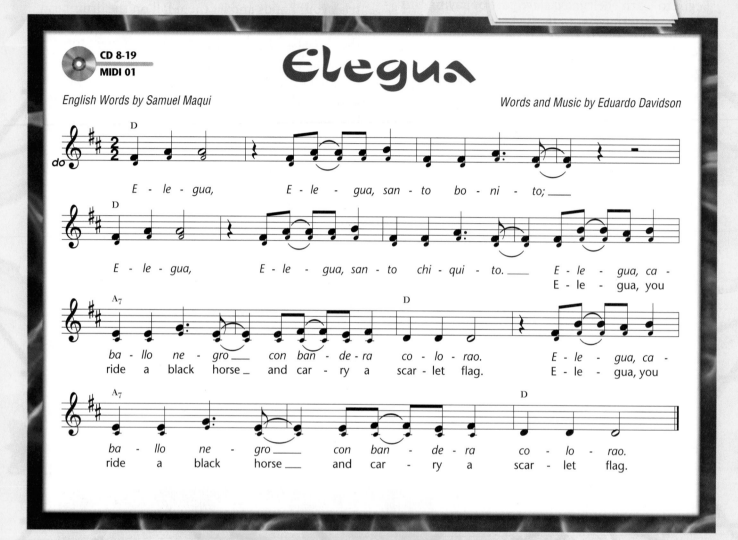

CD 8-19
MIDI 01

# Elegua

English Words by Samuel Maqui

Words and Music by Eduardo Davidson

E - le - gua, E - le - gua, san - to bo - ni - to; ___

E - le - gua, E - le - gua, san - to chi - qui - to. ___

E - le - gua, ca - ba - llo ne - gro ___ con ban - de - ra co - lo - rao.
E - le - gua, you ride a black horse ___ and car - ry a scar - let flag.

E - le - gua, ca - ba - llo ne - gro ___ con ban - de - ra co - lo - rao.
E - le - gua, you ride a black horse ___ and car - ry a scar - let flag.

◀ Giovanni Hidalgo from the Conga Kings, a contemporary Cuban group.

# Rockin' *Rumbas*

The Cuban *rumba* comes in three basic forms. *Yambú* [yahm-BOO], the slowest form, is what you just learned to play. *Guaguancó* [wah-wahn-KO] is a faster courting dance, and *columbia* [coh-LOOM-bee-ah] is an acrobatic dance.

**Listen** to the Conga Kings sing and play *Guaguancó pá las tumbadoras*. Notice how the three conga players respond to each other as they perform.

### *Guaguancó pá las tumbadoras*
**8-23**
**by Ray Santos**
**as performed by the Conga Kings**
The Conga Kings are Candido Camero, Giovanni Hidalgo, and Carlos Valdez.

## Note This

Candido Camero, one of the most famous conga players in Cuba, began his career playing guitar, bass, and mandolin. He later moved from Cuba to New York City.

# Shake It!

**Play** the *rumba* ensemble to accompany the Puerto Rican song *"Cheki, morena"* ("Shake It!"), which is printed on page I-16 in the Performance Anthology.

# Do the Mambo

The *mambo* is another popular Cuban dance that has become the driving force behind much of contemporary *salsa*.

**Listen** to *¡Cubanismo!* play *Mambo UK*. **Describe** how the *mambo* is similar to and different from the *rumba*.

### *Mambo UK*
**8-24**
**by Jesús Alemañy**
**as performed by *¡Cubanismo!***
The leader of *¡Cubanismo!* is trumpet player and composer Jesús Alemañy. The group is known for their "get up and dance now" performances of traditional Cuban dance music.

**Take It to the Net** Go to *www.sfsuccessnet.com* and read "Music of Cuba" to learn more about Cuba's musical history and culture.

▼ ¡Cubanismo!

# 4

# Sounds of South Africa

Traditional music of South Africa is rich with the culture and languages of its many tribes. Bells, rattles, xylophones, and drums are a part of everyday life. Music entertains, celebrates, and teaches. The Bantu word *ngoma* [ng-GOH-mah], is a generic term for "drum" in South Africa. The Zulu hide drum is played in many regions.

**Listen** to "*Nampaya omame.*" **Identify** the instruments in the accompaniment. Then **sing** the song with the recording.

◀ Zulu hide drum

**CD 8-25**

# Nampaya omame

## (There Come Our Mothers)

*Traditional Song from South Africa*
*Arranged by J. Shabalala*

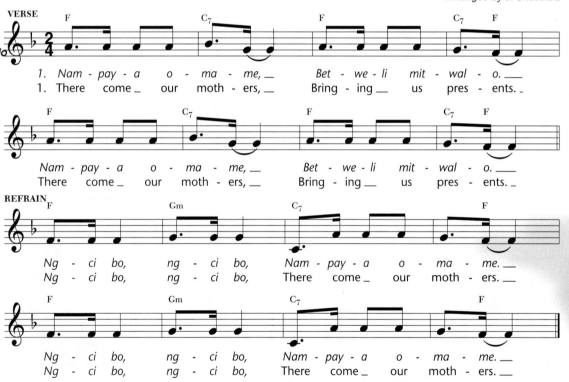

**VERSE**

1. Nam - pay - a  o - ma - me, ___  Bet - we - li  mit - wal - o. ___
1. There come _  our  moth - ers, __  Bring - ing _  us  pres - ents. _

Nam - pay - a  o - ma - me, ___  Bet - we - li  mit - wal - o. ___
There come _  our  moth - ers, __  Bring - ing _  us  pres - ents. _

**REFRAIN**

Ng - ci bo,  ng - ci bo,  Nam - pay - a  o - ma - me. ___
Ng - ci bo,  ng - ci bo,  There come _  our  moth - ers. ___

Ng - ci bo,  ng - ci bo,  Nam - pay - a  o - ma - me. ___
Ng - ci bo,  ng - ci bo,  There come _  our  moth - ers. ___

2. *Sabona ngoswidi*
   *Sabona nama keke.* (Repeat)
   Refrain

2. We can see sweeties,
   We can see cookies.  (Repeat)
   *Refrain*

3. *Sabona ngobanana,*
   *Sabona ngama-apul.* (Repeat)
   Refrain

3. We can see bananas,
   We can see apples.  (Repeat)
   *Refrain*

## South African-Style Ensemble

**Play** this South African-style ensemble to accompany "*Nampaya omame.*" The *shekere* [SHEH-keh-reh] rattle is played between the thigh and the palm of the free hand. Hold the rattle in your dominant hand and strike it on the thigh of the opposite leg to play low notes. For high notes, place your free hand above the thigh with your palm down. Lift the rattle to strike the palm of your free hand. **Play** the *shekere* part.

Now practice the medium drum part. Notice that the bass tone falls on every beat. Add the open tone after the second beat.

The low drum plays the bass tones on the first two beats, followed by two beats of silence. Practice the low drum bass tones and add the open tones. **Play** the low drum part with the medium drum.

Next **play** the high drum part. Notice that the sixteenth notes sound during the silences of the low drum part. The low and high drum parts fit together like puzzle pieces. **Play** the three drum parts together and add the *shekere*/rattle part.

Learn to play the double bell part by vocalizing the pitches in rhythm as you practice it on your forearm. Finally, layer all of the parts and **perform** the ensemble with "*Nampaya omame.*"

▲ Zulu drums at festival

◀ *ngoma*

### Note This

There is a traditional Zulu saying that "singing makes all the sad people happy because it is the voice of happiness."

## South African Ensemble

*Music in the Style of South Africa*

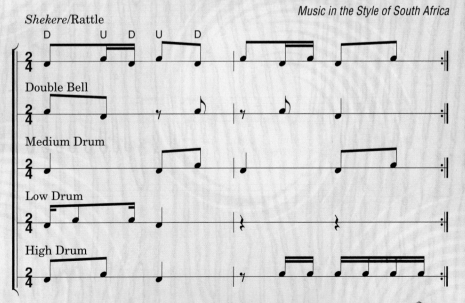

# 5

# West African HIGHLIFE

People all over the world love to dance, and new types of dance music are emerging all the time. In Ghana's capital city of Accra, the Ga people created a type of dance music called *highlife*. Highlife, which had an influence on *Afro-pop* or *juju*, grew out of traditional Ghanaian music and was influenced by jazz and the music of Cuba. Sometimes it is played on traditional drums and other acoustic instruments, but it is also played on synthesizers and electronically amplified instruments such as guitars and basses.

**Sing** the Ghanaian-style song "Friends Today."

### Note This

Originally created in Ghana and on the Ivory Coast, *adinkra* symbols are figures that may represent a range of subjects, from animals to philosophy. They are often printed on fabric.

▲ Many *kpanlogo* drums feature *adinkra* symbols carved on the side.

CD 8-29

## Friends Today

New Words by Will Schmid

Folk Melody from Ghana

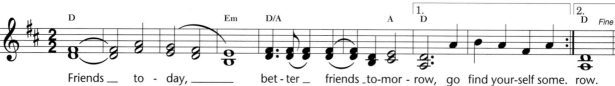

Friends __ to - day, _____ bet - ter _ friends _to-mor - row, go find your-self some. row.

If you want to make _ a friend, __ go and find some - one. ___

Lend a help - ing _ hand _ to them to - day. If you day, go find your-self some.

*Kpanlogo* [pahn-LO-go] was a type of youth music of the 1960s that has become a part of highlife. Practice each part of the "*Kpanlogo* Highlife Ensemble." The time line for this style is played on the bell.

The *axatse* [ahks-AHT-see] part is played between the leg and an upper hand. Some highlife music features the *axatse* part going twice as fast.

The *kpanlogo* (medium) drum is carved from the trunk of one tree. The drumhead is often made of antelope skin. **Play** the three open tones followed by the fingertip muted tones in the center of the drumhead. Say the syllables as you play.

**Perform** "*Kpanlogo* Highlife Ensemble" to accompany "Friends Today."

▲ Man printing an *adinkra* cloth

**Arts Connection**

▲ *Sankofa* is one of the best-known *adinkra* symbols from Ghana and the Ivory Coast. It pictures a mythological bird and represents this saying: "It is no taboo to return and fetch it when you forget. You can always undo your mistakes."

## *Kpanlogo* Highlife Ensemble

*Traditional Music of Ghana*

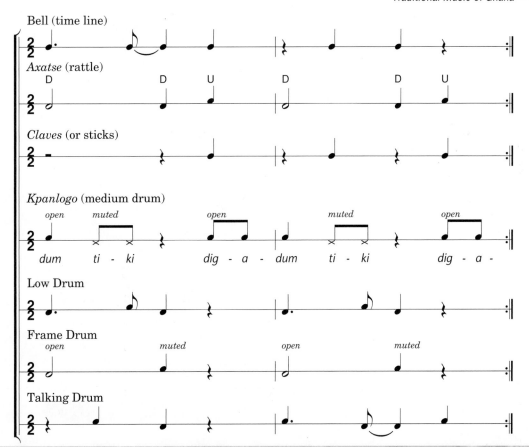

## Highlife Flute

Ghanaians also play a recorder-like flute made of bamboo covered with leather. **Play** the melody of "Friends Today" on a soprano recorder or flute.

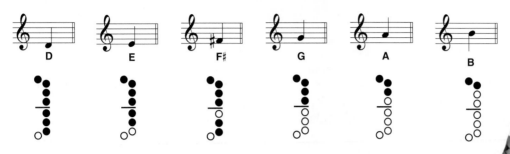

D  E  F♯  G  A  B

## A Highlife Awakening

**Listen** to Osei Tutu perform *Awakening*, a highlife piece from Ghana. Is the rattle playing faster or slower than the other parts?

### Awakening

**by Osei Tutu**

8-31  Osei Tutu is named after a great king who was the leader of the Asante people of Ghana in the late 1600s and early 1700s. This recording features the typical West African call-and-response alternation between a soloist and chorus.

**Take It to the Net** Go to *www.sfsuccessnet.com* and read "West African Drumming and Vocal Styles" for more information about West African music and instruments.

## Dancing Highlife

**Listen** to Angélique Kidjo sing *Tumba*, a highlife-style song for dancing. **Identify** the rattle part.

### Tumba

**by Angélique Kidjo and C. Brown**

8-32  as performed by Angélique Kidjo and ensemble
The word *tumba* means "conga drum" in Beninese.

◄ Ghanaian flute

Court drummers of the Timi of Ede. By varying the tension of the drumhead, the drummers can alter the pitch of the heads to reproduce the tonal structure of spoken Yoruba. ▼

MUSIC IS NOT ONLY EMOTION AND GROOVE. IT'S SOMETHING THAT SPEAKS FOR A CULTURE AND ITS PEOPLE.

—Angélique Kidjo

# Music MAKERS
# Angélique Kidjo

**Angélique Kidjo** (born 1960) is originally from Benin, a country near Ghana in West Africa. She now divides her time between Paris, France, and Brooklyn, New York. In her home village of Ouidah, she grew up surrounded by both Beninese and Portuguese-speaking Brazilian kids. This multicultural mix later encouraged her to cross musical boundaries in her own music. In 1996, while touring in Bahia, Brazil, with Malian guitarist, Ali Farka Touré, she rediscovered the richness of the Africa-Brazil connection and followed that path on her album *Black Ivory Soul.*

## Play More Highlife

**Play** the "*Kpanlogo* Highlife Ensemble" along with the song "Ev'rybody Loves Saturday Night," which is printed on page I-24.

## Checkpoint

Demonstrate drum-playing techniques, including the proper hand positions. **Play** patterns from the "*Kpanlogo* Highlife Ensemble," demonstrating correct technique and accurate rhythm.

- Conga drum open and bass tones—play the low drum or *kpanlogo* part.
- Rattle—play the *axatse* part as written or at double speed.
- Single bell—play the bell part.
- Frame drum open and muted tones—play the frame drum part.
- Talking drum stick technique—play the talking drum part.

# 6

# KUMI-DAIKO

One of the most exciting styles of drumming is *taiko*. Although Japanese *taiko* drums have a very long history, *taiko* drum groups only began in the 1950s. Today there are more than 5,000 *kumi-daiko* (drum ensembles) in Japan and more than 150 in North America. The choreographed performances feature movement and music that is powerful, exciting, and wild to watch!

**Listen** to the group *Kodo* perform *Nanafushi*. How many different drums do you hear? **Identify** the meter of this composition.

◀ *Odaiko* drums are often played by more than one person.

### Nanafushi

by Tetsuro Naito
9-1    as performed by *Kodo*
The word *kodo* can mean both "heartbeat" and "children of the drum."

## Music MAKERS KODO

**Kodo** is probably the best-known *taiko* group in the world. In 1971 about a dozen young people who were dissatisfied with Japanese life in the city moved to the small island of Sado to devote themselves to *taiko* drumming. In 1981 several of these people formed the group *Kodo*.

Today, Kodo members live and train communally in the Kodo Village. One-third of their year they spend practicing, another third they spend touring Japan, and during the remainder of the year they tour internationally.

**Video Library** Watch the episode *Kodo–Japan* to see and hear *Kodo* perform live.

## Home-Grown *Taiko*

The instruments used in *kumi-daiko* performances are built by hand and take a long time to make. For instance, the *odaiko*, which means "big drum," is carved from a single huge log. Many groups use old wine barrels that have been specially sealed, strengthened, and refinished.

Plastic pails and buckets can be used as substitutes for various *taiko* drums. Cleaned 20-gallon plastic garbage cans can be turned over and struck with wrapped mallets. For higher-sounding *taikos*, use 5-gallon plastic pails turned over and hit with dowel rods or snare drumsticks.

## Your Turn to *Taiko*

**Perform** the "Bucket O'Taiko Ensemble." Have everyone tap the beat with one foot. **Play** the shaker part and 5-gallon bucket part of section **A** first. Then add the cymbal and 20-gallon bucket part. Repeat the process for the **B** section. **Practice** going from the **A** section to the **B** section without stopping. Then practice playing the piece in **A A A A B B** form. Finally, **play** the coda to end the piece. Perform the entire ensemble, ending with a loud *hah!*

### ON YOUR OWN

Create your own patterns to replace either the **A** or **B** sections of "Bucket O'Taiko Ensemble." Add interest by using more stick clicks and other physical movements. Add various-sized plastic buckets on solo parts. Arrange a longer composition by adding additional sections to change the form, for example **A B A** *Coda* **A B A** .

### PRO TIPS

When playing barrel drums without stands, professional players often put one foot under the bottom of the drum to help make the pitch of the drum more audible. Place the side of your foot under the bottom of the pails and buckets when playing to improve their sound quality.

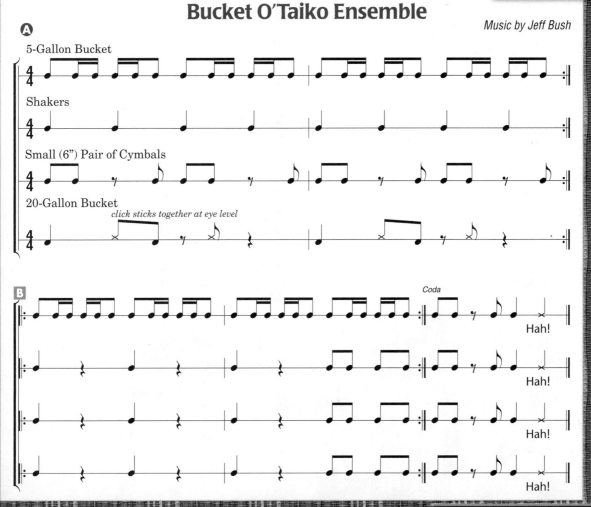

## Bucket O'Taiko Ensemble

*Music by Jeff Bush*

**A**

5-Gallon Bucket

Shakers

Small (6") Pair of Cymbals

20-Gallon Bucket
*click sticks together at eye level*

**B**

*Coda*

Hah!

Hah!

Hah!

Hah!

# 7

# CARIBBEAN SOUNDS

The music of the Caribbean is a lively and historical mix of the sounds of West Africa, Europe, and the islands. Because the Caribbean Islands are close together, these communities share many of the same styles, dances, and musical instruments. **Listen** to the rhythm of the *clave* in *"Panamam tombé."* This music, originally from Haiti, has rhythms and sounds that are typically found in Caribbean music.

CD 9-2
MIDI 02

# PANAMAM TOMBÉ

*Calypso Song*

◄ Members of the Papaloko Band performing during a Haitian Carnival celebration at the Tap Tap restaurant.

## Flavor of the Islands

In order to learn to play the *clave* rhythm for *"Panamam tombé,"* practice this pattern. Clap loudly on the accented notes and lightly tap the unaccented notes. Begin at a slow tempo, and then gradually get faster. You will begin to hear the *clave* rhythm on the accented notes.

Practice Clap

When you can accurately perform the rhythm with accents, leave out the unaccented notes. Now you are clapping the *clave* part! **Play** this rhythm with the song.

Clave

Haitian women returning from the market ▼

Now prepare to play this ensemble to accompany *"Panamam tombé."* **Play** the repeated rhythm of the maracas part. Use two maracas, one high and one low. Place the low maraca in your dominant hand and the high maraca in your other hand. Layer this part over the *clave* part.

In the low drum part, your non-dominant hand will play a bass tone on each beat. Hold a stick in your dominant hand, and add the stick rhythm by striking the rim of the drum. This stick technique is used by various percussion ensembles in Haiti. Prepare the high drum part by saying *boom* for the low bass tone and *dig-a* for the higher open tones. Practice the gesture on your knees as you say the syllables. Play the *guiro*, using a slow down stroke, followed by a quick up-stroke. Layer all of the parts and **perform** the ensemble with *"Panamam tombé."*

## Caribbean Island Ensemble

*Music by Anne Fennell*

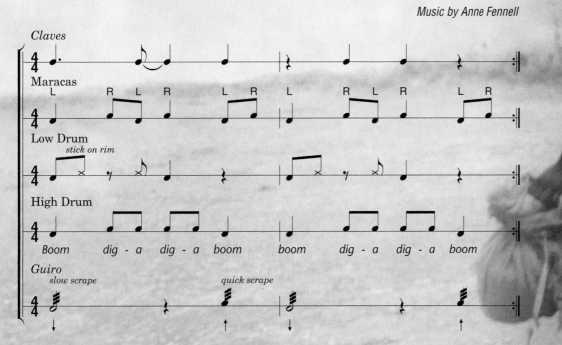

# 8

# Calypso Heat

Calypso is one of the many types of Caribbean music that has been influenced by a combination of African and European traditions. Although it began in Trinidad, you can now hear calypso throughout the Caribbean and around the world. The lyrics of calypso songs deal with matters of interest to the people, typically political or social issues. Today's calypso music combines many different African and Latin rhythms and is performed with the addition of brass and electronic instruments.

Every year, from New Year's until *Carnaval,* calypso music is performed in auditoriums and large tents all over Port-of-Spain, the capital of Trinidad and Tobago. Calypso artists perform their latest songs in front of appreciative audiences. These events can last several hours and usually include special late-night appearances from favorite calypso singers of the past. Radio stations play the best new calypso recordings almost non-stop so that when *Carnaval* finally arrives, everyone in Trinidad and Tobago knows all of the best songs. In a competition just before *Carnaval* begins, the songs are performed live for a huge audience and a "Calypso Monarch" is chosen for that year.

**Listen** carefully to the lyrics of the calypso song *Jump for Joy* and follow the story told by the singer, Superblue, whose real name is Austin Lyons. He is one of Trindad's most famous calypso performers. His songs have won many awards.

▲ Superblue

## Jump for Joy

**by Superblue**

9-4 This calypso song celebrates the anniversary of the steel band festival known as *Panorama.* (Another name for steel drums is "pans.")

▲ The steel drum band Exodus

## Play Calypso

**Play** the "Carnaval Calypso Ensemble." Begin with the cowbell part and then add the congas. When you can play the cowbell and conga parts comfortably, add the maracas and *guiro*. Finally, add the bongos and triangle parts. You may find it useful to tap your foot on beats one and three if you are playing the triangle part.

## Carnaval Calypso Ensemble

*Music by Jeff Bush*

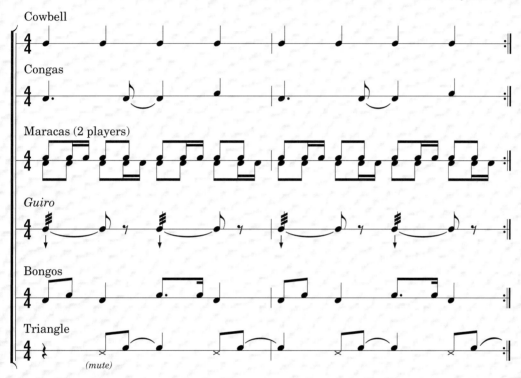

▲ Member of Exodus

## Sing Calypso

Sing the songs "Feliz Navidad," printed on page I-28 and "Pay Me My Money Down," printed on page I-46. Then **play** the "Carnaval Calypso Ensemble" to accompany the song.

### ON YOUR OWN

Listen to the recording of "Pay Me My Money Down." Pay particular attention to the words. Then choose a theme and write song lyrics based on that theme. Make your lyrics fit the melody of "Pay Me My Money Down." Your new song is called a parody. Perform your new lyrics along with the stereo performance track.

◄ Member of Exodus

# 9

# BAMBOO BAND

Wherever bamboo grows in the world, it is used to make musical instruments. Many years ago in Trinidad, players began using bamboo tubes of varying lengths and diameters for drumming. They formed groups called *tamboo bamboo* bands. Players would pound large bamboo tubes, called "basses" or "booms," on the ground, and strike smaller bamboo pieces, called "cutters," "fullers," and "chandlers," with a stick.

Another popular homemade instrument in Trinidad is the bottle-and-spoon. A glass bottle is partially filled with water and played with a metal spoon, creating a bright sound. Sometimes it is used in conjunction with *tamboo bamboo* bands.

**Listen** to *Fire Brigade Water the Road.* How many different bamboo pitches can you hear? **Identify** the other instruments in this recording.

### Fire Brigade Water the Road
**by Vasco de Freitas**
**9-5  as performed by Vasco de Freitas and the Tamboo Bamboo**

This is a protest song. The fire brigades, a powerful symbol of colonial authority, often used their hoses to spray disruptive groups.

## Play *Tamboo Bamboo*

Use homemade *tamboo bamboo* instruments and **play** the "Boomin' Bamboo Ensemble."

## Boomin' Bamboo Ensemble

*Music by Jeff Bush*

Cutters (12" PVC Tube)

Fullers (24" PVC Tube)

Low Bass Boom (6' PVC Tube)

High Tenor Boom (3' PVC Tube)

High Bass Boom (5' PVC Tube)

Low Tenor Boom (4' PVC Tube)

Bottle-and-Spoon

## Homemade *Tamboo Bamboo*

Build your own *tamboo bamboo* instruments out of PVC tubing, which is readily available in plumbing supply stores. The large booms can be various lengths of 4-inch diameter tubing. The smaller cutters and fullers can be shorter lengths of 2-inch diameter tubing.

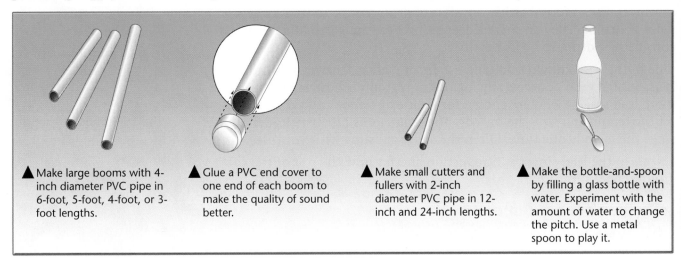

▲ Make large booms with 4-inch diameter PVC pipe in 6-foot, 5-foot, 4-foot, or 3-foot lengths.

▲ Glue a PVC end cover to one end of each boom to make the quality of sound better.

▲ Make small cutters and fullers with 2-inch diameter PVC pipe in 12-inch and 24-inch lengths.

▲ Make the bottle-and-spoon by filling a glass bottle with water. Experiment with the amount of water to change the pitch. Use a metal spoon to play it.

## Steel Drums

*Tamboo bamboo* bands gradually added instruments made of metal containers such as garbage cans and lids, old oil drums, cookie tins, and paint cans. Sometime in the late 1930s musicians discovered that dents in metal cans often had a definite pitch. After much experimentation, people learned how to tune the bottoms of old oil drums. These instruments developed into the steel drums of today.

**Listen** to this solo steel drum performance by Liam Teague. **Identify** and **describe** the musical elements that he manipulates to accomplish the sound of raindrops.

### Raindrops

**by Liam Teague**

9-6    Liam Teague plays a lead "pan" that has approximately 28 pitches.

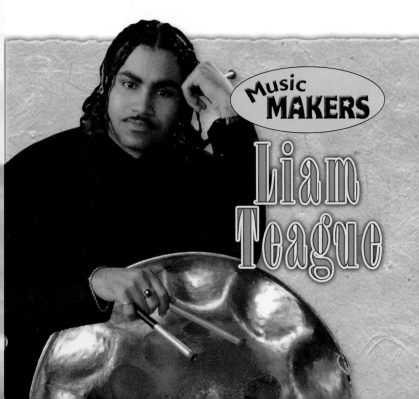

## Music MAKERS
## Liam Teague

**A**fter winning many awards in Trinidad, **Liam Teague** (born 1975) came to the United States to study music in the 1990s. Since that time, Teague has completed a bachelor's and master's degree and has continued to improve his impressive skills on the steel drum. Teague has performed for royalty and has appeared as soloist for the M.C. Hammer tour of Trinidad. Besides recording several albums, he has also played with orchestras, jazz groups, steel bands, and as a soloist in the United States, Italy, France, Germany, the Czech Republic, Taiwan, Korea, Canada, Panama, Barbados, and Jamaica. When he is not touring, Teague teaches at Northern Illinois University.

# 10

# Heartbeat OF THE Earth

The First Nation people of North America have been using drums for centuries. Each group has its own style of drumming and uses its own types of drums. They all share a deep respect for the Earth and most consider the drum to be its heartbeat.

One of the best-known traditional styles of Native American drumming is associated with powwow singing. A drum group is headed by one or more lead singers who are chosen for their experience and skills. They set the tempo and sing the melody. The group joins after the leader sings the melody one time. Often the songs are sung with **vocables.**

**Listen** to the lead singer's introduction and for how the rest of the group echoes him.

### Men's Fancy Dance

9-7
**by Irvin Waskewitch**
**as performed by the Red Bull Singers**
The Red Bull Singers are a world champion drum group. They sing in a northern plains powwow style that is associated with the Cree nation.

## Innu Music today

While keeping traditional music alive, many First Nation musicians also enjoy and perform popular music styles. **Listen** to *Akua Tuta*, an example of contemporary First Nation music. **Identify** the various musical styles that influence the music.

### Akua Tuta

9-8
**by Florent Vallant, Claude McKenzie, and Eric Poirier**
**as performed by Kashtin**
Kashtin members are from the Innu Nation in northern Quebec, Canada. They sing in the Innu language, which is spoken by approximately 12,000 people. Their music is a mixture of traditional, rock, folk, country, and Cajun styles.

**vocables** Syllables such as *hey, ya,* or *loi* that do not have a direct translation but nonetheless have meaning in the culture.

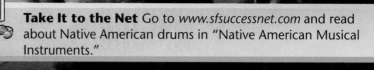

**Take It to the Net** Go to *www.sfsuccessnet.com* and read about Native American drums in "Native American Musical Instruments."

▲ George Saddleback from Samson Cree Nation sings a ceremonial song.

# First Nation Trio

**Listen** to *Ulali* perform *Mahk jchi*. **Compare** this selection to the other listening examples in this lesson. **Classify** the musical style(s) performed in this song.

### *Mahk jchi*

**by** *Ulali*

**9-9** In this song *Ulali* sings in unison, in harmony, and in canon.

## *Arts* Connection

Navajo rugs are entirely handwoven using wool on an upright loom. The maker's choice of color, objects, and patterns is a personal statement.

## Music MAKERS

# ULALI

Pura Fé (Tuscarora), Soni Moreno (Mayan, Apache, Yaqui), and Jennifer Kreisberg (Tuscarora) formed this *a cappella* (plus drums and rattles) trio in 1987. These women have created a unique sound by combining their First Nation musical roots with a variety of contemporary popular styles. Their unusual vocal harmonies and dynamic performance presence have made them popular with audiences and fellow musicians around the world. *Ulali* has become the model for the formation of many other First Nation women's groups. They have performed with a long list of musicians, including the Indigo Girls, Sting, Bonnie Raitt, and Buffy Saint Marie.

## On Your Own

Musicians sometimes use other works of art as inspiration. Create a composition based on patterns found in Native American art. For example, create a rhythmic pattern for each section of a Navajo weaving. Organize your composition by playing the patterns in the order they appear in the weaving. Teach your composition to other students and perform it in class.

## Note This

In ancient times, a Tuscarora woman with a beautiful voice was called *ulali*.

# 11

# Clang, Ding, Gong, Ring, Chime!

Metal can produce sounds that sing, sustain, and carry above other sounds. Metal objects can also produce different pitches, determined by their weight and size. This enables them to play melodies.

Find an old bell, a metal cabinet, a large can, legs of a chair, or maybe a desk. The metal around you can become musical instruments! **Listen** to the sounds as you tap each object with different beaters or mallets. If you choose sticks, pencils, rulers, twigs, chopsticks, dowels, or PVC pipe as mallets, how does it change the dynamics and timbre when you strike a metal object?

Clap the rhythm for each part in the "Mainly Metal Ensemble." Vocalize the high and low pitches when you practice each part. Say the syllables under the notes, and then **play** each part on a found object or standard metal instrument. Find ways to play higher and lower pitches.

Cameroon Agogo Bells ▲

## Mainly Metal Ensemble

*Music by Anne Fennell*

## Musical Metallurgy

**Arrange** the "Mainly Metal Ensemble" for a group of four players. Choose the type of metal instrument to use for each part and plan when each should enter and exit. Decide where to play loud and soft dynamics and where to perform *crescendos* or *decrescendos*. Complete the form for your arrangement by adding an introduction, *coda*, or an improvised solo section. **Notate** your score on paper, and **perform** your arrangement for the class.

## Bells from Benin

**Listen** to this bell ensemble, which opens a Circle Dance from Benin. **Identify** the instruments and the number of layers you hear. Clap the repeated rhythms you hear and determine when each bell part enters. **Play** this piece by imitating the rhythms you hear on the recording.

### *Gahu*

**Circle Dance from Benin**

9-10    *Gahu* is now also performed in Nigeria and by the Ewe people of Ghana.

## Musical Metal Tines

The *mbira,* found in many countries of Africa, has metal tongues or tines attached to the surface of a hollow resonator box of wood or a gourd. The metal tines are plucked by the thumb and sometimes the fingers. Often metal beads or bottle caps are attached to the resonator box to produce a buzzing sound.

**Listen** to *Katura.* **Describe** how interlocking melodies and rhythms are created when *mbiras* play repeating melodies.

### *Katura*

**by Ephat Mujuru and Dumisani Maraire**

9-11    The opening solo, played by a single *mbira,* is the repeated melody.

▲ Matepe *mbira* from Zimbabwe

▲ *Frikyiwa* from Ghana

▲ *Atoke* bell from Ghana

▲ *Gankogui* double bell from Ghana

# Metal Melodies

Some metal instruments have definite pitches that can be used to play melodies. **Listen** to the opening line of *Return to Misty Mountain*.

## Return to Misty Mountain

**by Richard Cooke and Michael Caporale**

**9-12**  The opening melody of this improvisation is played on the Moonlight Cyls, invented by Richard Cooke, designer and inventor of unique percussion instruments.

**Play** the opening **motive** of *Return to Misty Mountain* on a melodic metal instrument such as a vibraphone. Use this motive to begin your own improvisation.

**motive** A rhythmic or melodic fragment that can serve as the basic element from which a more complex musical structure can be created.

Richard Cooke playing the Moonlight Cyls ▶

## *Arts* Connection

*Sun Seeks Shadow*, a mixed media sculpture by Edwin White ▶

## Art–Music Connection

Study the large shapes and overlapping smaller shapes of the sculpture *Sun Seeks Shadow* by Edwin White. Notice the repetition in pattern and line. How might you relate this to repeating rhythm patterns and dynamics in music?

**Create** a composition using the sculpture as your guide. Study the metal sculpture as a musical map. The circle, diamond, and triangle shapes can represent rhythm or beat patterns. What could the rivets and the twelve bent metal tines represent?

Begin with the center cloverleaf pattern, which represents leaves, and **play** four quarter notes on a low metal instrument.

Choose another metal instrument to play a rhythm that represents the diamond shapes. Perhaps the four corners and sides of the diamond shapes can be represented by rhythm patterns that have multiples of four.

How do the size of the sculpture and its various parts relate to dynamics? **Create** a diagram or a score that identifies the shapes and sizes associated with your composed rhythms and dynamics. **Perform** your composition. Layer your ensemble, one rhythm pattern at a time, and have a conductor point to the area or shape in the sculpture that represents the music to be played.

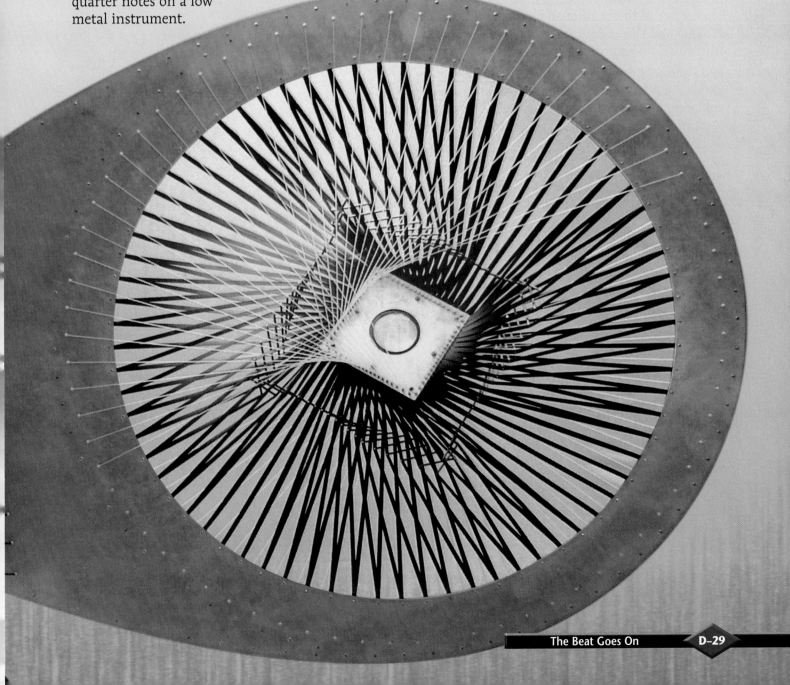

# 12

# Doumbek Drumming

In North Africa, the Middle East, and parts of southeastern Europe, people play goblet-shaped drums called by a variety of names such as *doumbek, tonbak, darabuka,* or *tarambuka. Doumbek* drums are popular in Arab, Turkish, Armenian, Persian, and Balkan music. The center of the drumhead produces a deep bass tone (*doum*) and the edge yields a high sharp tone (*bek*)—thus the name doumbek.

Read about the *doumbek* playing techniques on page D-31. Then **listen** to *Spaceville,* which features the *doumbek.* **Identify** by name any of the techniques you recognize.

### *Spaceville*

**9-13** **written and performed by Mick Rossi and Steve Holloway**
This selection also features the *bodhrán,* an Irish wood-frame drum.

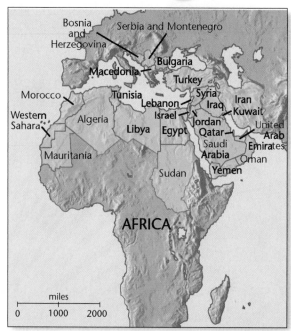

▲ Arab Musicians

▲ *Darabuka* player

Note This

Arab rhythmic patterns are called *iqa*. When performers improvise at the beginning of a piece, it is called *taqsim*.

▲ *Doumbek*

## *Doumbek* Technique

Play the *doumbek* sitting down. Hold the drum horizontally across your lap with the open end extending behind you. This will feel natural and give you the best sound.

Play with a relaxed motion. Strike the drumhead in different areas to get a variety of sounds. Play *rest strokes* by leaving your hand on the drumhead after striking it, and play *free strokes* by letting your hand bounce back up after striking the drumhead. Here are a few traditional Arab drum strokes.

- *dum*—[doom] a deep, resonant sound, played with your dominant hand by striking the center of the drumhead with a strong free stroke.
- *tak*—[tawk] a high, sharp sound, played by the dominant hand striking the drum on the edge of the drumhead. It will have the characteristic tones of the drum shell as well as the skin.

- *ka*—[kah] higher than *dum* and without the drum shell sound of the *tak*. It is played with the non-dominant hand by striking the skin just inside the rim. Many players consider it an "in-between" stroke.
- *ruff*—three fingers (ring, middle, and index) of either hand strike the drum in rapid succession.

**Play** these patterns using the strokes described above. Repeat the patterns until you can do them by feel rather than by reading them. Take turns with your classmates and **improvise** your own drum rhythm while the others play the basic pattern. **Notate** the patterns using standard notation.

## Doumbek or Hand Drum

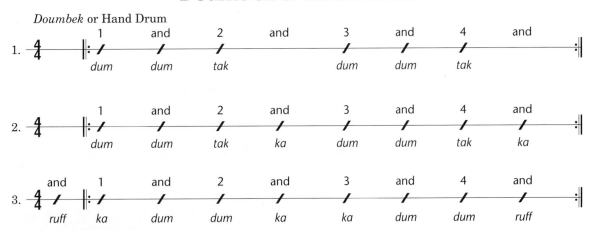

# 13

# MARIMBA MAGIC

African mallet instruments consist of hardwood bars set above resonator tubes. They are arranged in scales and struck with rubber-tipped mallets. African marimbas are named according to their range, from bass to soprano. Numerous players in an ensemble play the entire range together. They play interlocking melodies that complement each other.

**Listen** to the recording of *Nyoka*. **Identify** the four different voices of the marimbas and notice when each part enters. Clap the *hosho*, or rattle, part as you listen.

### Nyoka

**9-14**
by Walt Hampton
as performed by students from Marcus Whitman Elementary School, Richland, Washington

*Nyoka* is a Zimbabwe-style piece arranged for four marimbas.

## Harvest Melodies

Marimbas are members of the xylophone family. The modern xylophone is similar in structure to the marimba but its bars are much thinner and its range is much higher.

**Listen** to the melodies from the Bawa Harvest Festival of Ghana. **Describe** the timbre of the xylophones. **Compare** this piece to *Nyoka*.

### Bawa

**9-15**
Harvest Dance of the Dargati of Ghana as performed by Sowah Mensah, Marc Anderson, and Bernard Woma

The xylophones on this recording are called *gyils*.

## Note This

The *hosho*, or rattle, is the time keeper of the marimba ensemble. It is made of a dried gourd from the *maranka* plant. The *hosho* is filled with dried *hota* seeds or small pebbles.

◀ *hosho*

Xylophone from Ghana ▼

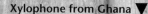

 **Video Library** View the video episode *Marimba Ensemble–Zimbabwe* to observe a marimba performance.

## Aural Tradition

In many cultures of the world, including Zimbabwe, traditional music is learned by ear. It is passed from generation to generation through listening, observation, and imitation. **Listen** to *Nyoka* again. **Sing** the melody played by the first marimba, using a neutral syllable such as *la*. Now **play** the parts of the melody you remember on a xylophone. Begin on C, one octave above middle C.

Learn to **play** each part of "*Nyoka*" on xylophones in traditional aural fashion. Refer to the printed notation only if necessary. Then add the *hosho* part and **perform** "*Nyoka*."

Bernard Woma, master of the Ghanaian xylophone ▶

## PRO TIPS

In the last two measures of *"Nyoka"* the xylophone 3 part has three notes that are played in the space of two beats. To practice this rhythm, have a friend clap one of the counting patterns below while you clap the other. Accent the beats that are bold.

Part 1    **1**-2-3-**4**-5-6

Part 2    **1**-2-**3**-4-**5**-6

## Nyoka

*Music by Walt Hampton*

# Review and Assess

Throughout The Beat Goes On, you have

- Listened to drumming ensembles from all over the world.

- Learned to play some representative examples of several important drumming traditions.

Your performance during this module has focused on ensemble playing. Ensemble playing is an important part of making music. It requires you not only to play your own part well, but also to listen and play together with other members of the ensemble to produce an effective performance.

## Review What You Learned

Review what you have studied and practiced. Consult with your teacher and select drumming pieces that allow you to demonstrate excellent musicianship. Selecting the right music to perform is an important part of becoming a successful musician.

Not everyone will be able to play all of the parts in every ensemble piece. Some

require different skills than others. What is most important is that you perform accurately, musically, and beautifully.

For this assessment you will form percussion ensembles to rehearse and perform for your class and for other audiences. Select an ensemble piece to perform from the following list.

| Ensemble | Number of parts | Instrumentation/Origin/Style |
|---|---|---|
| "Hambone Ensemble" | 4 | body percussion |
| "Box A-Rockin' Ensemble" | 4 | found instruments |
| "*Rumba* Ensemble" | 5 | Caribbean drumming |
| "South African Ensemble" | 5 | South Africa |
| "*Kpanlogo* Highlife Ensemble" | 7 | highlife |
| "Bucket O'Taiko Ensemble" | 4 | Japanese drumming |
| "Caribbean Island Ensemble" | 5 | Caribbean drumming |
| "Carnaval Calypso Ensemble" | 6 | calypso |
| "Boomin' Bamboo Ensemble" | 7 | Caribbean drumming |
| "Mainly Metal Ensemble" | 4 | found instruments |
| "*Nyoka*" | 4 | keyboard percussion instruments |

## Show What You Know

With the help of your teacher, select several pieces to perform in which you can do at least two of the following well.

- Conduct the ensemble, providing clear starting and stopping cues, a clear, steady pulse throughout, and cues for changing dynamics.
- **Play** a single-instrument part that defines the pulse of the music.
- **Play** a part with multiple sounds that remains steady throughout the piece.
- **Play** an improvised solo percussion part along with a small ensemble recording.
- **Play** a mallet instrument part.

In choosing the pieces to perform, your goal is to show all of the qualities of good musicianship. You want performances of which you can be proud; and not just something that is hard to do. The goal for this assessment is quality, not difficulty.

## Share What You Know

Select one of the recorded pieces from the module that is your personal favorite. Prepare a presentation for a class of younger children or your peers that will help them understand the music and why you like it. You may use poster board, overhead transparencies, or slides made with presentation software. Your presentation should include basic facts about the piece—title, composer or arranger (if known), the approximate time of its composition, the instruments used—and explanations of how the music plays a part in the culture of the society from which it comes. Also, be sure to include four aspects of music description that you will use this year: the actual sounds that make up the music (timbre); the organization of the sounds (rhythm, pitch, dynamics); the emotional effects that the sounds elicit from the listener; the cultural function of the music. In your presentation, you should play excerpts from the piece to illustrate your points. Some of these may be from recordings while others may be live performances.

## What to Look and Listen For

Excellent musicians often record themselves so they can evaluate their own work and refine their performances. You may wish to record your performances using digital audio, cassette tape, or video tape.

Ask yourself whether all these things are true about your performance. Use this checklist to see how you're doing and to identify aspects of your playing and singing that are in need of further refinement.

### Drumming

- Posture is upright and relaxed.
- Sticks (when used) are held loosely and comfortably.

- Arms, hands, and fingers move easily (no tension evident).
- Strokes, whether with hands, fingers, or sticks are even and relaxed.
- Playing motion is efficient and smooth.
- Instrument tone is open and resonant.
- Notes are accurate (keyboard).
- Tempo is steady and even.
- Rhythm is accurate.
- Volume level is balanced with other members of the ensemble.
- Dynamic and rhythmic changes are used to create expressive effects.

# A HANDFUL OF KEYS

**Playing Keyboard Chords and Progressions**

◄ Clavicytherium

"I cannot tell you how much I love to play for people... sometimes when I sit down to practice and there is no one else in the room I have to stifle my impulse to ring for the elevator man and offer him money to come in and hear me."

—Arthur Rubinstein (1887–1982)

◄ Psaltery

Harpsichord ▲

George Gershwin ▶

Billy Joel ▶

# POWER KEYS

"*Kou ri lengay*" is a game song from Tanzania, a country on the east coast of Africa. The last line is a direct translation of the Kikuyu words.

**Sing** the song and clap your hands every time you see a **chord** symbol above the notation.

CD 9-16
MIDI 3

## KOU RI LENGAY
### (The Strength of the Lion)

Words by Ague Commari

Game Song from Tanzania

Kou ri len - gay! Ka - len - gan - a chum, chum, pah!

Kou ri len - gay! Ka - len - gan - a chum, chum, pah!

Kou ri len - gay! Ka - len - gan - a chum, chum, pah!

Kou ri len - gay! Ka - len - gan - a chum, chum, pah!

*Perform four times*

O the strength of the li - on is in his tail.

**chord** Three or more pitches in a scale that are played or sung simultaneously.

# More Chord Moves!

You can also play chords in **inversion,** by playing the same notes but in different order. Each three-note chord has three positions: root position, **first inversion,** and **second inversion.**

**Play** the C and D♭ chords in first inversion.

**Play** the C and D♭ chords in second inversion.

Play "Fiddler on the Roof" with the chords in first inversion. Then play it again in second inversion.

**First Inversion**

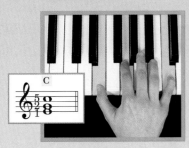

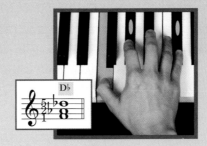

**Second Inversion**

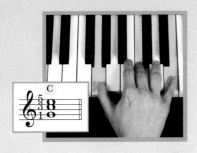

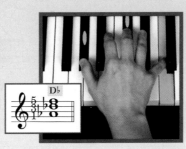

The actor Topol played Tevye in ▶ the stage and film version of *Fiddler on the Roof.*

---

**inversion** A chord in which a pitch other than the root is the lowest pitch.

**first inversion** A chord in which the pitch called the third is the lowest note of the chord.

**second inversion** A chord in which the pitch called the fifth is the lowest note of the chord.

# Play All IV-I

"All for One" is a song about working together to solve problems.
You can play it with just two chords—C(I) and F(IV).

CD 9-21

# All for One

*Words and Music by Bryan Louiselle*

**VERSE**
C(I)

*do*

1. When you've got a prob - lem that you can't solve a - lone, __
2. No one's born an ex - pert; We all can use a hand. __

F(IV)

Send a friend an e - mail or try the tel - e - phone. __
When you're in a quan - dary you just don't un - der - stand, __

C(I)                                              F(IV)

One brain might be ef - fec - tive, but two are much _ more fun.
An ex - tra cer - e - bel - lum can help to crack _ the code.

C(I)                                              F(IV)

Put - ting heads to - geth - er is the way __ to get _ things done.
One more pair of hands _ can help to light - en up __ the load.

**REFRAIN**
F(IV)                                              C(I)

One for all and all for one. _____

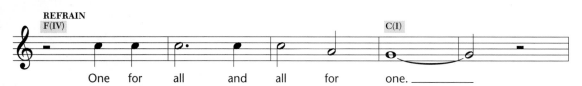

C(I)                          F(IV)          2nd time to Coda 𝄌
                                             C(I)

Put - ting heads to - geth - er is the way __ to get _ things done.

*Play four times*                *Last time* 𝄌 Coda
F(IV)          C(I)    *D. C. al Coda*  C(I)          F(IV)          C(I)

We're all _____ "IV _____ I!"   "IV I!"

## Play All Together

Review the C chord. Then **play** the C chord and the F chord in root position.

Moving from the C chord to the F chord is much easier when the F chord is played in second inversion.

This allows you to move from chord to chord with as little movement of the hand as possible. This is called playing the chords in closest position.

Practice this pattern, playing the chords in closest position.

**Play** "All for One," following the chord symbols in the song notation and playing the chords in closest position. Play the chord on the second beat of each measure.

### PRO TIPS

When you move from the I chord in root position to the IV chord in second inversion, hold finger 1, move finger 3 up a half step, and move finger 5 up a whole step.

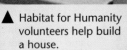
▲ Habitat for Humanity volunteers help build a house.

## Add the Bass

Make an accompaniment for "All for One" more interesting by adding a left-hand bass part. **Play** C with your left pinky. Then play the C chord with your right hand in root position.

Next, play F with the index finger of your left hand, and play the F chord in second inversion. This is how your accompaniment would look in notation.

When you are comfortable, **play** and **sing** the song with your two-hand accompaniment.

## Comping Is the Real Deal

Pianists who play in restaurants and clubs often play from "fake" books—large books containing hundreds of songs. Only the melody of the song, chord symbols, and lyrics appear in these books. Performers use the chord symbols to improvise interesting arrangements of the songs. Here is an example of a **lead sheet** from a fake book.

FLIP, FLOP AND FLY
(EXCERPT)

WORDS AND MUSIC BY CHARLES CALHOUN
AND LOU WILLIE TURNER

SWING

NOW WHEN I GET THE BLUES I GET ME A ROCK - IN' CHAIR.___

WHEN I GET THE BLUES I GET ME A ROCK - IN' CHAIR.___

WHEN THE BLUES O - VER-TAKE ME GON-NA ROCK RIGHT A-WAY FROM HERE.___

**lead sheet** A shorthand score or part, which can provide melody, chord symbols, accompaniment figures, or lyrics.

**ON YOUR OWN**
Visit a restaurant or shopping center where a pianist or small group of musicians is performing. Talk to the pianist about comping and ask to see the book the pianist is using.

▲ George Gershwin playing piano on the roof of his hotel while on vacation

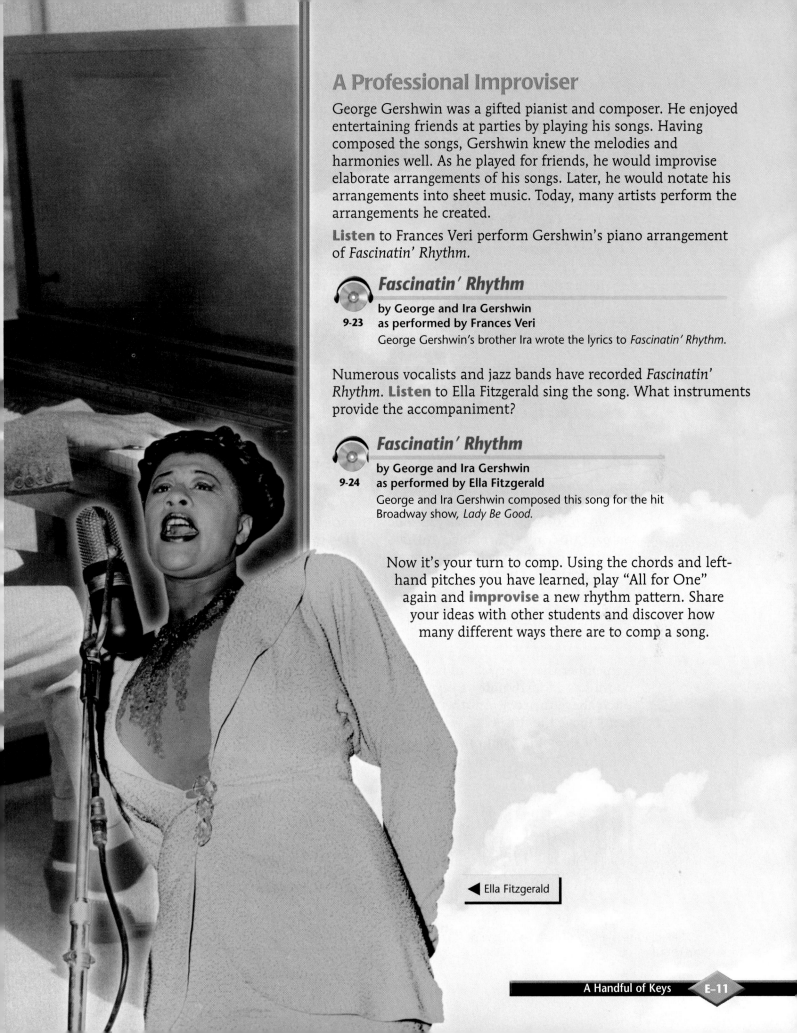

# A Professional Improviser

George Gershwin was a gifted pianist and composer. He enjoyed entertaining friends at parties by playing his songs. Having composed the songs, Gershwin knew the melodies and harmonies well. As he played for friends, he would improvise elaborate arrangements of his songs. Later, he would notate his arrangements into sheet music. Today, many artists perform the arrangements he created.

**Listen** to Frances Veri perform Gershwin's piano arrangement of *Fascinatin' Rhythm*.

### Fascinatin' Rhythm

9-23

**by George and Ira Gershwin**
**as performed by Frances Veri**
George Gershwin's brother Ira wrote the lyrics to *Fascinatin' Rhythm*.

Numerous vocalists and jazz bands have recorded *Fascinatin' Rhythm*. **Listen** to Ella Fitzgerald sing the song. What instruments provide the accompaniment?

### Fascinatin' Rhythm

9-24

**by George and Ira Gershwin**
**as performed by Ella Fitzgerald**
George and Ira Gershwin composed this song for the hit Broadway show, *Lady Be Good*.

Now it's your turn to comp. Using the chords and left-hand pitches you have learned, play "All for One" again and **improvise** a new rhythm pattern. Share your ideas with other students and discover how many different ways there are to comp a song.

◀ Ella Fitzgerald

# Stairway to Seven

**4**

There are many folk songs that have simple harmonies. *"Cheki, morena"* is a singing game from Puerto Rico. It uses only two chords, G(I) and $D_7$ ($V_7$). Play the G and $D_7$ chords below. Practice playing them until you can move smoothly back and forth.

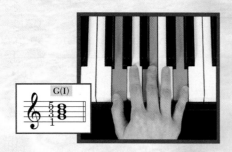

**Listen** to *"Cheki, morena"* as you follow the song notation. It is printed on page I-16 in Performance Anthology. Pat your knees on the beat when you hear the G chord and snap your fingers on the beat when you hear the $D_7$ chord.

Learn more about key signatures and how to identify the key of a song on page H-17 in Musical Tool Kit.

## Seventh Chords

Remember that every chord has a root, a third, and a fifth. The $V_7$ chord has a fourth note—a seventh. The seventh is the flatted seventh pitch above the root. Another way to think of the seventh is three half steps above the fifth.

Look at the $D_7$ chord in first inversion at the top of the page. When you play the $V_7$ chord in inversion, which pitch is eliminated?

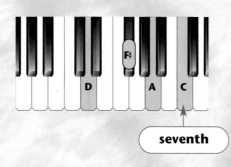

seventh

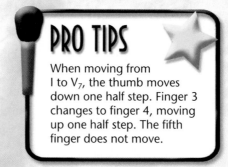

### PRO TIPS

When moving from I to $V_7$, the thumb moves down one half step. Finger 3 changes to finger 4, moving up one half step. The fifth finger does not move.

## Play a Chord Progression

Practice this **chord progression**, playing the chords you just learned .

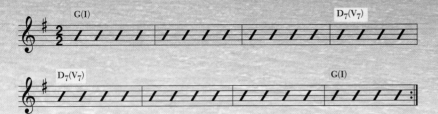

When you are comfortable, **play** *"Cheki, morena,"* following the chord symbols in the song notation on page I-16.

## An Alternating Bass

You can **perform** *"Cheki, morena"* with a bass accompaniment in the left hand. Alternate playing the root and the fifth of the chord as you play the chords with the right hand. This is called an alternating bass accompaniment. Practice this pattern.

**Play** *"Cheki, morena"* with your alternating bass accompaniment.

For another song played with I and V₇ chords, see page I-46, "Pay Me My Money Down."

## Island Music

Piano music is popular all over the world. **Listen** to a piano composition that was written in the style of Puerto Rican folk music.

### Vano empeño

9-25

**from *Danzas Puertorriqueñas***
**by Juan Morel Campos**
**as performed by Jesus Maria Sanroma**
This is one of the more than 300 *danzas,* or dance songs, written by Campos.

Statue of Juan Morel Campos,
Ponce, Puerto Rico ▶

---

**chord progression**  The order in which chords are played in a piece of music.

# Two Chords Tomorrow

"*Mañana*" is a folk song from Spain. It is in triple meter. Tap a three-beat pattern as you **sing** "*Mañana*" with the recording.

## Mañana

(Tomorrow)

*English Words by David Eddleman*

*Folk Song from Spain*

F(I)

Ma - ña - na, por _____ la ma - ña - na pa - sas - te,
My Jua - na, dear _____ when to - mor - row's here, _____ will you

F(I)          C₇(V₇)

Jua - na, por _____ mi ta - ller, la ran - le. Te
please ap - pear _____ while the sun is still high. Though

C₇(V₇)          F(I)

ju - ro que _____ ten - go ga - na de _____ ver - te,
it may be _____ that I'll on - ly see _____ just a

C₇(V₇)          F(I)

Jua - na, la pun - ta del pie. _____
toe or three _____ pass - ing by. _____

▲ Batllo House, designed by architect
Antonio Gaudi y Cornet (1905)

E-14

## Two Chords—A New Key!

"*Mañana*" is written in the key of F and uses two chords, F(I) and C$_7$(V$_7$). Learn more about keys and key signatures on page H–17 in Musical Tool Kit. You already learned how to play the F chord in root position. Now play C$_7$ in first inversion.

## Progress with Progressions

Practice this chord progression until you can move smoothly between the F and C$_7$ chords.

Now you can **play** a left hand accompaniment, using the roots of the F and C$_7$ chords. Play F with your fifth finger, and C with your thumb.

Practice the chord progression in a new way. **Play** the root of the chord on beat 1 and the chord on beats 2 and 3. **Play** this pattern as you follow the song notation. Watch for chord changes. For another song using F and C$_7$ chords, see page I-36, "He's Got the Whole World in His Hands."

## Checkpoint

Learning to recognize patterns in music helps you make sense of what you hear. **Listen** as your teacher plays these chord progressions. Choose which progression is the one you heard. **Play** the chords on your keyboard to help you make your choice.

| | | | | | |
|---|---|---|---|---|---|
| **1.** a. | C | F | C | F | C |
| b. | C | C | F | F | C |
| **2.** a. | G | D$_7$ | D$_7$ | D$_7$ | G |
| b. | G | G | G | D$_7$ | G |
| **3.** a. | C | C | C | D♭ | C |
| b. | C | D♭ | C | D♭ | C |

▲ Titanium-clad Guggenheim Museum, Bilbao, Spain. It was designed by Frank Gehry and built in 1997.

# Music MAKERS
# Franz Liszt

**Franz Liszt** (1811–1886) was a Hungarian pianist and composer who dazzled audiences with his dramatic, emotional performances. A flamboyant character, he dressed for his performances in fancy military uniforms covered with medals, velvet gloves, and a jeweled sword at his side. Until Liszt's time, musicians were mostly thought of as servants. Liszt created a new category of musician—superstar.

Liszt is thought of as the finest pianist of the nineteenth century. He was the first to play most of his performances by memory. He was also very generous. He taught many students for free, and supported a number of struggling composers.

If people in the nineteenth century had owned car radios, *Hungarian Rhapsody No. 2 in C♯ Minor* is one of the pieces they might have listened to.

*Arts* Connection    ▲ Caricature of Liszt playing before an enthusiastic audience by Adolf Brennglass (1842)

## Pipes Make It Big

We know that by the year A.D. 1100, large pipe organs were used in churches. Two people were needed to play these organs. An organist played the keyboard, and a calcant (often a friend or family member of the organist) pumped the bellows—not an easy job. Many calcants were probably happy when their jobs were taken over by electric motors around the turn of the twentieth century.

Sounds on the organ, called *stops*, are called by several of the same instrument names as those in an orchestra. You will find flute stops, trumpet stops, and string stops. There are also sounds unique to the organ.

There is usually one pipe for each key and each of its stops. A pipe organ can have up to seven keyboards, and each keyboard can have up to 61 keys. A large organ has thousands of pipes!

Though pipe organs are best known for sacred music, they are found in other places too. You often hear an organ at a baseball game. One of the largest organs in the world is at the Lord & Taylor department store in Philadelphia.

 **Take It to the Net** Learn more about the history of the organ at *www.sfsuccessnet.com*.

### Note This

Foot pedals were first added to the pipe organ in Spain and France in the early 1300s. The organist uses the pedals to play the lowest pitches.

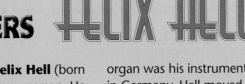

## Music MAKERS — FELIX HELL

In many ways, **Felix Hell** (born 1985) is an ordinary person. He likes to go to parties, eat pizza, and go rollerblading. In other ways, however, he is most extraordinary. When he was seven, Hell sat down at the piano and played a Bach piece he had heard, even though he had never had a piano lesson. He started piano lessons, but a year or so later, when he heard an organ recital, he knew the organ was his instrument. Born in Germany, Hell moved to New York City at age 14 to attend the Juilliard School of Music and then The Curtis Institute of Music in Philadelphia. He spends his weeks practicing, and his weekends giving organ recitals all over the United States. It's hard work. Though his last name sounds odd in English, *hell* means *light* or *bright* in German.

## Organ Pizzazz

This piece demonstrates the powerful and majestic sound of the pipe organ.

 ### Toccata and Fugue in D Minor

10-8 **by Johann Sebastian Bach**
**as performed by Felix Hell**
The dramatic *Toccata and Fugue in D Minor* has been used as background music for a number of scary movies. It is also played in the movie score for *Fantasia*.

# Rockin' Keys

The Beach Boys were at the top of the rock 'n' roll charts in the 1960s. Their music was based on California sunshine and life at the beach. As you **listen** to "Surfin' U.S.A.," **identify** measures where chords change. The song notation is found on page I-58 in Performance Anthology.

Review the C(I), F(IV) and $G_7(V_7)$ chords. Then practice this chord progression, playing the root of the chord on beat 1 and the chord on beat 2.

## Rock the Accompaniment

**Play** an accompaniment for the song using this lead sheet. You can **sing** the first measure and start your accompaniment with the $G_7$ chord on the second measure. Use the pattern given in the chord progression you just learned.

### Surfin' U.S.A.

*Words by Brian Wilson*                                    *Music by Chuck Berry*

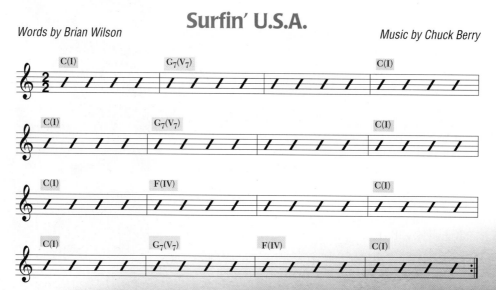

## Rockin' Syncopation

Notice that "Surfin' U.S.A." contains **syncopation** in the background vocals. Clap this syncopated rhythm.

Which words use this syncopated rhythm?

**Create** a rhythm pattern you will use to play your accompaniment for "Surfin' U.S.A." Will it be steady beat or syncopated? **Play** your accompaniment one more time while the rest of the class sings the song.

## Checkpoint

Here are some of the chords you have played.

C   F   G   D♭

**Play** each chord in root position, first inversion, and second inversion. You and a partner can take turns playing the chords and checking each other for accuracy. Then you can take turns challenging each other to play any of the chords in any inversion.

### Note This

"Surfin' U.S.A." is in duple meter. Look at the song notation. This time signature means that the half note gets one beat.

**syncopation** A rhythm where the note that is stressed comes between two beats.

# 11

# What A MINOR Difference

You learned about the C major scale in Lesson 7. Review the half steps and whole steps in the scale in Musical Tool Kit on pages H–22 and H-28. For every major scale, there is a parallel minor scale. In the minor scale, the third, sixth and seventh degrees are lowered by a half step.

Every major chord has a minor version as well. **Play** these chords. Which finger moves to play the second chord?

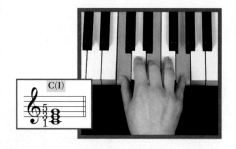

A lowercase *m* after the chord letter indicates the chord is minor.

## A New Take on an Old Chord

You already know how to play F major in second inversion. Here is the F minor chord in second inversion.

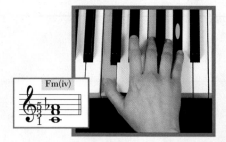

**Play** minor chords on F, G, and D by lowering the third of the major chord one half step. Practice moving between the i and iv chords until you can make the change smoothly.

## PRO TIPS

When moving from Cm to Fm, the thumb stays on the root of the Cm chord. Finger 3 moves up a whole step. Finger 5 moves up a half step.

## Play in Minor

"Let's Get the Rhythm of the Band" uses Cm and Fm chords. Follow the notation and play a root-chord accompaniment as you **listen** to the recording.

**CD 10-10**

# Let's Get the Rhythm of the Band

*Based on a Children's Rhyme*

*New Words and Music by Cheryl Warren Mattox*

Let's get the rhy-thm of the band, oh yeah, _ We got the rhy-thm of the band. _

Let's get the rhy-thm of the hand, clap your hands now, We got the rhy-thm of the hand. __
snap your fin - gers,
wave your hands high,

Let's get the rhy-thm of the feet, stomp it out with me, We got the rhy-thm of the feet, ___
jump up high __ now,
march in time __ now,

Let's get the rhy-thm of the band. Let's get the rhy-thm of the band.

## Move It!

Tap this rhythm. Use your left hand for the stems pointing down and your right hand for the stems pointing up.

Then pair up with a classmate to play the song. One partner plays the chord roots with the left hand rhythm pattern, and the other partner plays the chords with the right hand rhythm pattern.

 **MIDI** Using the MIDI file for "Let's Get the Rhythm of the Band," transpose to A minor, E minor, and D minor.

# 12

# WIRED FOR SOUND

Being a "one-person band" is a lot easier today than it was 40 years ago. Until the mid-twentieth century, the only way to make musical sounds was on acoustic instruments. No matter whether the instrument was brass, voice, woodwind, string, or percussion, something had to move or vibrate for sounds to be created. Today, a small keyboard controller, connected to a synthesizer or sampler, can trigger sound that resembles a musical instrument or voice by generating electronic signals.

## Sound You Can See

Sound can be graphically represented as a **waveform.** The parts of sound—timbre, pitch, and amplitude—can all be viewed with a computer and dedicated software. Scientists have discovered that different sound timbres produce different **sonograms.**

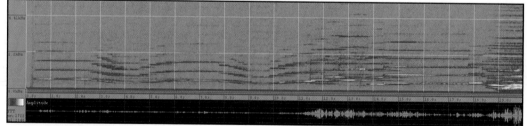

▲ While a waveform shows amplitude (green area), a sonogram shows timbre (blue area).

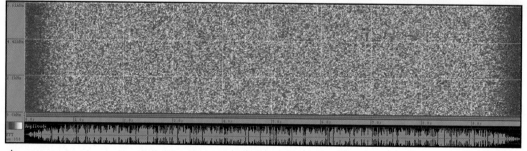

▲ White noise is shown here by a random waveform and sonogram.

**waveform** A graph that visually describes the volume of a sound over time.
**sonogram** A graph that describes the volume, pitch, and timbre of a sound over time.

| 0–5 decibels | the softest sound a human ear can hear |
|---|---|
| 20 decibels | a whisper |
| 60 decibels | normal conversation |
| 120 decibels | loud rock music |
| 140 decibels | sound causes pain |

The **frequency** of a waveform is equivalent to its pitch—the higher the frequency, the higher the pitch, and vice versa. In physics, frequency is measured in vibrations per second. This scale of measurement is known as Hertz (Hz). Human hearing extends from 20 Hz to 20,000 Hz. Sounds below 20 Hz are called subsonic, or infrasounds. Sounds above 20,000 Hz are termed ultrasonic, or ultrasounds.

The **amplitude** of a sound is shown by the height of the waveform. Louder sounds are taller and carry more energy than softer ones. Very high energy levels can damage ear drums, so be cautious of the volume when you play or listen to music. Sound is measured in decibels. The chart above gives the number of decibels for different kinds of sounds. Repeated exposure at or above 85 decibels causes hearing loss.

## Sound Samples

Many musicians and scientists can now accurately reproduce acoustic sounds electronically. A machine called an *analog-to-digital converter* is used to chop sounds into tiny pieces and store them in a sampler or computer as a file, just like e-mail and other documents. Once sounds have been digitized and saved in a sampler, musicians can experiment with the sounds in many ways.

**Listen** to this recording to hear sampling.

### Onomatopoeia Study No. 2
**by Timothy Polashek**
**10-12** All of the sounds you hear on this recording are samples of a human voice.

Keyboard controllers provide one way in which musicians can perform, using the sounds they have "sampled." Many of the kinds of recorded music we listen to today are made up of series of samples including compacts discs and MP3s.

Samples are used commonly in popular forms of music such as rock and pop. Sometimes it is difficult to tell what parts of songs are real and what are sampled. Listen to this recording. **Identify** which parts are real and which are sampled or synthesized.

### The Magnificent Tree
**written and performed by Hooverphonic**
**10-13** This Belgian trio is known for using a combination of electronic and organic sounds in their songs.

**frequency** A scientific term for the speed of a sound wave. The musical term is pitch.

**amplitude** The amount of movement that occurs in a vibration. In sound, this movement is related to volume.

### Note This
Compact discs (CDs) are made up of samples of sound that are converted 44,100 times per second. An audio CD holds approximately 74 minutes of stereo music.

## What to Look and Listen For

Excellent musicians often record themselves so they can evaluate their own work and refine their performances. Record your performance using digital audio, cassette tape, or video tape.

Use this checklist to see how you're doing and to identify aspects of your playing and singing that are in need of further refinement.

### Keyboard

- Seat is positioned so that shoulders are relaxed and forearms are parallel to the floor.
- Posture is upright and relaxed.
- Wrists are comfortably straight.
- Fingers are curved.
- Tone is resonant and even.
- Notes and rhythms are played accurately.
- Dynamic levels of the chord pitches are balanced.

- Accompaniment is softer than the melody.
- Accompaniment reflects the character of the music.
- Dynamic and rhythmic changes are used to create expression.

### Singing

- Posture is upright and relaxed.
- Jaw and mouth are relaxed and open.
- Breath is inhaled with natural, relaxed expansion of the body.
- Tone is free, open, and even throughout range.
- Singing is accurate and in tune.
- Diction is clear (all words are understood).
- Dynamic and rhythmic changes are used to create an expressive effect.

# Guitars Unplugged

**Playing Guitar Chords, Progressions, and Strums**

Sonny Landreth ▶

◀ Susan Tedeschi

"Yes, we three were so happy, my wife, my guitar, and me."

—Big Bill Broonzy (1893–1958)

▲ Adrian Legg

## More Chord Changes

The song "My Home's Across the Blue Ridge Mountains" has a chord progression that requires you to change chords more often than in the song "Pay Me My Money Down." As you **listen** to the recording of "My Home's Across the Blue Ridge Mountains," **read** the notation of the song. Notice the timing of the chord changes. Point your index finger upward when you hear the D chord and open your hand when you hear the A₇ chord. Pulse the beat with your hand.

**Listen** to the recording again and practice grabbing the chords on the beat. Then **play** the chords, using the thumb-strum or a flat pick to strum the chords. To add variety, use your index finger or your index finger and thumb pressed together to strum the chords downward.

**CD 10-22**

*Collected by Louis Land Bascom*

*Folk Song from the Southern United States*

**REFRAIN**

My home's_ a-cross _the Blue Ridge Moun-tains. My home's_ a-cross _the Blue Ridge Moun-tains.

My home's_ a-cross _the Blue Ridge Moun - tains. And I may nev-er see you an-y - more.

**VERSE**

1. I'm go-in' back to North Caro-li - na. I'm go-in' back to North Caro-li - na.
2. I'm gon-na leave here Mon-day morn-in'. I'm gon-na leave here Mon-day morn-in'.
3. One __ more kiss be-fore I leave __ you. One __ more kiss be-fore I leave __ you.

*D. C. al Fine*

I'm go-in' back to North Caro-li - na.
I'm gon-na leave here Mon-day morn-in'. } I may nev-er see you an-y - more.
One ___ more kiss be-fore I leave __ you.

## Down-Up Strumming

Another way to strum the guitar is to first strum downward with your thumb. Then strum upward, using your index finger or index and middle fingers. You can also use a flat pick to strum down and up. First, use this strum to play

"Pay Me My Money Down." Then, play it with "My Home's Across the Blue Ridge Mountains." Accent the first and third beats by playing stronger down-strokes on beats 1 and 3.

You can also strum faster, twice on each beat, using a *down-up-down-up* strumming pattern.

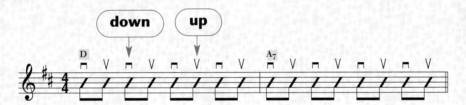

## Bluegrass to Newgrass

Now **listen** to the group Chesapeake perform in a style known as "newgrass." **Compare** this playing style to the recording of "My Home's Across the Blue Ridge Mountains." List ways they are similar and ways they are different.

### The Last Thing on My Mind

**10-24**

**by Tom Paxton**
**as performed by Chesapeake**

This musically adventurous group is known for recording folk, country, and pop songs with their unique arrangements in "newgrass" style.

## A Pro Strummer

Guitarist David Bromberg uses two different strumming-hand techniques in these two excerpts of *Mr. Bojangles.* In the first excerpt Bromberg plays a modified *down-up-down-up* strum. In the second excerpt he plays melodic lines and plucks individual strings.

### Mr. Bojangles

**10-25**

**by Jerry Jeff Walker**
**as performed by David Bromberg**

David Bromberg began his career as a backup musician in the 1960s. His reputation as a leader earned him a recording contract with Columbia Records in the 1970s. In the 1980s he stopped performing and began making and repairing instruments. In the 1990s Bromberg returned to recording and performing.

# 3

# Acoustic Guitar

Many different styles of music use various types of **acoustic** guitars. Acoustic guitars come in a variety of shapes and styles. The number of strings and material from which they are made can also vary. Each type of guitar has a unique tone quality that determines its suitability for certain styles of music. Here are a few of the most common types of acoustic guitars. Where have you seen them played? What styles of music were performed on them?

## Steel-String Guitars

The **dreadnought** is the most popular type of acoustic guitar. It is very versatile and balances well with the voice and other instruments.

The **12-string guitar** produces a brighter, fuller sound and is mostly used for playing the rhythm part. The strings are tuned to the same pitches as a six-string guitar, but every string is doubled. Each pair is tuned an octave apart except for the B and the high E, which are tuned in unison. This guitar is usually strummed with a pick or plucked with individual finger picks. The 12-string usually has a dreadnought-style body.

The **cutaway** design allows players to reach the higher frets more easily. This is especially helpful for guitarists who play melodies, or "lead style." Cutaway guitars usually have a low action, which means that the strings are quite close to the frets, making it easier to press down on the strings while you play chords or solos.

▲ Dreadnought          ▲ 12-string          ▲ Cutaway

**acoustic** A term describing instruments that project sound naturally and do not require an amplifier.

# Classical Guitar

▲ Classical

The **classical guitar** has nylon strings and a wider neck than the steel-string acoustic guitars. The nylon strings give the classical guitar a softer, more delicate tone. The classical guitar is the oldest design, dating back to the eighth century C.E. in Spain. It is often the favored guitar of longtime players.

## Note This

Before the invention of nylon, guitar strings were made of material called "cat gut." When nylon became available to the public after World War II, musicians began to use nylon fishing line to string their guitars. Soon thereafter manufacturers began to produce nylon strings designed specifically for guitar.

**Listen** to Adrian Legg play "Carolina Sunday Waltz" from his album *Waiting for a Dancer*. In this example, he plays in **arpeggio** style, which means that his fingers play the individual notes of a chord in a sequence. How does Legg use technology to make his acoustic guitar sound like an electric guitar? **Describe** the sound of these effects and **identify** where they occur on the recording.

**arpeggio** A style of playing chords where the pitches are sounded in succession rather than simultaneously.

 **Carolina Sunday Waltz**

**by Adrian Legg**

10-27 Although many musicians enjoy writing about their music for the CD sleeve—or liner notes—Adrian Legg says, "If I could write about the pieces, I wouldn't have to play them."

## Music MAKERS
## Adrian Legg

**Adrian Legg** (born 1948) is a guitarist from England who plays fingerstyle guitar. He often appears on many "best player" lists, has won top awards from *Guitar Player* magazine, and was voted "Guitarist of the Decade" (1984–1994) by *Guitarist* magazine. Other guitarists listen to his recordings because his technique, or method of playing, is unusual. He is known for creating complex and beautiful music. Legg is also well-known as a storyteller, and he gives concerts that combine stories and music.

# 4

# Shake it in G

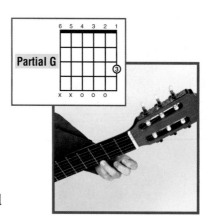
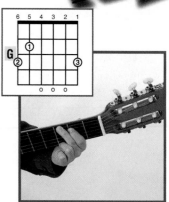

**Partial G**

**G**

The more chords you learn, the more songs you will be able to play. The song *"Cheki, morena"* (Shake It!), which is printed on page I-16 in *Performance Anthology*, is a street song from Puerto Rico. In order to accompany this song you will play the D chord that you already know and a new chord—G.

There are two ways to play the G chord. It is easy to play the partial G chord but you must avoid strumming strings 6 and 5. Use your 3rd finger on string 1 at fret 3.

Play the full G chord with your 2nd finger on string 6 at fret 3, your 1st finger on string 5 at fret 2, and your 3rd finger on string 1 at fret 3. Notice that your 2nd and 3rd fingers are at the same fret on the two outside strings.

## Grabbing and Strumming

- Grab the G chord four times. Arch your fingers to avoid touching other strings.
- Strum the G chord, using a downward stroke.
- Make sure that all of the strings sound clear, not buzzy.

## Changing from G to D

It is easier to change from G to D if you use the partial G chord. If you use the full G chord, practice moving from G to D. Notice that your 2nd finger has the farthest distance to travel when changing from G to D. One at a time, practice moving each finger from its G chord position to its D chord position several times.

- Start with the 2nd finger.
- Then move the 1st and 3rd fingers.
- Finally, practice moving all three fingers simultaneously.

▼ *Cuatro* group, Old San Juan, Puerto Rico

# Working Out the Changes

To prepare for accompanying a song, practice changing from G to D as follows.

- Grab the G chord four times.
- Grab the D chord four times.
- Repeat.
- Strum four beats of G followed by four beats of D and then four beats of G.

Now **play** the G and D chords to accompany the song "Cheki, morena." Use this chord chart as a guide. Play along with the recording, alternating downward and upward strums on the beat.

**PRO TIPS**

Make sure that you get to the new chord on time. Leave the old chord early if you have to. Think ahead.

## Cheki, morena

*Folk Song from Puerto Rico*

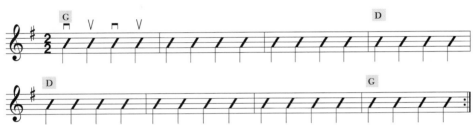

When you can move between the G and D chords smoothly, explore other ways of strumming. Practice these strum patterns. Then play them with the recording of "Cheki, morena."

- Accent beats 2 and 4 throughout.
- Strum two times per beat, alternating downward and upward.
- Accent the upward strokes.

Now **listen** for the down–up strumming pattern played by guitarists in the accompaniment of this Puerto Rican folk song.

### Pasodoble

**Pasodoble from Puerto Rico**

10-28    Notice the way the lead guitarist picks the melody in this recording. Henrietta Yurchenko recorded this when she was researching and collecting songs in Puerto Rico.

◄ Folk Dancer in Puerto Rico

### Note This

Notice the collar on the dress of the dancer. It is made of lace, or *mundillo* (bobbin lace in Spanish). *Mundillo*-making is a craft that exists only in Spain and Puerto Rico, and its history goes back about five centuries.

# 5

# A Three-Chord Song

The folk song, "Goin' Down the Road Feelin' Bad" was popular among the people of the United States who were affected by the Great Depression. The lyrics of the song express the feelings of despair shared by the entire nation during those troubled times. As you learn to play the song, think of ways that you can show these feelings through the music.

Prepare to play the song, using the three chords D(I), G(IV), and $A_7(V_7)$. Build finger muscles and finger memory of chord positions by playing this guitar workout.

1. Begin on the D chord. Choose any strum to play for eight beats.

2. Anticipate the fingering for the G chord. Strum for eight beats on G.

3. Return to D and strum for eight beats.

4. Go to A7 and strum for eight beats.

5. Return to D and strum for eight beats.

6. Play the exercise again, this time strumming for four beats on each chord.

7. Then play the exercise strumming for two beats on each chord.

## Listen for Three Chords

**Listen** to the **slide** guitar playing in Susan Tedeschi's recording of *Gonna Move*. **Identify** the 3-chord structure in the song.

### Gonna Move

**written by Paul Pena**

**10-29 as performed by Susan Tedeschi**

Tedeschi recorded this song in 2002 for her album *Wait For Me*.

## Music MAKERS

# Susan Tedeschi

**G**uitarist and singer **Susan Tedeschi** (born 1970) burst on the scene in 2000 with a Grammy nomination for "Best New Artist" and was nominated for "Best Female Rock Vocal Performance" in 2003. In 2004, her album *Wait for Me* was nominated for "Best Contemporary Blues Album." She describes her eclectic style of music as American roots—music that comes from the soul. Tedeschi has performed with Willie Nelson, Sheryl Crow, John Mellencamp, B.B. King, and the Allman Brothers Band.

**slide** A technique of playing guitar with a metal or glass tube worn on one finger of the chording hand. The tube allows the player to produce vibrato and to slide between notes and chords. It is also known as *bottleneck*.

## Strummin' "Down the Road"

**Analyze** the chord changes in the notation for the song "Goin' Down the Road Feelin' Bad." Then **listen** to the recording of "Goin' Down the Road Feelin' Bad." As you listen, silently grab the chords. Then use your favorite strum to play the chord changes with the recording.

▼ Stalled migrant car in Arizona, May 1937

### PRO TIPS

Musicians sometimes use Roman numerals to show chord progressions. If D (the first note of the scale) is I, $A_7$ (the fifth note) will be $V_7$, and G (the fourth note) will be IV.

## GOIN' DOWN THE ROAD FEELIN' BAD

CD 10-30
MIDI 04

*Adapted, Collected, and Arranged by John A. Lomax and Alan Lomax*

1. I'm goin' down the road feel-in' bad,
2. I ain't got but one old lous-y dime,
3. I'm goin' where the cli-mate suits my clothes,

Lord, I'm goin' down the road feel-in' bad,
Lord, I ain't got but one old lous-y dime,
Lord, I'm goin' where the cli-mate suits my clothes,

Well, I'm goin' down the road feel-in' bad, Lord,
Well, I ain't got but one old lous-y dime, Lord,
Well, I'm goin' where the cli-mate suits my clothes, Lord,

Lord, And I ain't gon-na be treat-ed this-a-way.
Lord, But I'll find me a new dol-lar some old day.
Lord, 'Cause I ain't gon-na be treat-ed this-a-way.

TRO—Copyright 1947 (Renewed) Ludlow Music, Inc., New York, NY. Used by Permission.

# 6

# 12-Bar Blues

When guitar players get together to "jam," they frequently turn to the blues. The blues is an important African American style of music that is now popular around the world. Blues guitarists often trade off (take turns) playing the rhythm guitar (chords) and lead guitar (solo melody) parts.

Twelve-bar blues is the most common form of the blues. **Play** this rhythm-guitar strum, using the D, G, and A₇ chords that you already know.

## 12-Bar Blues

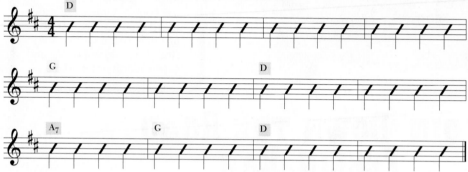

## 12-Bar Blues Form

The lyrics for 12-bar blues songs are usually organized into three rhyming phrases in Ⓐ Ⓐ Ⓑ form. The second line is a repeat of the first line. The last word of the third line rhymes with the last word of the first and second lines. **Listen** for the rhyming pattern in the traditional blues song *Sun Gonna Shine*. Here are the first three lines of the lyrics.

> *Sun gonna shine on my back door **someday**.*
>
> *Sun gonna shine on my back door **someday**.*
>
> *Wind gonna rise up and blow my blues **away**.*

Big Joe Turner ▶

### Sun Gonna Shine

**Traditional Blues**

11-1   As is typical of many blues songs, each phrase in *Sun Gonna Shine* is four measures long.

The chord progression in the rhythm guitar strum you played above is used in the classic blues song "Flip, Flop and Fly." **Listen** to "Flip, Flop and Fly" and follow the listening map on the next page. Each box contains one **bar**, or measure, of four beats. The Ⓐ Ⓐ Ⓑ lyrics in both the verse and refrain are labeled. Notice how the lead guitar solos fill the time between phrases of lyrics. Both the verse and refrain follow the 12-bar blues form.

___

**bar** Another word for *measure,* a grouping of beats set off by bar lines.

 **CD 11-2**

# FLIP, FLOP AND FLY

*Words and Music by Charles Calhoun
and Lou Willie Turner*

**VERSE**

**(A)** | **D** Now when | I get the blues | I | get me a rock - in' chair, |_____ |_____ LONG | SOLO _____ | When
1 | | 2 | 3 | 4

**(A)** | **G** I get the blues | I | get me a rock - in' chair, | **D** |_____ LONG | SOLO _____ | When the
5 | | 6 | 7 | 8

**(B)** | **A₇** blues o - ver-take me gon - na | **G** rock right a - way from here. | **D** |_____ LONG | SOLO _____ | Now
9 | | 10 | 11 | 12

**REFRAIN**

**(A)** | **D** flip, flop and fly; |_____ _____ SHORT SOLO _____ | I | don't know the rea - son why. |_____ _ SHORT SOLO _ | Now
1 | | 2 | 3 | 4

**(A)** | **G** flip, flop and fly; |_____ _____ SHORT SOLO _____ | I | don't know the rea - son why. |_____ _____ SHORT SOLO ___
5 | | 6 | 7 | 8

**(B)** | **A₇** Don't ev - er leave me, | **G** don't ev - er say good-bye. | **D** |_____ _____ LONG | SOLO _____
9 | | 10 | 11 | 12

## Play the Blues

**Sing** and **play** "Flip, Flop and Fly," which is printed in Performance Anthology on page I–32.

Now **play** these lead guitar solos with a flat pick on string 2, using just two notes (C and D).

- Place your 1st finger at fret 1 and your 3rd finger at fret 3.
- Press both fingers at the same time and pluck the note D.
- Then lift your 3rd finger (leave your 1st finger down) and play the note C.

You can play the same solos an octave higher on string 1 at frets 8 and 10. Practice these long and short solos. Then **play** them along with the recording where shown in the above map.

### Long Solo

### Short Solo

## ON YOUR OWN

Working alone or in a group, compose your own 12-bar blues song. Use the chord progression and the information on page F-14 to make sure that your song follows the form correctly. Perform your song for the class.

# 7

# Go Electric

**N**ew technology can enhance the sound of or add features to existing instruments. The electric guitar is one of the most widely developed instruments. The string vibrations of electric guitars are converted into an electric signal. Then the sound can be electronically modified in new and interesting ways. Through the use of amplifiers and effects processors, guitarists can add extra dimensions to their music.

Many different types of electric guitars, amplifiers, and effects processors can be combined to produce a variety of distinctive sounds.

Look at the picture to learn about the features of electric guitars that make them different from acoustic guitars.

Here are some common types of electric guitars.

◀ Solid-body electric

## Solid Body

Solid-body electric guitars are by far the most commonly used. Although there were only a few makers when electric guitars first appeared in the early 1950s, now there are many brands available. Fender™ guitars are favorites of both professional musicians and new players because they are durable, economical, and versatile, and they sound great.

pickups

tremolo bar

pickup selector switch

volume and tone control knobs

bridge

cord jack

## Hollow Body

Hollow-body acoustic-electric guitars are favored by jazz players and vintage or "retro" groups such as the Brian Setzer Orchestra. The most common style has *f*-shaped sound holes. They are especially effective for producing **feedback**.

Hollow-body electric ▶

**feedback** A sound that occurs when the amplified sound vibrations from the strings are detected by the guitar pickups and amplified again.

## The "Rickenbacker Sound"

One of the most easily recognized features of "vintage rock" is the "Rickenbacker sound" introduced in the 1960s by the Beatles in England and by the Byrds in the United States. Since then, such artists as John Mellencamp and Tom Petty have revived this sound.

◀ Rickenbacker electric

**Music MAKERS**

# The Byrds

The folk-rock band, **The Byrds,** formed in Los Angeles in 1964, performing a mixture of styles that combined British rock (The Beatles and The Rolling Stones) with the topical lyrics of American songwriters like Bob Dylan and Pete Seeger. Two of The Byrds' biggest hits were Dylan's "Mr. Tambourine Man" and Seeger's "Turn! Turn! Turn!" The Byrds were originally composed of Roger McGuinn (Rickenbacker guitar), David Crosby, Gene Clark, Chris Hillman, and Michael Clarke. The Byrds were inducted into the Rock and Roll Hall of Fame in 1991.

**Listen** to The Byrds perform *It Won't Be Wrong.* This performance highlights the "Rickenbacker sound." Listen to the sound of the electric guitar and **analyze** its role in the performance. Does it play lead or rhythm parts?

### It Won't Be Wrong

**11-3** **by Roger McGuinn and Harvey Gerst as performed by The Byrds**

The original version of this song, recorded a year before this version, was titled *Don't Be Long.*

## A New Sound—"Touch" Guitars

The "touch" guitar is played by tapping on the frets with both hands, which gives the instrument a more percussive sound. This new playing technique allows players to experiment with new musical ideas. The touch guitar shown has ten strings so that it can be used as both guitar and bass.

**Listen** to bass player Trey Gunn play the touch guitar. **Identify** the bass line and **describe** how it balances with other instruments in the group.

### *Dziban*

**by Trey Gunn**

**11-4** The long and sustained sounds in this recording are played by band member Joe Mendelson on a 8-string touch guitar.

▲ 10-string touch guitar

▲ Trey Gunn

## Amplifiers

Amplifiers (amps) allow you to control the volume and tone of your electric guitar. Some are powered by transistors and are called solid-state amps. Others are powered by glass tubes and are called tube amps. Tube amps give the rich, warm sound of "classic rock." Hybrid amps combine the circuitry of both types and are also very popular. Amps come in several sizes.

▲ The combo amp combines the amplifier circuitry and speaker in a single cabinet.

▲ The head-and-cabinet amp has two separate cabinets for the amplifier and speaker.

# Effects Processors

Effects processors are used by guitar players to expand the variety of sounds they can make with their instruments. These special electronic circuits are usually contained in a little metal box that is placed on the floor so that the guitarist can turn it on and off with a foot switch. Sometimes effects processors are wired directly into the circuitry of an amplifier. These are some types of popular effects processors.

**Distortion** makes a dirty, driven sound by overloading one of the amplifier channels.

**Wah-wah** produces the "crybaby" effect that was made famous by Jimi Hendrix.

**Compression** increases the **sustain** by capturing the string signal and then letting it through the amp at a rate that a player can adjust.

**Reverb** creates an atmosphere of a large concert hall by increasing the depth of the guitar sound.

**Delay** produces an echo. The speed of the echo can be adjusted from very fast (called a "slapback") to very slow, so that entire phrases can be heard again after they are played.

**Chorus** produces a time delay across channels so that the guitar sound is richer, similar to a 12-string guitar.

▲ Distortion box

◄ wah-wah pedal

## Effects at Work

**Listen** to Lyle Workman play his *Rising of the Mourning Sun* on electric guitar. **Identify** as many effects as you can in the music.

### *Rising of the Mourning Sun*

**by Lyle Workman**

**11-5** Workman plays electric and acoustic guitars, as well as keyboards, on this recording.

---

**sustain** The duration of a sound.

Lyle Workman ►

# 10

There are many different ways to strum guitar chords. Learning a variety of strums can make accompanying songs more interesting. The way you strum the guitar can set the mood and style of a song. The strumming patterns for the three songs in this lesson are well suited to their styles and cultural backgrounds.

Practice this strum, using your thumb to play the down strums and your index and middle fingers to play the up strums. Then place a capo at fret 3 and **play** the strum along with the recording of "This Land Is Your Land." The song is printed on page I-66 in Performance Anthology.

## This Land Is Your Land

*Words and Music by Woody Guthrie*

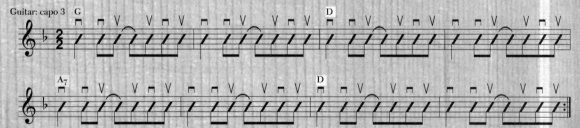

## Holiday Strumming

The song "*Stille Nacht*" (Silent Night) is printed on page I-54 in Performance Anthology and can be played with this strum.

- First, play this pattern, using all down strums.
- When you are ready for more challenge, play the bass note with your thumb and the other notes with down strums, using your index finger.
- Now place a capo at fret 3 and play the G, C, and D₇ chords to accompany the song.

## Latin Strumming

Here is a strum to play with the song *"Feliz Navidad"*, which is printed on page I-28 in Performance Anthology. Use the G, C, and $D_7$ chords that you have already learned. Give it a Latin sound by using this strum based on the *huapango*, which is very well-known in Mexican music. Notice the diamond shape above beats 2 and 4. This indicates that you should "slap" or gently tap your palm on all of the strings directly over the sound hole.

Practice this strum without the chords until you can play it without having to concentrate on counting strums. Memorize the feel of the strum. The down strums on beats one and three should be heavier than the up strums and slaps. Notice how the strum fits with the word accents in the lyrics!

# Checkpoint

**Compose** your own 12-bar blues song, using the chord progressions you have learned so far. Use this chart to make sure that your composition follows 12-bar blues form.

| 1 I | 2 I | 3 I | 4 I |
|---|---|---|---|
| 5 IV | 6 IV | 7 I | 8 I |
| 9 V | 10 IV | 11 I | 12 I |

Add a part for drums and have a classmate play it. Practice together so that the guitar and drums are "tight" or well rehearsed. Invite some classmates to interpret the music using dance movements, and ask them to create a name for the dance. **Perform** the music and dance together. Then make a music video of your performance.

## PRO TIPS

This strum is a little tricky, but it can be easier if you practice this way. Silently count *1-and-2-and-3-and-4-and* over and over. Play only the bass note with your thumb on beats 1 and 3. Do this over and over until it becomes easy. Then add the slap on beat 2. Finally, add the up strum after the slap on the *and* after beat 2 so that the pattern is *thumb-slap-up-thumb-slap-up.* Use the 1st and 2nd fingers for the up strum.

# 11

# Strummin' and Slidin'

One of the most exciting things about guitar playing is learning new techniques. Before you learn how to play them, it is good to know how they sound when performed by professionals. Examples of some techniques are slide, or bottleneck, and fingerpicking style.

**Listen** to Sonny Landreth's guitar artistry in his instrumental piece *Native Stepson*.

### Native Stepson
**11-10**
by Sonny Landreth
Landreth's trademark is being able to fret notes behind his slide on the fretboard.

### Music MAKERS

## Sonny Landreth

Born in Canton, Mississippi, **Sonny Landreth** (born 1951) has earned his reputation as the ultimate southern slide-guitar/bottleneck player. As Bonnie Raitt said about his fifth album *Levee Town*, "[It's] a killer record by one of the most astonishing guitarists I know." Landreth has spent his career developing his own unique blues guitar voice by successfully combining zydeco rhythms, swamp pop, and Cajun music.

While using a bottleneck on the fretboard, Landreth plays with a combination of fingerpicking, palm, and thumb-pick techniques to achieve his virtuosic solos. He is also known for the way he slurs notes. He explains, " . . . [by] slurring you make the most of the phrase . . . and [it] ends up behind the beat: you anticipate it sometimes and you're on the back of it other times. . . You elongate even that one beat. . . if something tastes really good, you can either just scarf it down or you can take your time and reeeaaaaallly stretch the moment."

Now **listen** to the blazing speed of jazz guitarist Pat Metheny's soloing on *Take Me There*. At age 18, Metheny was the youngest teacher to ever join the faculty at the

### Take Me There
**11-11**
by Pat Metheny and Lyle Mays
as performed by the Pat Metheny Group
The other musicians featured on this

## E Minor Bass Strum

Examine the diagram for the E minor (Em) chord to determine which strings, frets, and fingers you will need to play this chord. Practice grabbing the chords, remembering to lift your fingers just above the strings after you strum.

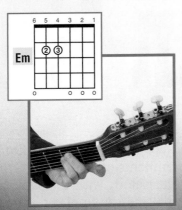

Here is a new strumming pattern. This technique requires you to play the bass note of the Em chord with your thumb (string 6) and then strum the remaining strings with your fingernails. This is called the "bass-strum" pattern.

**Play** this new strumming technique along with the recording of "Shortnin' Bread."

# Shortnin' Bread

CD 11-12

*African American Folk Song*
*Arranged by Linda Tillery*

**REFRAIN**

I do love short-nin' bread. I do love short-nin' bread. Ma - ma loves short-nin' bread.

Pa - pa loves short - nin' bread. Ev - 'ry-bod-y loves short - nin' bread.

**VERSE**

1. Two lit - tle ba - bies lay - in' in the bed; one play' sick and the oth - er play' dead.
2. Old la - dy Di - nah's sick __ in the bed;

Called the doc - tor, the doc - tor said, "Oh, _____ she needs some short - nin' bread!"

# Mountain Guitar

Since the early days of American country music, the guitar has been one of the most important instruments of that style. In the Appalachian Mountains the guitar, along with the banjo and fiddle, was used to accompany great ballads and to play for dances.

Now that you know the Em chord, combine it with the D, G, and A₇ chords for a new chord progression. This chord progression can be played to accompany the traditional Appalachian mountain song "Man of Constant Sorrow." Play along with the song recording, using a basic down strum.

CD 11-14

## MAN OF CONSTANT SORROW

*Appalachian Folk Song*

| Em | | | | | | D |
|---|---|---|---|---|---|---|
| 1. I am a man | | of con - stant sor - row _____ |
| I'll bid fare - well | | to old ___ Ken - tuck - y, _____ |
| 2. All through this world _____ | | I'm bound__ to ram - ble, _____ |
| I'm bound to ride _____ | | the North - ern Rail - way, _____ |

| G | | | | | A₇ |
|---|---|---|---|---|---|
| ____ And I've seen trou - bles all my days. _____ |
| ____ The state where I _____ was born and raised. _____ |
| ____ Through sun and wind _____ and driv - ing rain, _____ |
| ____ Per - haps I'll take _____ the very next train. |

## Guitar Workout

Add variety to your strumming by playing these two patterns. On the first example, pick string 4 on beats 1 and 3, and then strum strings 3 through 1 on beats 2 and 4. **Play** this bass-strum pattern with the D and Em chords to accompany "Man of Constant Sorrow."

Practice the next strum variation to make the song sound more like country rock. Then **perform** the song, using this strum.

## Oh, Brother—Bluegrass

Norman Blake is a master of the bluegrass steel-string guitar. **Listen** to him play *I Am a Man of Constant Sorrow*, one of the songs from the soundtrack of the popular film *Oh Brother, Where Art Thou?* Notice Blake's use of a technique called a *hammer-on*, which guitar players call a *slur*. How is the melody the same as, or different from, the one you sang?

### *I Am a Man of Constant Sorrow*

**Folk Song from Appalachia**
**11-16   as performed by Norman Blake**

This recording features variations on the melody, combining both melody and chords.

## Checkpoint

Strum the rhythm guitar part below, using a down-up strum.

- Play three single notes: E on open string 1, and D and F♯ shown at the right.
- Improvise your own guitar solos over the chords, using these three notes.
- Trade off playing rhythm and lead guitar with a classmate.

◀ Norman Blake

# 13

# Doo-Wop PROGRESSION

Doo-wop is a popular style where backup singers sing syllables such as *doo-doot-n-doo* or *a-hoopa-hoopa-hoopa* to imitate the sounds of instruments. "Little Darlin'" was the first hit single made by doo-wop group the Diamonds, in 1957. It was one of the most-played songs on the radio that year.

Prepare to play along with the recording of "Little Darlin'" by practicing this chord progression. Notice that this progression has four chords—G, Em, C, and D$_7$. Then **play** along with the recording. As you play, experiment with various strumming patterns until you find one that works well with the style.

▲ 1950's microphone

## PRO TIPS

Many guitarists look for "shortcuts" or ways to make their guitar playing easier. When changing chords in this progression, remember that each successive chord has a common fingering with the previous chord. When changing from G to Em, keep the 1st finger on string 5, fret 2; from Em to C, keep the 2nd finger on string 4, fret 2; from C to D$_7$, keep the 1st finger on string 2, fret 1. When starting over, slide the 3rd on string 1, fret 2, up to fret 3.

CD 11-17

## Little Darlin'

*Words and Music by Maurice Williams*

Eye, _____ yi - eye-eye - eye _____ Yi - eye-eye -

eye _____ Ya - ya-ya - ah Hey, lit - tle

dar-lin', oh, lit-tle dar-lin', oh ho-oh where

are __ you? My __ hon-ey,

I was wrong to __ try to __ love __ two. A - hoo-pa hoo-pa hoo-pa. Know __ well-a that my love-a was __ just for __ you, oh, on - ly you. _____

**INTERLUDE**

My __ dear - a,

*(Spoken during Interlude—optional)*
My dear, I need your love to call my own
And never do wrong;
and to hold in mine your little hand.
I'll know too soon that I'll love again.
Please come back to me.

◄ The Diamonds

# 14

# SURF GUITAR

**1960s** rock 'n' roll was dominated by the "British Invasion," which included rock groups such as the Beatles and the Rolling Stones. The United States also had its share of bands that were equally important. The song "Surfin' U.S.A." was a big hit by the Beach Boys, a group from southern California. Their music influenced many of the most famous rock bands, including the Beatles.

Prepare to accompany the song "Surfin' U.S.A.," which is printed on page I-58 in Performance Anthology. First, place a capo at fret 5. Then strum the chords G, C, and $D_7$, which will sound as C, F, and $G_7$. **Play** the chord progression, using this strum with your thumb (T) and index finger (I) or using a pick.

▲ The Beach Boys

Now **play** along with the recording of the song. Once you can keep time with the strum and the chord changes throughout the song, play this more challenging strum, which uses the thumb for the bass note and the index finger for the down and up strums.

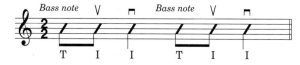

Finally, **play** this new strum to capture the spirit of 1960s "surfer music."

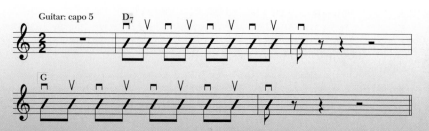

### Note This

The Beach Boys and their music were associated with a unique clothing style called the "surfer look." Young people nationwide wanted to look like surfers. This trend continued for many years.

### PRO TIPS

Notice that you must wait for an entire measure before beginning to strum. Begin strumming on the word O-cean and alternate with the vocals. You will strum during the longer notes in the melody.

The Surfaris from left to right are Pat Connolly at age 15, Jim Fuller at age 15, Ron Wilson at age 17, and Bob Barryhill at age 15. ▶

## Single-Note Soloing

There are two basic characteristics of surfer music.

• The lyrics are about surfing.

• It has guitar-led instrumental sections.

Lyrics are the easy part, but you have to practice soloing. Use a pick to perform a single-note melody on the guitar. With the capo still set at fret 5, **play** these notes on strings 3 and 4. Notice that finger and fret numbers are shown in the staff next to the notes. At first, pick the strings downward only.

Next, play eighth notes, picking downward and upward as shown in the notation.

Now add a new note on string 2.

**Listen** to this popular surfer tune by the Surfaris. How would you describe the sound of the lead guitar solos?

### *Wipe Out*

**by the Surfaris**

11-19 One of the most popular parts in this recording is the drum solo.

## On Your Own

Jam with another guitarist, using the chord progression G-C-D₇. Play your single notes while the other guitarist strums. Play back and forth, keeping time and listening to each other. Either guitar can improvise new melodies, or play new strumming patterns that keep the basic beat. "Jamming" is an essential part of playing in a band.

## Review and Assess

Throughout Guitars Unplugged, you have

- learned to play the guitar and sing.
- learned a number of different chords.
- practiced different accompaniment patterns with a variety of songs.

Playing and singing the notes and rhythms and remembering the words to the songs are just the first steps of excellent music making. Real musicianship involves playing and singing beautifully, using all of the good habits that you've been practicing. It's not so important *what* you play; it's *how well* you play and sing that matters.

## Review What You Learned

Review what you have studied and practiced. With your teacher, review and choose performance activities that permit you to demonstrate excellent musicianship. Selecting the right music to perform is an important part of becoming a successful musician.

Not everyone will be able to play a rhythmic accompaniment and sing at the same time. What is most important is that you perform accurately, musically, and beautifully. Think about the songs that you enjoy and that you can play and sing well.

| Song | Key | Chords | Progression |
|---|---|---|---|
| "My Home's Across the Blue Ridge Mountains" | D major | D, $A_7$ | $I$-$V_7$ |
| "Cheki, morena" | G major | G, D | I-V |
| "Goin' Down the Road Feelin' Bad" | D major | D, G, $A_7$ | $I$-$IV$-$V_7$ |
| "Flip, Flop and Fly" | D major | D, G, $A_7$ | $I$-$IV$-$V_7$ |
| "Do Wah Diddy Diddy" | A major (capo 2) | G, C | I-IV |
| "The Midnight Special" | G major | G, C, $D_7$ | $I$-$IV$-$V_7$ |
| "Stille Nacht" ("Silent Night") | C major (capo 3) | G, C, $D_7$ | $I$-$IV$-$V_7$ |
| "Feliz Navidad" | G major | G, C, $D_7$ | $I$-$IV$-$V_7$ |
| "Shortnin' Bread" | E minor | Em | i |
| "Man of Constant Sorrow" | D major | D, Em, G, $A_7$ | $I$-$ii$-$IV$-$V_7$ |
| "Little Darlin'" | G major | G, C, $D_7$, Em | $I$-$IV$-$V_7$-$vi$ |
| "Surfin' U.S.A." | C major (capo 5) | G, C, $D_7$ | $I$-$IV$-$V_7$ |

## Show What You Know

With the help of your teacher, select several songs to perform in which you can do at least two of the following well:

- Play the accompaniment chords and strum with your thumb on the beat while your classmates sing.

- Play a rhythmic guitar accompaniment while your classmates sing.

- Play the accompaniment chords by strumming on the beat with your thumb; a partner plays a different accompaniment rhythm and you sing with your classmates.

- Play a rhythmic guitar accompaniment as you sing with your classmates.

In choosing the songs to perform, your goal is to show all of the qualities of good musicianship. You want performances of which you can be proud; not just something that is difficult to do. The goal for this assessment is quality, not difficulty.

# What to Look and Listen For

Excellent musicians often record themselves so they can evaluate their own work and refine their performances. Record your performance using digital audio, cassette tape, or video tape.

Ask yourself whether all these things are true about your performance. Use this checklist to see how you're doing and to identify aspects of your playing and singing that are in need of further refinement.

## Guitar

- Posture is upright and relaxed.
- Face of the guitar is perpendicular to the floor.
- Guitar is positioned so that right and left hands remain relaxed.
- Wrists are comfortably straight.
- Fingers are curved.
- Left hand fingertips contact the fingerboard.
- All strings vibrate with a clear, resonant tone.
- Accompaniment chords and rhythms are played accurately.

- Chords change in tempo.
- Dynamic levels of the chord voices (individual strings) and bass notes are balanced.
- Accompaniment is softer than the melody.
- Lengths of individual notes and strums reflect the character of the music.
- Dynamic and rhythmic changes are used to create expressive effects.

## Singing

- Posture is upright and relaxed.
- Jaw and mouth are relaxed and open.
- Breath is inhaled with natural, relaxed expansion of the body.
- Tone is free, open, and even throughout range.
- Rhythm is precise and sung with inflection.
- Singing is accurate and in tune.
- Diction is clear (all words are understood).
- Dynamic and rhythmic changes are used to create expressive effects.

# Lift UP Your VOICE

*"I think for every situation there is a song."*

—Björk Gudmundsdóttir (born 1965)

▼ Jeff Barry and Ellie Greenwich

Dolly Parton▲

Youssou N'Dour ▲

proud? Yeah, — we need a change, yeah, — do it to-day, — yeah. —

I can feel — my spir-it ris-ing. Change, yeah, — we need a change, yeah, — do it to-

day, — yeah. — 'Cause I can see — a clear — hor-i-zon.

What have you done to-day — to make you feel proud?

The photographs on these pages show people who believed in themselves enough to accomplish great things.

▲ Oprah Winfrey

Dolly Parton ▲

▲ Youssou N'Dour

# British Connection

**Listen** to *Search for the Hero* by M People, a British band whose members are Mike Pickering, Paul Heard, Heather Small, and Andrew Lovell.

### Search for the Hero

**by Mike Pickering and Paul Heard**
**11-22   as performed by M People**

This song became a hit after being used in an automobile commercial in Great Britain.

## Music MAKERS

# Heather Small

**Heather Small** (born 1965) is the lead singer for M People. She was born in London, England, and began singing at an early age. Though she did not consider herself particularly talented, she enjoyed singing more than anything else, and she performed regularly in various local venues. Small was singing with a different band when she was asked to sing a couple of songs with M People. She quickly became their permanent lead singer.

M People got its start in Manchester, England in 1990. Small has made several albums with the group, and now she also records as a soloist. Her first album, *Proud,* was released in 2000. Small is a songwriter and co-writes many of her songs with Simon Climie and Peter-John Vettese. Her musical style is a blend of dance, soul, and pop music.

# Your Changing Voice

**2**

Is your singing and speaking voice lower than it was a year ago, or even just a few months ago? All voices change and grow during adolescence. Good singing habits help your voice adapt and improve during these changes.

## Female Voices

Voice changes for females are more subtle than for males. Noticeable, but temporary, changes may include

- unsteadiness or breathiness.
- change in range either higher or lower.
- a shift in the transition between chest and head voice.

Proper breath support and control will strengthen your voice as it matures.

## Male Voices

Vocal changes for males are usually much more obvious than for females. Initial changes include

- cracking or shifting between pitches in speaking or singing.
- lowering of the range.
- weak or non-sounding pitches in the transition from higher to lower notes.

Some voices change quickly, while others change gradually. Some voices will not experience a change until high school, and others might experience the change in upper elementary school.

## Make the Transition

The transition in all voices requires good breath support so that the vocal cords are free to vibrate. Here are some rules for good singing as the voice matures.

- **Take a full breath just before singing a phrase.** Keep the breath moving. Check your breathing by placing your hands on your lowest rib and inhaling through your mouth or nose. If your ribs expand under your hands, you're filling your lungs with air.
- **Start each pitch with breath.** You can check yourself by starting on an *h* followed by a vowel the first few times to get the breath moving. Eliminate the *h* as you gain confidence.
- **Sing with a relaxed, open sound**. Forcing a loud sound is very hard on the vocal cords.
- When singing in parts, **experiment with singing different parts on a song.** If you sing part 1 on song 1, sing part 2 for song 2. Stretch the range of your voice whenever possible.

## Start Your Sound

Singing vocal exercises before you sing a song is an excellent way to wake up and prepare the voice. Here are some exercises to get the voice moving. Notice that you will sing through the transition in the first two exercises, taking your voice through the break. Use your breath to make the sound.

Sing this exercise on an *n* sound. Slide from the top note down to the bottom note. Continue the exercise, moving down in half steps, five more times. Your bottom note will be middle C.

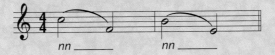

## Shape Your Sound

The next exercise picks up where the last one left off. *Me* has a bright, forward vowel, and *you* has a more rounded vowel. As you sing this pattern, notice how *me* is focused right behind your front teeth. As you move to *you*, make a space as if you have a gumball in your mouth. Sing this pattern up in half steps until you reach another C. Then come back down.

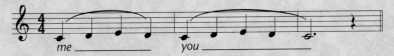

## Sing Across the Range

This exercise stretches the bottom of the voice. Place your hand as if you were going to say the Pledge of Allegiance. Then sing this pattern. You should feel a "buzz" in your chest where your hand is resting.

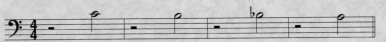

(breathe) *eeyah* (breathe) *eeyah* (breathe) *eeyah* (breathe) *eeyah*

## Get the Words Out

Tongue twisters, such as "Peter Piper picked a peck of pickled peppers" are often used for improving diction. Sing this tongue twister, going up by half steps eight times. As you sing, be aware of where the pitches resonate in your head and chest.

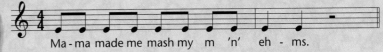

Ma - ma made me mash my m 'n' eh - ms.

◀ David at ages 6, 8, 10, 12, 14, 16, and 20

# 3

# I Hear an Echoooo

"⊚ver My Head" is an African American spiritual that contains echo parts. Spirituals could be called religious folk songs. Many spirituals had double meanings for enslaved African Americans. For example, a reference to reaching heaven in a song might actually refer to reaching freedom in the North. Read the third and fourth verses of "Over My Head." What might the word *victory* refer to?

## Singing Tips

Look at the song notation and notice that there is a bass part and a treble part. Males with lower voices can sing part 2. Females and unchanged voices can sing the echo, written as part 1.

**Sing** "Over My Head" in a **legato** style. Each two-measure phrase should be sung in one breath.

## Reading Music Tips

Hold the whole and dotted-half notes in "Over My Head" for their full value.

## Knowing the Score

In echo singing, singers are divided into two groups. One group sings a phrase, while the other repeats, or echoes, the phrase. Follow the score to see where your part begins.

---

***legato*** An Italian word that means "smoothly." In *legato* singing style, the words flow smoothly together.

## PRO TIPS

To practice taking in a full breath, breathe in as if you were drinking a milkshake through a straw.

## African American Spirituals

Spirituals such as "Over My Head" were created by African people enslaved in the United States. The music was influenced by African musical traditions, as well as by the folk and church music they heard in the United States. The words of many spirituals reflected hope and a longing for freedom. Some of the songs went even further—they were coded instructions about how to escape. Because slaves were rarely taught to read and write and had no printed music, they learned songs by memory. Often, the songs were in call-and-response form. A leader sang first, and the group either echoed the leader or sang a different, short response. Spirituals remain one of the most popular types of American folk music.

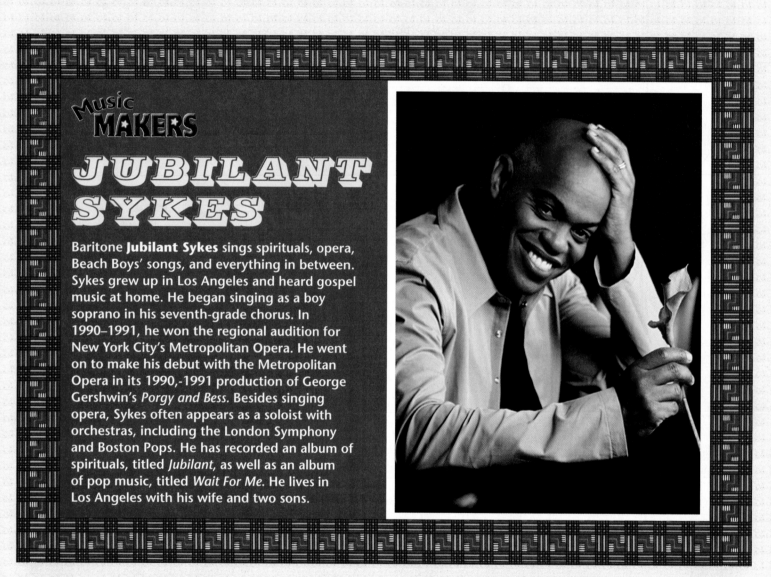

**Music MAKERS**

**JUBILANT SYKES**

Baritone **Jubilant Sykes** sings spirituals, opera, Beach Boys' songs, and everything in between. Sykes grew up in Los Angeles and heard gospel music at home. He began singing as a boy soprano in his seventh-grade chorus. In 1990–1991, he won the regional audition for New York City's Metropolitan Opera. He went on to make his debut with the Metropolitan Opera in its 1990,-1991 production of George Gershwin's *Porgy and Bess*. Besides singing opera, Sykes often appears as a soloist with orchestras, including the London Symphony and Boston Pops. He has recorded an album of spirituals, titled *Jubilant*, as well as an album of pop music, titled *Wait For Me*. He lives in Los Angeles with his wife and two sons.

## Jubilant Sounds

**Listen** to Jubilant Sykes sing an African American spiritual about freedom.

### Go Down, Moses

**African American spiritual**
11-25 **as performed by Jubilant Sykes**

This spiritual refers to the biblical character Moses and his quest for freedom.

**Arts Connection** ▲ African American artist Aaron Douglas (1899-1979) was part of the Harlem Renaissance of the 1920s. He painted murals for public buildings and illustrations for African American magazines. He later moved to Nashville, Tennessee, where he taught at Fisk University, home of the famous African American vocal group, the Fisk Jubilee Singers, for almost 30 years. Douglas painted this work, *Into Bondage,* in 1936.

# 4

# ✴ MELODIES ✴
## from the Congo

The music of the Congo has its roots in the African rainforest. As the Congolese culture developed, forest peoples took the music from the jungles to the savannahs. Many rhythms particular to Congolese music are identified with names such as *moana binge, mbayeh, hamba,* and *bonganga*.

*"Si, si si"* is a song from the Congo in western Africa. It has three separate parts that can be sung alone or together.

## Singing Tips

**Sing** the melody that best fits your vocal range. **Perform** the song by having each part sing in order. Sing part 1. Then add part 2. Finally, sing all three parts together. Continue singing until all three parts are sung together twice. How many times will each part be sung?

Dotted rhythms and syncopation are very important to the vocal character of *"Si si si."* When singing dotted rhythms, lift slightly between the dotted-quarter note and the following eighth note to make the rhythm more prominent. For the syncopated rhythms, accent the initial consonants of each word to emphasize the off-beat feeling.

## Reading Music Tips

In most music, the emphasis is on the beat. In music containing **syncopation**, the emphasis falls between the beats. Measures 3 and 7 of each melody in *"Si si si"* contain syncopation. Read the rhythms in these measures.

A pickup, or anacrusis, is one or more notes that occur before the first strong beat of a phrase. The rhythmic value of the pickup is "borrowed," or taken away from the final measure of the piece. Which part for *"Si si si"* begins singing on a pickup?

---

**syncopation** A type of rhythm where the note that is stressed comes between two beats.

**Village in the Ruzizi valley in the Republic of Congo (Zaire), Africa** ▼

# Si si si

Folk Song from the Congo

## Knowing the Score

Part 1 of "Si si si" contains five pitches, from *do* to *la*. Part 2 begins with a three-note melodic sequence that happens three times. **Analyze** part 3 to identify the pitches. Note that it is written in bass clef.

## Hear the Music of Congo

**Listen** to *Kyrie*. **Compare** it to "Si si si."

### Kyrie

12-3

from *Missa Luba*
arranged by Guido Haazen
as performed by the Muungano National Choir

*Missa Luba* contains elements typical of traditional Congolese music.

# 5 Harmonies of Spain

"*Con el vito*" is a famous composed song from Spain. A *vito* is a fast, fiery dance. The song contains melodies, harmonies, and rhythms typical of Spanish music.

## Singing Tips

"*Con el vito*" moves at a lively tempo. Sing it lightly to keep the tempo moving. Determine whether the melody or harmony is best suited for your vocal range, and **sing** that part.

## Reading Music Tips

As you **read** "*Con el vito*," look for repeated melodic patterns. For example, the third and fourth lines are identical to the first and second lines. Also, watch for notes that have been altered with accidentals, and remember them when you repeat the passage.

Find examples of two types of repeating rhythm patterns in the song. **Practice** clapping and counting these rhythms.

**homophonic texture** Melody supported by harmony.

## PRO TIPS

Take advantage of the eighth rests in the melody to get quick and deep breaths. Notice the different rhythms for the word *vito* and perform them accurately.

## Knowing the Score

"*Con el vito*" is in binary form, which means it has an **A** and a **B** section. Find the beginning of the **B** section in the printed notation. Which section of "*Con el vito*" is in unison and which contains harmony?

Notice that while the melody and harmony parts of "*Con el vito*" have different pitches, they have the same rhythm. This is called **homophonic texture.**

## More Spanish Flair

**Listen** to this choral work by the Madrid Community Orchestra and Chorus. What instrumental timbres and style characteristics do you hear?

### Viva Madrid, que sí, que sí

from *Don Manolito*

12-4 written by Pablo Sorozabal
as performed by The Madrid Community Orchestra and Chorus

This chorus is from a popular Spanish opera from 1943 called *Don Manolito*. It was first performed at the *Teatro Reina Victoria* in Madrid.

▲ Plaza España, Seville, Andalusia, Spain

# Con el vito

*English Words by Aura Kontra*

*m, f, s, si,(l) t, d r m*

*Folk Song from Spain*
*Arranged by Darrell Peter*

**A**

Con el vi - to, vi - to, vi - to,

Con el vi - to, vi - to, va. _____

Con el vi - to, vi - to, vi - to,

Con el vi - to, vi - to, va. _____ *Fine*

**B**

U - na ma - la - gue - ña fue a
To the bull - fights in Se - vi - lla,

Se - vi - lla a ver los to - ros;
Went the Span - ish la - dy rid - ing;

Y en la mi - tad del ca - mi - no
She was cap - tured on the high - way

La cau - ti - va - ron los mo - ros.
By some Moor - ish ban - dits hid - ing. *D.C. al Fine*

# 6

# We Are Family

Composer Joanne Hammil wrote "One Family" in the style of an African community song, in which several short, independent melodies can be sung both separately and together. When the melodies are sung together, they create a **polyphonic** texture.

## Singing Tips

Sing each of the four parts to find one in your range. Note that part 4 can be sung as notated by unchanged voices, or down an octave for changed voices.

## Reading Music Tips

Read through the score for "One Family" to find when your part comes in. Count the measures and beats accurately so that the parts come together on the words *one family*.

## Knowing the Score

Repeat signs let performers know when to repeat a phrase or section of music. Look for the repeated sections in "One Family." Read through the score to discover what sections are repeated in your part.

## A Rock Family

Sly and the Family Stone was an important rock and funk band in the late 1960s. The band included Sly Stone, his younger brother Freddie, his sister Rosie, Cynthia Robinson, Jerry Martini, Greg Errico, and Larry Graham. It was one of the first to include people of different races, and both men and women, as part of a musical family.

**Listen** to *Everyday People*. What message does the song send?

### Everyday People

**by Sly Stone**
12-10 **as performed by Sly and the Family Stone**
*Everyday People* was a hit single in 1969.

▲ Sly and The Family Stone

**polyphonic** A musical texture in which two or more melodic lines occur at the same time. This creates layers of harmony.

# One Family

*Words and Music by Joanne Hammil*

We may dis - a - gree, but we are one fam - i - ly. ___

One fam-i-ly, ___ with man-y dif-f'rent voic-es. One fam-i-ly. ___

The world is ___ one fam-i-ly ___ to pro - tect and love. The world is ___ one fam-i-ly. ___

# 7

# JA-DA JAZZ

In music, some words are used for meaning, and others are used simply for sound. For example, jazz singers sometimes use scat syllables instead of words when they perform. "Ja-Da," written in 1918, is a popular song that uses scat syllables. This catchy tune has been used often through the years in musicals, movies, and commercials.

## Singing Tips

Find the half steps in the melody of "Ja-Da." **Listen** to the half steps played on a keyboard or other instrument. Then **sing** or hum softly until you are singing the half steps in tune with confidence.

Hold the tied notes for their full rhythmic value.

## Reading Music Tips

"Ja-Da" contains many accidentals. These symbols alter a pitch for one measure. In the next measure, the note returns to normal. How many accidentals occur in "Ja-Da"? Do they usually occur on the same pitch? To help you read more easily, find all the accidentals in the song notation before you sing.

## Knowing the Score

"Ja-Da" is arranged in three parts for mixed choir, which includes both male and female singers. Notice that each voice part has its own staff. **Identify** the sections of the song where parts 1 and 3 both sing the melody.

**CD 12-13**
**MIDI 10**

# Ja-Da

*Words and Music by Bob Carleton*
*Arranged by Susan Brumfield*

# 8

# A Song for the Soul

"You Were on My Mind" is a popular song from the 1960s. It was performed by the group We Five in a folk/rock style. This version is arranged in two parts for male voices.

## Singing Tips

The vocal style for "You Were on My Mind" is primarily *legato*. Use strong consonants when you **sing** the phrases that contain repeated notes (*When I woke up this mornin'*).

## Reading Music Tips

**Read** verse 1 of "You Were on My Mind" using pitch syllables. **Identify** any repeating melodic three-note patterns. How many times is each pattern repeated in the song?

## Knowing the Score

The first section of "You Were on My Mind" is sung in unison. **Identify** the measure where the harmony part begins. Notice the smaller "cue notes." Those notes can be performed by a second group of voices as another harmony line.

Hi! We Five    Pete-Fullerton    Bob Jones

◄ We Five

M. Stewart    Jerry Burgan

Bev Bivens

# YOU WERE ON MY MIND

Words and Music by Sylvia Fricker

## 1960s on My Mind

**Listen** to this version of *You Were on My Mind*.

### You Were on My Mind

**by Sylvia Fricker**
**12-17   as performed by We Five**

The We Five rendition of this song went to Number Three on the charts in 1965.

### Folk/Rock Style

Folk music and rock 'n' roll were both popular in the 1960s. Although popular performing groups of the 1960s sang arrangements of true folk songs, they also performed songs that were composed in the folk style.

Sylvia Fricker composed "You Were on My Mind" in the folk style, but when We Five recorded the song, they broke with the tradition of using only acoustic instruments to accompany their singing. They added drums and an electric 12-string guitar to their accompaniment. Their million-selling version of the song matched the arrival of a new style of music that became known as folk/rock—a blend of rock 'n' roll with folk music. They led the way for other groups such as the Mamas and the Papas, Simon and Garfunkel, the Association, and many others to perform in this new style.

Ian Tyson ▶

Sylvia Fricker ▶

## Music MAKERS
## Sylvia Fricker

Singer/songwriter **Sylvia Fricker** (born 1940) is the composer of "You Were on My Mind." She is from Canada. Her music was inspired by the social and folk/rock movements of the 1960s. Fricker's early compositions influenced folk/rock musicians such as Jefferson Airplane and the Mamas and the Papas. Fellow Canadians Neil Young, Gordon Lightfoot, and Joni Mitchell were also inspired by her music. She has recorded the song "You Were on My Mind" twice, once as a duo with Ian Tyson and once on a solo album.

# 10

# Turn to Freedom

Freedom is experienced in many forms, such as freedom of speech, thought, and movement. Freedom from oppression was dreamed about by African American slaves until the end of the Civil War. "Oh, Freedom" is a song from the time of slavery that was sung during the time of the Civil Rights Movement.

## Singing Tips

Sing "Oh, Freedom" with a warm, full tone. Reflect the meaning of the words in the vocal quality of your singing.

Find the syncopations in the notation. Accent the initial consonants of syncopated words.

## Reading Music Tips

All voice parts have the same rhythms for the entire song. Clap and speak the text for each phrase, and then read the rhythm of the entire song.

## Knowing the Score

This song is in strophic form. There are four verses set to the same melody and harmony, which makes it simple to learn.

The top staff of each system is a descant written for a soloist or a small group of singers. The descant is performed only on the last verse. The middle staff of each system is divided into two parts and should be sung by unchanged voices. Males with changed voices should sing notes on the third staff. Which voice part has the melody? Choose a part to sing, and then **perform** the song with the recording.

CD 12-20
MIDI 13

# Oh, Freedom

*Gospel Song*
*Arranged by Joan R. Hillsman and Linda Twine*

# 11

# Believe in Song

"I'm a Believer" has been recorded by several artists, including the Monkees and Smash Mouth. **Listen** to this version of *I'm a Believer*. **Compare** it to the version in this book. What differences do you hear?

### I'm a Believer

**written and performed by Neil Diamond**

12-22 This is the original version of this popular song.

## Singing Tips

**Analyze** pop music sound. What makes pop vocal style? Consider timbre, pronunciation, rhythm, and voice placement. Use pop style when singing "I'm a Believer." Think about the meaning of the words as you sing. Enunciate the words so that the story can be understood.

## Reading Music Tips

The rhythmic patterns for each measure in the verse are different. However, each measure contains syncopation. Find the syncopations, and **describe** how each one is different.

## Knowing the Score

"I'm a Believer" is in verse-and-refrain form. Identify where the verse and refrain start on B♭, the **tonic** of the song.

Find the measures where part 1 divides into two parts. The upper notes of those divisions can be sung by a small group of singers. The solo beginning on the last page can be sung as written or an octave lower. Determine which part best fits your vocal range, and then **sing** the song with the recording.

---

**tonic** The key note in a scale.

◄ Neil Diamond

▼ Smash Mouth

▲ The Monkees

# I'm a Believer

Words and Music by Neil Diamond
Arranged by Susan Brumfield

# A CHANGE IN THE WEATHER

Science tells us that birds fly south in the late fall because they know winter is coming and they migrate to find a steady food supply. **Describe** what the poet suggests in "Something Told the Wild Geese."

Choral groups sing from octavos. Octavos are music scores that show both the vocal and keyboard accompaniment parts on the same page. Singers, accompanists, and conductors are able to stay together by following along with the other parts. "Something Told the Wild Geese" is an octavo arranged for mixed voices. Males with changed voices sing part 3, changing voices and females sing part 2, and unchanged voices and females with higher voices sing part 1. Study your part, and then **sing** the song with the recording.

## Singing Tips

**Analyze** the lyrics to determine what words and syllables should receive emphasis to portray the feelings described in the poem. Then sing the song expressively.

## Reading Music Tips

**Listen** to the right hand part of the piano accompaniment in the introduction. Listen to it a second time and follow part 1 in measures 7–10. Describe what you see and hear.

## Knowing the Score

"Something Told the Wild Geese" is through-composed. **Read** the notation to find the repeat of the opening phrase at the conclusion of the song.

CD 12-25
MIDI 15

# SOMETHING TOLD THE WILD GEESE

Words by Rachel Field

Music by Sherri Porterfield

*Legato*

*mp*

*poco rit.*  *a tempo*

*mp*

Some-thing told the wild geese it was time to go.

But be-neath warm feath-ers, some-thing cau-tioned, some-thing cau-tioned, "Frost." _____

But be-neath warm feath-ers, some-thing cau-tioned, some-thing cau-tioned, "Frost." _____

But be-neath warm feath-ers, some-thing cau-tioned, some-thing cau-tioned, "Frost." _____

All the sag-ging or - chards steamed with am-ber spice.

All the sag-ging or - chards steamed with am-ber spice.

All the sag-ging or - chards steamed with am-ber spice.

## Meet the Lyricist

**Rachel Field** (1894–1942), an American author and poet, is best known for her books and poetry for children. She was born in New York City, but spent most of her childhood in Massachusetts. Field first achieved fame by winning the Newbery Medal with *Hitty*, a story of an early American wooden doll purchased in an antique shop. *Calico Beach*, the story of the experience of a French servant girl, is considered by critics to be one of Field's best books.

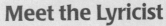

## Sherri Porterfield

**Sherri Porterfield** (born 1958) is an award-winning middle school choir teacher and a well-known composer. She has devoted her career as a composer to writing and arranging music for junior high and middle school voices. "Something Told the Wild Geese" is one of her most popular compositions.

Porterfield was born in Missouri. She began her teaching career in her home state, but later moved to Kansas. Under her direction, the choirs at her junior high school won many awards and performed at numerous state and national conventions.

Porterfield has composed or arranged more than 100 choral compositions, and is in demand as a clinician and guest conductor of elementary, junior high, and high school honor choirs throughout the country.

# Lift UP Your VOICE

## Review and Assess

Throughout Lift Up Your Voice, you have

- sung unison and two-, three-, and four-part music in a variety of styles.
- listened to vocal music in a variety of styles.
- learned how interesting and varied vocal music can be.

Singing notes and rhythms and remembering the words to the songs are just the first steps of excellent music making. Real musicianship involves singing with appropriate style, using all of the good habits of singing that you've been practicing. No matter what style of music you sing, how well you sing matters the most.

## Review What You Learned

Review what you have studied and practiced. With your teacher, choose performance activities that demonstrate your excellent musicianship. Make careful choices that show your vocal skills and range. Selecting the right music to perform is an important part of becoming a successful musician.

Choose songs from this list that you like and sing well.

| Song | Features |
| --- | --- |
| "Proud" | unison |
| "Over My Head" | echo song |
| "Si si si" | three-part singing in Congolese style |
| "Con el vito" | two-part singing in Spanish |
| "One Family" | four-part singing in African community style |
| "Ja-Da" | three-part singing in jazz style |
| "You Were on My Mind" | two-part boys singing |
| "Chapel of Love" | three-part girls singing |
| "Oh, Freedom" | three-part gospel singing with a descant |
| "I'm a Believer" | three-part popular singing with solo descant |
| "Something Told the Wild Geese" | three-part singing in minor mode |

# Show What You Know

1. Think about the songs that you enjoy and can sing well. With the help of your teacher, select several songs from the list to sing. Each one should demonstrate one of these skills.

   • Sing a unison melody with classmates and a live or taped accompaniment.

   • Sing the melody of a two- or three-part arrangement with classmates and a live or taped accompaniment.

   • Sing a harmony part in a two- or three-part arrangement with classmates and a live or taped accompaniment.

   • Sing a melody alone with a live or taped accompaniment.

   • Sing a harmony part in a two- or three-part arrangement with one person on each part.

2. Compare and contrast three songs from the list. You may also choose to review the listening selections in the module. In a two-paragraph essay, consider the following.

   • style of selections

   • number of vocal parts

   • difficulty of the melody

   • range

   • language or diction challenges

## What to Look and Listen For

Excellent musicians often record themselves so they can evaluate their own work and refine their performances. Record your performance using digital audio, cassette tape, or video tape.

Ask yourself whether all these things are true about your performance. Use this checklist to see how you're doing and to identify aspects of your playing and singing that are in need of further refinement.

• Posture is upright and relaxed.

• Jaw and mouth are relaxed and open.

• Breath is inhaled with natural, relaxed expansion of the body.

• Tone is free, open, and even throughout range.

• Singing is accurate and in tune.

• Rhythm is precise and sung with inflection.

• Diction is clear (all words are understood).

• Dynamic and rhythmic changes are used to create expressive effects.

# Musical TOOL KIT

## Music Theory and Fundamentals

> "I know that twelve notes in each octave and the varieties of rhythm offer me opportunities that all of human genius will never exhaust."
>
> —Igor Stravinsky (1882–1971)

# 1 Rhythm Basics

Have you ever tapped your foot or nodded your head to music? If you did, you were probably moving to the **beat.** One way to represent one sound per beat is with a **quarter note (♩).** Silence instead of sound for one beat can be represented by a **quarter rest(𝄽).** Tap the beat as you **read** quarter notes and quarter rests using rhythm syllables.

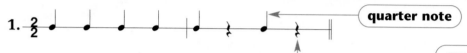

Music with only sounds or rests on the beat would be very boring. Combinations of different sounds are **rhythms.** In the music below, two even sounds on a beat are represented by two **eighth notes (♪♪).**

Tap the beat while you **read** the rhythm.

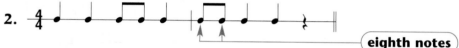

Turn to "Rock Around the Clock" on page B-18 for more practice reading quarter notes, quarter rests, and eighth notes. Note how the style of the music changes the feeling of the eighth notes from even to uneven.

# 2 Longer Sounds, Longer Rests

Some notes last longer than a beat. How would you represent these sounds using notation? If a quarter note equals the beat, you can use a **tie ( ⌣ )** to connect two quarter notes (♩ ♩) to show one sound that lasts for two beats. You can also write the same rhythm using a **half note (♩).** Tap the beat as you **read** these examples. What do you notice about them?

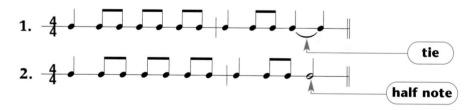

For more practice reading half notes, go to "Bear Dance" on page I-10.

How would you represent two beats of silence using notation? You have a choice! You could write two quarter rests(𝄽 𝄽) or one **half rest (▬).**

Tap the beat as you **read** this rhythm. Then look for more half rests in *"Cheki, morena"* on page I-16.

half rest

3.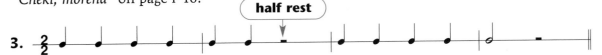

Experiment with ties to make even longer sounds. If the quarter note equals one beat, tying three quarter notes together creates a three-beat sound. ♩‿♩‿♩ = ♩· This symbol ( ♩· ) is a **dotted-half note. Read** this new note in the rhythm below and in *"Fiddler on the Roof"* on page E-5.

dotted-half note

4.

Here's a trick question. How many ties are needed to make a four-beat sound using quarter notes? ♩‿♩‿♩‿♩ = 𝅝 In this example, a **whole note ( 𝅝 )** sounds for four beats. Tap the beat as you **read** the rhythm below. Look for a similar rhythm in *"Over My Head"* on page G-9.

5.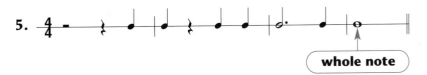

whole note

# 3 Syncopation

**Listen** to *"Let's Get the Rhythm of the Band"* on page E-29 or *"Cheki, morena"* on page I-16. Both of these songs have **syncopation.** What is syncopation? Syncopation happens when an accented rhythm or long rhythm happens in an unexpected place or off the beat.

- Tap your foot to the beat as you clap four eighth notes. (♫ ♫)
- Now accent the second eighth note. (♫ ♫)
- Tie the second and third eighth notes. (♫‿♫)
- Write the rhythm like this. (♪ ♩ ♪)

That's one kind of syncopation! Read the syncopation in the rhythm below and in *"Let's Get the Rhythm of the Band"* on page E-29.

## Meter and Measure

**Read** this line of rhythm. Then tap the beat while others clap the rhythm. **Identify** beats that sound and feel stronger. What patterns do you hear?

Here is the same rhythm with **accents (>).** Emphasize the notes and rhythms that have accent marks. How many beats do you hear from one accent to the next?

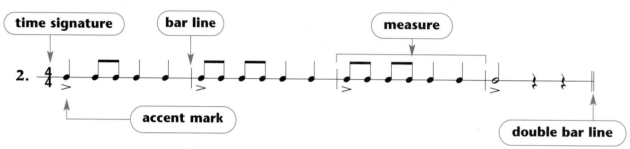

In the above example, the beats are grouped in sets of four. The first beat in each set sounds and feels stronger than the rest. A **time signature** indicates the grouping of beats or the **meter. Identify** the 4/4 time signature. The top number indicates that beats are grouped in sets of four. The beat note is a quarter note, so the bottom number is a four. Note that each set of four beats is separated by a **bar line.** The space between bar lines is a **measure.** A **double bar line** means you have reached the end of a section. **Read** the rhythm above. Then find similar rhythms in "Fiddler on the Roof" on page E-5.

## More Meter and Rhythm

Music is written in many kinds of meters. **Identify** the time signatures in the music below. Tap the beat as you **read** the rhythms. Accent the first beat in each measure to show the meter of the music.

Find and **read** similar rhythms in "Something Told the Wild Geese" on page G-39 and "Andante" from *Ten Little Ostinato Pieces* on page I-62. Look for other examples of rhythms written in triple or duple meter in your book.

**Create** rhythm pieces in 2/4, 3/4, or 4/4.

# 6 ▸ Repeat Signs

**Repeat signs** in music notation tell musicians to do exactly what the name says—repeat! Do it again! **Play** this rhythm on an instrument of your choice. Observe the repeat sign by repeating the rhythm. Then find this rhythm and the repeat signs on page E-2.

repeat sign

1.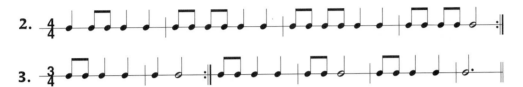

One repeat sign tells musicians to go back to the beginning and perform that part of the music again. **Read** these two examples.

2.

3.

Identify other examples of repeat signs on other pages of your book.

# 7 ▸ 1st and 2nd Endings

Sometimes a phrase or section of music that is repeated has two different endings. **Identify** the markings for 1st ending and 2nd ending below. **Perform** the rhythm below on a percussion instrument of your choice. When you get to the repeat sign, return to the beginning and perform the first measure again. Then skip the 1st ending and perform the 2nd ending.

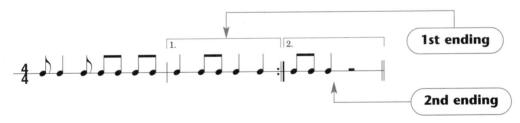

1st ending

2nd ending

You can find a similar rhythm with 1st and 2nd endings on page I-62.

# Basics of Melody

Hum or whistle your favorite song. You are humming or whistling a melody. A **melody** is the series of musical **pitches** that you recognize as a song or tune. If you created your own melody and wanted to write it down, how would you do that? One way to write a melody is to show the pitches on a **staff.** The musical staff, which has five lines and four spaces, is like a graph that shows musical pitches. The higher the pitch, the higher the placement of notes on the staff.

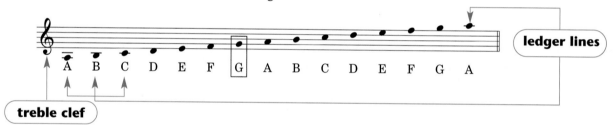

How will you and others know which pitch is which? Fortunately, pitches, or **notes,** have names that correspond to letters of the alphabet from A to G. There are only seven letters from A to G, and there are more than seven pitches so the musical alphabet starts over after G as pitches go upward. **Ledger lines** are placed above or below the staff to make room for higher and lower pitches. How many As can you find on the staff below? Which As are on ledger lines?

Notice the **treble clef** at the beginning of the staff above. Clefs provide cues about the letter names of pitches. The treble clef is also called the G-clef because the spiral of the clef circles around and ends on the second line. The note on line two is G!

# mi-re-do

You can identify pitches using letter names, or read them using pitch syllables. Singing pitch syllables will help you hear relationships between pitches. Hum or sing the first three notes of "Hot Cross Buns." Then sing the same pitches on the syllables *mi, re,* and *do.* Use hand signs as you **sing** these three notes again.

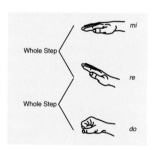

The mi-re-do pattern can appear anywhere on the staff. In the example below, *do* is G. What is the letter name for *re*? For *mi*? **Sing** the example using hand signs and pitch syllables. Then **sing** it again using letter names.

mi   re   do

**Analyze** the melody below. *Do* is G. Find the *mi-re-do* patterns. The **interval** or distance between *mi* and *re* is a **whole step** or **major second.** The interval from *re* to *do* is also a whole step. The interval from *do* to *mi* is a **major third. Identify** the major third in the melody. **Perform** the melody, first using hand signs and pitch syllables, and then using letter names. Find more *mi-re-do* patterns in the song "Little Darlin'" on page F-30.

**1.**

Remember, the *mi-re-do* pattern can start on any pitch and appear anywhere on the staff. In the next melody, *do* is C. What are the letter names for *re* and *mi*? **Sing** the melody, first using hand signs and pitch syllables, and then using letter names.

**2.**

mi   re   do   re   mi   re   do   mi   do

 ## More Melody: *fa*

The next pitch up from *mi* is **fa.** The interval from *mi* to *fa* is a **half step** or **minor second.** Half steps are smaller intervals than whole steps.

**Analyze** these melodies to find *fa*. **Sing** them using hand signs and pitch syllables. Then sing them using letter names. For more practice, find similar melody patterns in "Lean on Me" on page E-22.

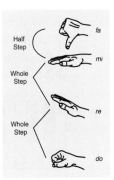

The mi-re-do pattern can appear anywhere on the staff. In the example below, *do* is G. What is the letter name for *re*? For *mi*? **Sing** the example using hand signs and pitch syllables. Then **sing** it again using letter names.

mi   re   do

**Analyze** the melody below. *Do* is G. Find the *mi-re-do* patterns. The **interval** or distance between *mi* and *re* is a **whole step** or **major second.** The interval from *re* to *do* is also a whole step. The interval from *do* to *mi* is a **major third. Identify** the major third in the melody. **Perform** the melody, first using hand signs and pitch syllables, and then using letter names. Find more *mi-re-do* patterns in the song "Little Darlin'" on page F-30.

**1.**

Remember, the *mi-re-do* pattern can start on any pitch and appear anywhere on the staff. In the next melody, *do* is C. What are the letter names for *re* and *mi*? **Sing** the melody, first using hand signs and pitch syllables, and then using letter names.

**2.**

mi   re   do   re   mi   re   do   mi   do

 ## More Melody: *fa*

The next pitch up from *mi* is **fa.** The interval from *mi* to *fa* is a **half step** or **minor second.** Half steps are smaller intervals than whole steps.

**Analyze** these melodies to find *fa*. **Sing** them using hand signs and pitch syllables. Then sing them using letter names. For more practice, find similar melody patterns in "Lean on Me" on page E-22.

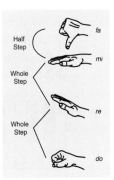

Musical Tool Kit          H-7

# Melody Review

**Sing** *do-re-mi-fa* with hand signs and pitch syllables to review the sound. Now, **sing** the melody below, first using hand signs and pitch syllables, and then using letter names. **Identify** the major seconds, minor seconds, and major thirds. The melody also has the intervals of a minor third (three half steps) and a perfect fourth. Find them. Turn to page I-66 for more practice reading these pitches.

# Step Up to *so*

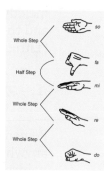

Look at the chart of hand signs and **sing** from *do* up to *so*. The interval from *fa* to *so* is a whole step or major second. **Sing** the next melody using hand signs, pitch syllables, or letter names. Then find and **read** similar melody patterns in "All for One" on page E-8.

# Five Notes in Two Places

**Read** the *do-re-mi-fa-so* pattern below the first keyboard. Now move *do* to G on the second line. **Read** the pattern below the second keyboard. **Compare** the keyboards. How is the interval from *mi* to *fa* different than the interval from *do* to *re*, *re* to *mi*, and *fa* to *so*?

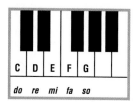

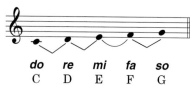

TRO © Copyright 1956 (Renewed) Ludlow Music Publishers, Inc., New York, NY Used by Permission.

**Sing** the next melody, first using hand signs and pitch syllables, and then using letter names. Then **play** it on a keyboard or a melody instrument of your choice.

 ## When *do* Is F

What happens when *do* is written as first space F? A problem develops. Look at the keyboard. The interval from A to B is a major second, or whole step. We need a minor second, or half step, between *mi* and *fa*. To solve the problem, play or sing B♭, the black piano key to the left of B. The **flat sign ( ♭ )** appears next to the letter name on the keyboard and before the B on the staff. B is now B♭. **Sing** or **play** *do-re-mi-fa-so* starting on F.

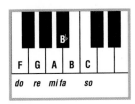 

**Sing** this melody using hand signs, pitch syllables, and letter names.

Writing in all of those flat signs is a lot of work. **Compare** the melody above to the melody below. All of the flat signs in the melody above have been moved to the **key signature** at the beginning of the music. This key signature tells you that every B in the melody will be B♭. **Sing** the melody, first using hand signs and pitch syllables, and then using letter names.

# 15 ▸ Conducting Meter

When an ensemble has a conductor, one of the conductor's responsibilities is to show the beat and meter of the music. The conductor looks at the time signature to find out which meter to show. When the time signature is $\frac{4}{4}$, conductors use this pattern. **Conduct** as you use rhythm syllables to **read** this example. Then turn to page E-29 and conduct "Let's Get the Rhythm of the Band."

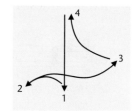

1.

When the time signature is $\frac{3}{4}$, conductors use this pattern to show the beat and meter. **Conduct** as you **read** this rhythm. For more practice, conduct and read "Something Told the Wild Geese" on page G-39.

2.

# 16 ▸ Dynamics

Hum your favorite tune quietly. Sing it loudly. You can perform at different volume levels. In printed music, **dynamic markings** indicate how loudly or softly to perform. The mark *p* indicates *piano*, an Italian word for soft. The mark *f* indicates *forte*, an Italian word for loud. A ***crescendo*** ⟨ indicates to perform gradually louder. A ***decrescendo*** ⟩ means gradually softer.

**Identify** the dynamic marks in this example. Then **perform** the rhythm with the dynamics indicated in the music.

# 17 Ties and More Ties

These rhythms may look easy, but the ties create rhythm challenges. Which examples include ties from an eighth note to a quarter note? Which examples include ties across the bar line? **Conduct** the beat as you **read** these rhythms. For more practice, look for ties in "Let's Get the Rhythm of the Band" on page E-29, "Lean on Me" on page E-22, and "*Cielito lindo*" on page I-20.

# 18 Eighth Rests

What is the difference between these two examples? The second example begins with an eighth rest. An eighth rest shows a half beat of silence when the meter is $\frac{2}{4}$, $\frac{3}{4}$, or $\frac{4}{4}$. **Read** both examples.

**Identify** the eighth rests in the music below. **Conduct** the beat as you **read** the rhythm. Then turn to "Flip, Flop and Fly" on page I-32 for more practice.

# ◆19◆ Anacrusis

**Conduct** a three-beat pattern. The first beat of the pattern is the strongest beat. A note that comes before the first strong beat is an **anacrusis.** Other words for anacrusis are **upbeat** or **pick-up note.** **Identify** the anacrusis in this example. Then conduct as you **read** the rhythm.

1.

In this example, the words show the strong beats. **Conduct** and **read** the music. Turn to "Fiddler on the Roof" on page E-5 for more practice.

2.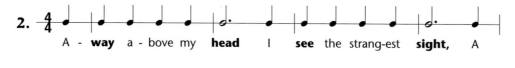

A - **way** a - bove my **head** I **see** the strang-est **sight,** A

**fid** - dler on the **roof,** who's **up** there day and **night.**

Some music has more than one note in the anacrusis. **Identify** the anacrusis notes in these examples. **Conduct** the beat as you **read** the rhythms. Find more anacrusis notes in "America, the Beautiful" on page I-4 and "Certainly, Lord" on page I-13.

3.

4.

# ◆20◆ Conducting in $\frac{2}{4}$

When the time signature is $\frac{2}{4}$, conductors use this pattern to show the beat and meter. **Conduct** and **read** these rhythms. Which rhythm includes an anacrusis? How do you know?

1.

2.

# 21 Dotted-Quarter Note

You already know that a dotted-half note has the same duration as three tied quarter notes.  Tap the beat as you **read** this rhythm.

1.

Now tap eighth notes while a friend **performs** this rhythm. Then switch jobs.

2.

Here are three ways to show the new rhythm. **Describe** each one. A **dotted-quarter note ( ♩. )** lasts for one and one-half beats.

3.    4.   5.

**dotted-quarter note**

**Identify** the dotted-quarter note in this example. **Conduct** the beat as you use rhythm syllables to **read** the rhythm. Then turn to "This Land Is Your Land" on page I-66 for more practice reading dotted-quarter notes.

6.

These examples are from the patriotic songs "America" and "America, the Beautiful." To practice the rhythms, conduct and read them here. Then turn to pages I-2 and I-4 and **read** the dotted-quarter and eighth note rhythm in the song notation.

7.

8.

TRO © Copyright 1956 (Renewed) Ludlow Music Publishers, Inc., New York, NY Used by Permission.

Dotted-Quarter Note

**Musical Tool Kit**   H–13

## 22 Moving Up to *la*

**Sing** *do-re-mi-fa-so* with hand signs and pitch syllables to review. Look at the hand sign chart. **Sing** *do-re-mi-fa-so-la* using hand signs and pitch syllables. The interval from *so* to *la* is a whole step. **Identify** the whole steps and half steps in *do-re-mi-fa-so-la*. Look at the two examples below. What is the letter name for *la* when *do* is C? When *do* is G?

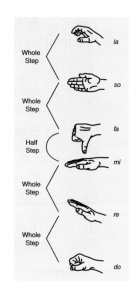

**Read** and **sing** these melodies, first using hand signs and pitch syllables, and then using letter names. Practice reading a similar melody in "I Love Peanuts" on page E-20. For a challenge, **read** a melody with *do* in a different place in "Pay Me My Money Down" on page I-46.

## 23 The Slur

This melody has five curved lines. Some of them are ties. Remember, a tie connects two notes of the same pitch. **Identify** the ties. What is different about the curved line in the second measure? A curved line connecting two or more different pitches is called a **slur.** A slur tells musicians to perform in a smooth, connected manner called *legato.* **Sing** or **play** this melody. For a challenge, **read** the same melody with *do* in a different place on page F-28.

**Identify** three slurs and one tie in this melody. How do you tell them apart? **Sing** or **play** the melody. Then turn to page I-2 for more practice.

**24** **Low *la-la*₁**

Sing from *do* up to *la* using hand signs and pitch syllables. You have just sung *la* above *do*. Now find *la* below *do* or **low *la* (*la*₁)**. The interval between *do* and low *la* is a **minor third**—the same as the interval between *so* and *mi*. **Analyze** the melody. **Identify** the minor third. **Read** and **sing** the melody, first using hand signs and pitch syllables, and then using letter names.

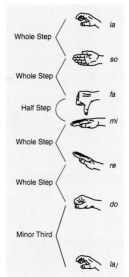

For an extra challenge, **read** "My Home's Across the Blue Ridge Mountains" on page F-6 with *do* in a different place.

**25** **Low *ti-ti*₁**

To sing or play from *do* to low *la* without skipping a pitch, you'll need a new syllable—**low *ti* (*ti*₁).** The interval between *do* and low *ti* is a half step or minor second. **Sing** these F-*do* and C-*do* melodies, first using hand signs and pitch syllables, and then using letter names.

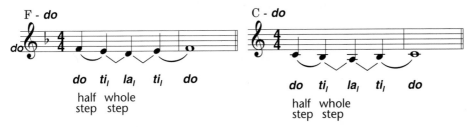

When G is *do*, the note F must change because the interval between F and G is a whole step. Remember, the interval between *ti*₁ and *do* is a half step. Placing a **sharp sign (♯)** before F raises the pitch a half step. F♯ (*ti*₁) to G (*do*) is a half step. **Sing** this melody using hand signs and pitch syllables.

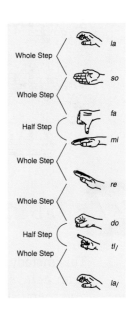

**1.**

The key signature of this melody indicates that every F will be F♯. **Read** and **sing** using hand signs and syllables. Then sing using letter names. **Read** a similar melody in "Ev'rybody Loves Saturday Night" on page I-24 with *do* in a different place.

**2.**

# 26 How Low Can You Go?

**Sing** *do-ti₁-la₁* using hand signs and pitch syllables. If you continue downward, what pitch syllable will you need next? It's **low so (so₁).**
**Sing** this melody using hand signs and pitch syllables. Then turn to page C-41 for more reading practice.

**1.**

**Conduct** the beat as you **read** the rhythm only. Next, **sing** using hand signs and pitch syllables. Then sing using letter names. Turn to page I-16 for more reading practice.

**2.**

Many melodies you have sung or played end on *do*. Melodies that end on low *la* sound different. **Read** and **sing** these melodies, first using hand signs and pitch syllables, and then using letter names. For an extra challenge, turn to page E-29 and **read** a melody with low *la* in a different place.

**3.**

**4.**

# 27 Going Up: High *do* and *ti*

This melody begins on **high *do* (*do*ᶦ).** The interval between *do* and high *do* is an **octave.** Sing this melody, first using hand signs and pitch syllables, and then using letter names. For more practice, **read** a similar melody with *do* in a different place on page I-13.

**1.**

**Identify** *ti* in the next melody. What is the interval between *ti* and high *do?* **Sing** the melody using hand signs and pitch syllables. Then sing using letter names. **Read** "I Love Peanuts" on page E-20.

 # Key Signature Check

**Play** *do-re-mi-fa-so-la-ti-do*ᴵ on a keyboard. Begin on C, then F, and then G. Now move *do* to D. Experiment to find the same pattern of pitches. What adjustments do you have to make to get the same sound?

 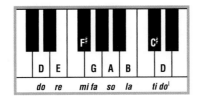

To maintain the pattern of whole steps and half steps between *do* and *do*ᴵ, you must raise F to F♯ and C to C♯. Sing *do-re-mi-fa-so-la-ti-do*ᴵ beginning on D and using hand signs and pitch syllables. Then **play** from *do* to *do*ᴵ on a keyboard starting on D.

How many sharps do you see in the key signature of these melodies? The key signature indicates that D is *do*. Every F is F♯ and every C is C♯. **Sing** the melodies, first using hand signs and pitch syllables, and then using letter names. **Play** the melodies on an instrument of your choice. Turn to page G-13 for more reading practice.

#  Move It: Sixteenth Notes

Tap your foot to the beat as you **improvise** eight-beat rhythms using quarter notes, quarter rests, and eighth notes.

The rhythm symbols above occupy one beat when written in $\frac{2}{4}$, $\frac{3}{4}$, or $\frac{4}{4}$. When four sounds occur in one beat, they are notated with four **sixteenth notes (**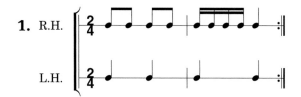**).**

**Perform** the rhythm below by tapping the beat with your left hand and the rhythm with your right hand. For an extra challenge, switch hands, or tap your foot while you clap the rhythm or perform it on an instrument of your choice.

# 30 Eighth and Sixteenth Combinations

Eighth and sixteenth notes occur in all kinds of combinations. Here is one.

**Identify** the eighth and two sixteenth note combination in the rhythms below. Tap a steady beat as you **read** these rhythms using rhythm syllables.

**Describe** how this combination of eighth and sixteenth notes is different than the one you have just learned.

**Identify** the two-sixteenth and eighth note combinations in the rhythms below. Tap a steady beat as you **read** these rhythms using rhythm syllables.

3.

4.

Put all of these sixteenth-note rhythms together! Tap the beat as you **read** the rhythms using rhythm syllables. Then **perform** similar rhythms in "Shortnin' Bread" on page F-27.

5.

## 31 Composing with Sixteenth Notes

**Create** and **perform** 8-beat rhythm compositions using your new rhythm vocabulary. Use at least one of each of these rhythms.

**Notate** your composition. **Perform** it on a nonpitched percussion instrument of your choice. Extend your composition by combining your ideas with those of one or two classmates. Experiment with layers of sound, dynamics, and tempo to create a longer piece.

# 32 Dotted Rhythms with Sixteenth Notes

Let's make more sixteenth note combinations by adding dotted rhythms. **Analyze** this rhythm. Will the sounds be even or uneven? This rhythm symbol is called a dotted-eighth and sixteenth note.

Tap the beat as you **read** these rhythms using rhythm syllables. Which example has ancrusis notes? For more practice, **read** the rhythms of "The Star-Spangled Banner" on page I-56.

**1.**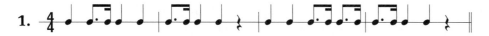

**2.**

Solve this rhythm puzzle. **Analyze** the rhythm to find the tie. Tap a steady beat as you **perform** the rhythm without the tie, then with a tie. How does the sound change? For more rhythm practice, **read** the rhythm of "*Nampaya omame*" on page D-10.

**3.**

## 33 Reverse the Rhythm

Reverse the rhythm you just learned. **Analyze** this new rhythm. Are the sounds even or uneven? Which sound is longer?

**Identify** the sixteenth and dotted-eighth note rhythm in these examples. Which example includes an anacrusis? Syncopation? Tap the beat as you **read** these rhythms. Then **perform** these rhythms in the songs on page F-6 and page F-13.

1.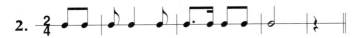

**Identify** the anacrusis, syncopation, and new rhythm in this example. Tap the beat as you use rhythm syllables to **read** this rhythm.

2.

## 34 More Composing with Sixteenth Notes

**Improvise** 8-beat rhythms on nonpitched percussion instruments. Include this rhythm at least once in each 8-beat improvisation.

Continue improvising 8-beat rhythms. Now include this rhythm at least once in every 8-beat improvisation.

Continue experimenting with different combinations of the eighth and sixteenth-note rhythms that you know. For example, what does a dotted eighth and sixteenth followed by a sixteenth and dotted eighth sound like? What happens if you reverse the order?

Now **create** a new rhythm composition using all of the sixteenth note combinations you know.

**Notate** your composition and **perform** it on a nonpitched percussion instrument of your choice.

# 35 ▸ Scales: They're Major!

Let's review. Starting on the pitch C, **sing** *do-re-mi-fa-so-la-ti-do¹* using hand signs and pitch syllables. Look at the keyboard below and sing the same pitches using letter names. You are singing the **C major scale.** **Play** the C major scale.

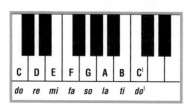

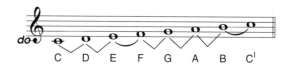

A **scale** is a particular arrangement of whole steps and half steps. In the **major scale** the half steps are between *mi-fa* and *ti-do¹*. **Play** the C major scale.

# 36 ▸ A Major Formula

A major scale can begin on any pitch. No matter where you begin, the order of whole steps and half steps is the same. The major scale formula is:

whole-whole-half-whole-whole-whole-half

**Analyze** the **G major scale** below. **Compare** the order of whole and half steps to the major scale formula. **Sing** the G major scale, first using pitch syllables, and then using letter names. **Play** it on a keyboard or other melody instrument.

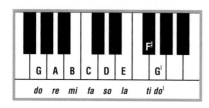

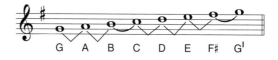

The G scale above has one sharp. What is its letter name? **Analyze** the D scale on the next page. Compare the order of whole steps and half steps to the major scale formula. How many sharps are in the **D major scale?** What are their letter names? What sharp is in both the G and D scales?

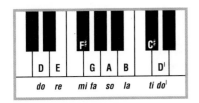

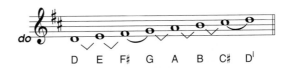

Solve this scale puzzle. What is the relationship between the last sharp in the key signature and the letter name of the scale? What is the letter name of the scale with three sharps—F♯, C♯, and G♯?

 ## Major Scales with Flats

Let's look at scales with flats. Remember the major scale formula: whole-whole-half-whole-whole-whole-half. **Analyze** the **F major scale.** **Compare** the order of whole and half steps to the major scale formula. **Sing** the F major scale, first using pitch syllables, and then using letter names. **Play** it on a keyboard.

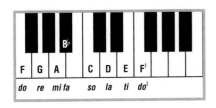

The **B♭ major scale** has two flats. Why are two flats needed? What are the letter names of the flats? **Sing** and **play** the B♭ major scale.

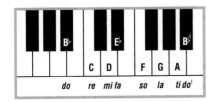

Solve this scale puzzle. The F major scale has one flat—B♭. The B♭ major scale has two flats—B♭ and E♭. What will be the name of the scale with three flats?

# Melodic Sequence

**Sing** this melody, first using hand signs and pitch syllables, and then **play** it on a melody instrument of your choice. **Compare** measures 1 and 2 to measures 3 and 4, then 5 and 6. A melodic phrase or pattern that is repeated, with each repetition starting on a different pitch, is called a **melodic sequence.** Find the melodic sequence in the song on page E-14.

1.

**Sing** or **play** this melodic sequence. In what measure does the repetition begin? Find this melodic sequence in the song on page D-18.

2.

# Intervals—Seconds and Thirds

Distances between musical pitches are called intervals. You already know whole steps or major seconds, and half steps or minor seconds. Work with a partner to **identify** as many major seconds and minor seconds as you can find on the keyboard shown below. Which type of second cannot be played with two black keys?

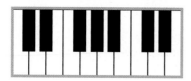

**Sing** this melody using hand signs and pitch syllables. Then sing it using letter names. **Play** it on a melody instrument of your choice. **Identify** the thirds—*do-mi* and *mi-so.*

1.

Thirds are written on consecutive lines or consecutive spaces. **Identify** the thirds in the melody below. Then **sing** or **play** it. Look for thirds in "Rock Around the Clock" on page B-18, with *do* in a different place.

**2.**

**Identify** the thirds in this melody. **Sing** or **play** the melody. Then find this melody in "Surfin' U.S.A." on page I-58.

**3.**

For an extra challenge, **analyze** the melodies in this lesson and **identify** major thirds (made up of two whole steps) and minor thirds (made of one whole step and one half step).

# More Intervals–Fourths, Fifths, Sixths and Sevenths

**Sing** this melody using hand signs and pitch syllables, or **play** it on a melody instrument of your choice. **Analyze** the melody to find the seconds, thirds, and **fourths.** **Read** a similar melody on page F-21.

**1.**

This melody uses intervals of a **fifth** and a **sixth.** **Identify** the fifths and sixths. Then **perform** the melody. Practice reading a melody with fifths and sixth on page E-2.

**2.**

**Analyze** this melody to find the interval of a **seventh.** **Read** and **sing** or **play** the melody. Then find and read this melody in "*Cielito lindo*" on page I-20.

**3.**

# 41 ▶ Three Major Chords

Find and **play** a C, E, and G that are close to each other on a keyboard. You have just played a **chord**—three or more pitches sounded simultaneously. A chord built from *do* includes the pitches *do-mi-so*. It is called the **tonic** chord or **I chord** because it is built from the first scale degree.

Look at the keyboard and C major scale. **Play** the first, third, and fifth pitches of the scale (*do-mi-so*) simultaneously. You played the I chord in the key of C. Note that scale degrees are Arabic numerals (1-7) and chord names are Roman numerals (I, IV, V).

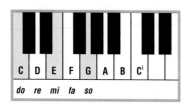

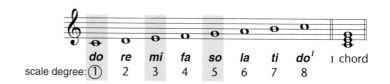

Find the pitches of the **IV chord** in the key of C. The lowest pitch is F (*fa*). Which other two pitches will you use? **Play** the IV chord.

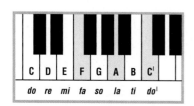

**Identify** and **play** the pitches for the **V chord** in the key of C.

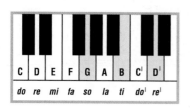

# 42 ▶ Chords in F

Sing or **play** the F major scale. Then **identify** and **play** the I, IV, and V chords in the key of F. In what other keys can you play these three chords? Wow! Those last two chords are pretty high in pitch. Solve the problem by using the pitches below *do* to build the IV and V chords.

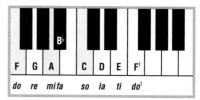

# 43 ▸ Reading Chord Symbols

Sometimes musicians read chord symbols when they perform. Each slash (/) in the music represents a beat. The I and V represent chords in the key of G. **Play** these chords on the beat. Change chords when the chord symbols change.

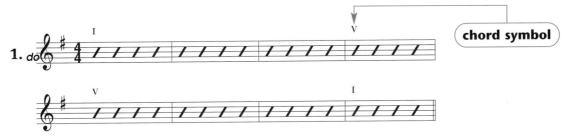

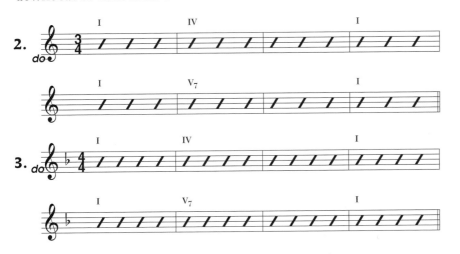

Practice the I, IV, and V chords in the keys of C and F. **Identify** and **play** the chords, changing when the chord symbols change. For an extra challenge, play the chord **root**—the lowest note in a chord—on the downbeat of each measure and the full chord on all other beats.

# 44 ▸ What Makes a Chord Major?

**Play** the I, IV, and V chords in the key of C. What is similar about them? Why are they called **major chords?** **Analyze** the chords. The interval between the lower two pitches is a major third, or two whole steps. The interval between the higher two pitches is a minor third, or a whole step plus a half step. This arrangement of thirds sounds like a major chord. What other major chords can you find on the keyboard?

# 45 ▸ Minor Scales

**Sing** or **play** a major scale from *do* to *do'*. Remember, the arrangement of whole and half steps in a major scale is whole-whole-half-whole-whole-whole-half. **Sing** or **play** the new scale below. It begins and ends on *la*. **Analyze** the order of whole and half steps.

1.

The **natural minor scale** begins and ends on *la*. The arrangement of half steps and whole steps is whole-half-whole-whole-half-whole-whole. **Play** the minor scale beginning on E below. **Compare** it to the minor scale beginning on A.

2.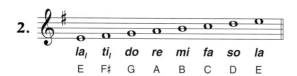

# 46 ▸ Minor Chords

You can build minor chords the same way you built major chords. **Play** the first, third, and fifth scale degrees of the **E natural minor scale** below. You have played a **minor i chord.**

1.

How are major and minor chords different from each other? Remember, a major chord has a major third as the bottom interval and a minor third as the top interval. **Play** the minor i chord you learned above. **Analyze** the thirds. The minor third is now on the bottom, and the major third is on the top! **Play** the minor i chord you have learned to accompany the song "Shortnin' Bread" on page F-27.

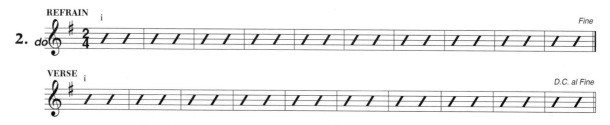

# 47 The Minor iv Chord

**Play** the **C natural minor scale.** Build and **play** a chord beginning on the fourth scale degree. This is the **minor iv chord.**

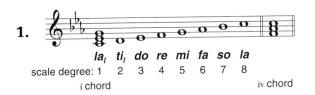

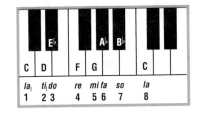

**Play** the i and iv chords in C minor to accompany "Let's Get the Rhythm of the Band" on page E-29. As a challenge **play** the root of the chord on the downbeat of each measure and the full chord on the remaining beats.

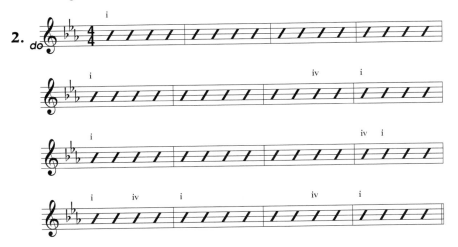

# 48 A Different Minor Scale

**Identify** the scale degree that has been changed in this minor scale. When the seventh scale degree is raised, the scale is called **harmonic minor. Sing** or **play** the harmonic minor scale. Then **sing** this harmonic minor melody. For more practice, **sing** or **play** the melody of "Con el vito" on page G-15.

## Share What You Know

Select one piece from the module that is your personal favorite. Prepare a presentation for the class that will help students understand the music itself and why you like the music. Your presentation may be placed on poster board, on overhead transparencies, or on presentation software. You should start your presentation with basic facts about the piece—title, composer, the approximate date of its composition—and explanations of how the sounds of the music convey the composer's intentions—the mood, the emotion, the picture, or idea. Be sure to include in your presentation the four aspects of music description that you've used before: the actual sounds that make up the music (timbre); the organization of the sounds (melody, rhythm, harmony, form, tempo, dynamics); the emotional effects that the sounds elicit from the listener; and the cultural function of the music. In your presentation, you should play excerpts from the piece to illustrate your points.

# PERFORMANCE ANTHOLOGY

Gene Autry ▶

▲ The Beach Boys

"When you play from your heart, all of a sudden, there's no gravity. You don't feel the weight of the world, of bills, of anything. That's why people love it. Your so-called insurmountable problems disappear and instead of problems you get possibilities."
—Carlos Santana (born 1947)

◀ Janis Joplin

John Lee Hooker ▶

# America in Harmony

The melody of "America" is older than the United States. During the American Revolution, the colonists knew this melody as "God Save the King." Today, British citizens sing "God Save the Queen." Around 1832, Samuel Francis Smith wrote new words to the melody for a Fourth of July celebration. **Sing** the melody of "America."

**CD 13-1**
**MIDI 16**

## America

*Words by Samuel Francis Smith*

*Traditional Melody*

1. My coun-try! 'tis of thee, Sweet land of lib-er-ty, Of thee I
2. My na-tive coun-try, thee, Land of the no-ble free, Thy name I
3. Let mu-sic swell the breeze, And ring from all the trees Sweet Free-dom's

sing; Land where my fa-thers died, Land of the Pil-grims' pride,
love; I love thy rocks and rills, Thy woods and tem-pled hills;
song; Let mor-tal tongues a-wake, Let all that breathe par-take.

From ev-'ry ___ moun-tain-side Let ___ free-dom ring!
My heart ___ with ___ rap-ture thrills Like ___ that a-bove.
Let rocks ___ their ___ si-lence break, The ___ sound pro-long.

I–2

# Voices

**Analyze** this harmony part for "America." Which measures include a dotted rhythm? Which measure contains a flatted pitch? Which measures include a skip of a third? **Sing** this harmony part, then **perform** it with the melody.

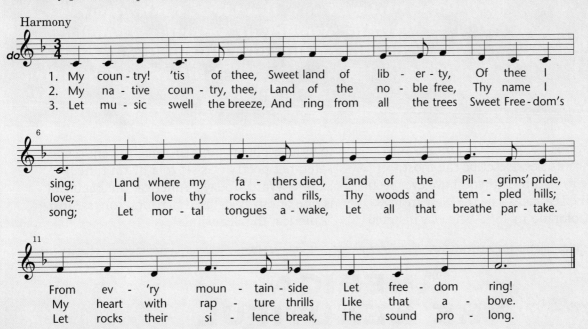

Harmony

1. My coun - try! 'tis of thee, Sweet land of lib - er - ty, Of thee I
2. My na - tive coun - try, thee, Land of the no - ble free, Thy name I
3. Let mu - sic swell the breeze, And ring from all the trees Sweet Free - dom's

sing; Land where my fa - thers died, Land of the Pil - grims' pride,
love; I love thy rocks and rills, Thy woods and tem - pled hills;
song; Let mor - tal tongues a - wake, Let all that breathe par - take.

From ev - 'ry moun - tain - side Let free - dom ring!
My heart with rap - ture thrills Like that a - bove.
Let rocks their si - lence break, The sound pro - long.

## Hand Bells or Choir Chimes

**Play** the melody and harmony for "America" on hand bells or choir chimes. **Read** the music and find the note or notes assigned to you. Then **perform** with the class.

## Conducting Challenge

How can you keep the melody and harmony parts together as you perform? One way is to listen to the other performers in your group. Another way is to follow a conductor. **Conduct** a triple-meter pattern as you sing. Take turns conducting performances of "America."

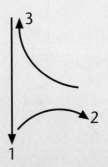

**Meter in 3 or Triple Meter**

## PRO TIPS

Listen for the balance between the melody and harmony parts when you conduct "America." Can you hear both parts? Which part is stronger? Decide how to adjust the dynamics of the performance to make the best possible balance between parts.

# O BEAUTIFUL LAND

"When I saw the view, I felt great joy. All the wonder of America seemed displayed there, with sea-like expanse."
—Katharine Lee Bates

▲ View from Pikes Peak, Colorado

Nature has inspired poets, writers, musicians, and artists for centuries. Describe the most beautiful scene in nature that you have ever seen. When Katharine Lee Bates saw the view from Pikes Peak in Colorado in 1893, she was inspired to write a poem about the magnificent scene. Later, her poetry was set to a hymn tune by Samuel Ward. Today, "America, the Beautiful" is one of our best-loved patriotic songs. **Sing** "America, the Beautiful."

CD 13-3
MIDI 17

# AMERICA, THE BEAUTIFUL

*Words by Katharine Lee Bates*

*Music by Samuel A. Ward*
*Countermelody by Buryl Red*

1. O beau-ti-ful for spa-cious skies, For am-ber waves of grain,
2. O beau-ti-ful for Pil-grim feet, Whose stern im-pas-sioned stress
3. O beau-ti-ful for pa-triot dream That sees be-yond the years

For pur-ple moun-tain maj-es-ties A-bove the fruit-ed plain!
A thor-ough-fare for free-dom beat A-cross the wil-der-ness!
Thine al-a-bas-ter cit-ies gleam, Un-dimmed by hu-man tears!

A-mer-i-ca! A-mer-i-ca! God shed His grace on thee
A-mer-i-ca! A-mer-i-ca! God mend thine ev-'ry flaw,
A-mer-i-ca! A-mer-i-ca! God shed His grace on thee

And crown thy good with broth-er-hood From sea to shin-ing sea!
Con-firm thy soul in self con-trol, Thy lib-er-ty in law!
And crown thy good with broth-er-hood From sea to shin-ing sea!

## Voices

**Read** the countermelody for "America, the Beautiful." Then **sing** it with the melody. Be sure to observe the rests.

## Hand Bells or Choir Chimes

Find all of the notes assigned to you in this harmony part for the hand bells or chimes. **Play** along with the recording of "America, the Beautiful." Count and **listen** to the other parts as you play.

## Bass

**Analyze** this bass part for "America, the Beautiful" before you play it. What is the key signature? What is the meter? What are the names of the notes in bass clef? Which measures have chromatic notes? Practice the bass part on a keyboard instrument or a bass instrument of your choice. **Play** the bass part to accompany "America, the Beautiful."

# Play Mariachi

Mariachi is a word for a particular style of music that originated in the state of Jalisco in Mexico. Mariachi ensembles have a special sound and "look." You can participate in a mariachi ensemble by singing or playing the guitar, bass, trumpet, or violin. **Listen** to the recording of "¡Ay, Jalisco no te rajes!" The song recalls the vitality and beauty of Mexico and is widely known around the world. This song can be found in the repertoire of most mariachi groups, regardless of regional origin. **Identify** the instruments in the accompaniment and where the chord changes occur. This song is a mariachi standard.

### Note This

Mariachi culture has become so popular that there are now mariachi conventions in the United States. Even the police force in Mexico City has adopted the characteristic charro costume worn by mariachi musicians.

CD 13-5
MIDI 18

## ¡Ay, Jalisco no te rajes!
### (Oh, Jalisco!)

Words by Ernesto M. Cortázar
English Words by Sandra Longoria Glover

Music by Manuel Esperón
Arranged by Buryl Red

¡Ay! Ja - lis - co, Ja - lis - co, Ja - lis - co, tú
Oh, Ja - lis - co, Ja - lis - co, Ja - lis - co, your

tie - nes tu no - via que es Gua - da - la - ja - ra.
great - est at - trac - tion is Gua - da - la - ja - ra. __

Mu - cha - cha bo - ni - ta, la per - la más ra - ra de
Beau - ti - ful land, __ the rar - est of pearls __ in

to - do Ja - lis - co, es mi Gua - da - la - ja - ra. __
all of Ja - lis - co, is Gua - da - la - ja - ra. __

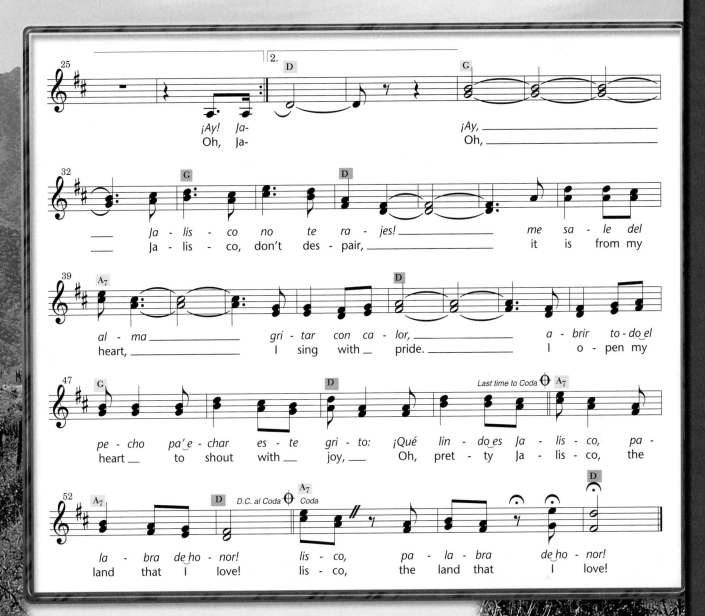

(lyrics under the music, verse 1 / verse 2)

¡Ay! Ja-
Oh, Ja-

¡Ay,_____
Oh,_____

____ Ja - lis - co no te ra - jes! _____ me sa - le del
____ Ja - lis - co, don't des - pair, _____ it is from my

al - ma _____ gri - tar con ca - lor, _____ a - brir to - do el
heart, _____ I sing with __ pride. _____ I o - pen my

pe - cho pa' e - char es - te gri - to: ¡Qué lin - do es Ja - lis - co, pa -
heart __ to shout with __ joy, ___ Oh, pret - ty Ja - lis - co, the

la - bra de ho - nor! lis - co, pa - la - bra de ho - nor!
land that I love! lis - co, the land that I love!

# The Sound of Mariachi

**Listen** to this recording of the song *Jarabe tapatío* made by *Mariachi Vargas de Tecalitlán*. When this group formed in 1898 the ensemble consisted of four musicians playing violins, harp, and a small guitar called a *guitarra de golpe*. This version of *Jarabe tapatío* is regarded as one of the premier *mariachi* recordings. Do you know this song by another name?

## *Jarabe tapatío*

**Mariachi song from Mexico**

**13-10** as performed by *Mariachi Vargas de Tecalitlán*

The beginning of this recording features trumpets and violins playing in harmony.

## On Your Own

Do a research project to find out more about *mariachi* music. Consider these questions: When were trumpets added to the ensembles? When did ensemble members start to wear *charro* costumes and why? What instruments were included in the first *mariachis*? What instruments were added later? Make a presentation for your class that includes pictures and recordings.

Voices • Drums • Keyboards • Guitars • Bass • Mallets • Mariachi • Bells and Chimes • Winds • Strings

## Guitars and Bass

**Play** guitar and bass parts to accompany "¡Ay, Jalisco no te rajes!" Before playing, **read** through the notation and make sure that you know what to do when you see the repeats, the 1st and 2nd endings, and the *coda*. When you see the symbol ✗, play the previous measure for the number of times indicated. The symbol is a multi-measure repeat sign. After some practice, play along with the song recording. Wait for the introduction and then start playing when the vocal line enters.

### PRO TIPS

When the guitar and bass parts are performed together, the pattern of their combined rhythms is a series of eighth notes. Guitarists strum on the offbeats and should feel the downbeat before playing. Bass players are responsible for keeping the beat steady.

# Winds and Strings

**Play** the trumpet and violin parts below. Notice that some measures require accented notes, while others have long held notes. **Identify** multi-measure rests at the beginning and at the end of the first line. In order to keep track of the measures of rest, count **1**-*2*, **2**-*2*, **3**-*2*, **4**-*2*, and so on until you have rested for the number of measures indicated. **Play** along with the recording and the other instruments.

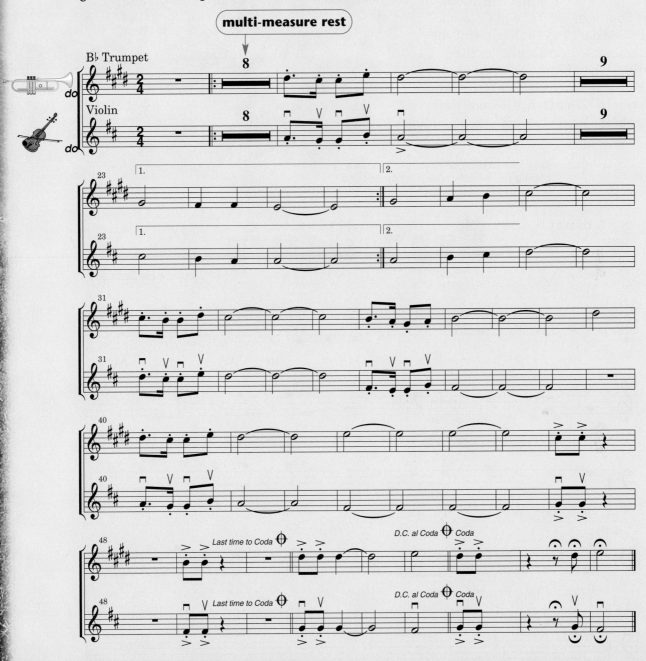

• Voices • Drums • Keyboards • Guitars • Bass • Mallets • Mariachi • Bells and Chimes • Winds • Strings

# 4

# MUSIC FOR WAKING BEARS

Depending on where you live, you may have special ways of recognizing or celebrating the seasons. The people of the Southern Ute Tribe of Colorado, New Mexico, and Utah perform the ceremonial "Bear Dance" in the spring, when bears and other animals are waking from winter hibernation. **Listen** to "Bear Dance." Study the **vocables**. Then **sing** with the recording.

Early 20th–century photo of Ute musicians ▶ playing the *morache*, a rasp instrument also known as a "bear growler."

 **CD 13-11**

## BEAR DANCE

*Southern Ute Dance Song*

Wey    le    yeh le    le    hey ya    hi ___ ya.    Wey    le ___ ha

hey    hey    ya    ha ___ hey    ya    ha    hey    ya    ha ___ hey    ya    ha    hey    ah    weh.

Ya    hey    ya    ha    hey    ya    hey.    Ya    hey    a    ha    hey    a

ha ___    hey    ya    ha    hey    ya    hey.    Ya    hey    ya    ha    hey    ya

1.    hey    heh    le.    2.    he    le    hey    le.

**vocables** Syllables such as *hey*, *ya*, or *loi* that do not have a direct translation but nonetheless have meaning in the culture.

## Drums

On the recording, the singer of "Bear Dance" is accompanied by an instrument that imitates the growling of a bear, known as a "bear growler." The musician places one end of a notched stick, or rasp, on the head of a large drum and then scrapes the rasp with another stick in an even rhythm. Experiment with drums and rasps to make your own bear growler. **Play** these ostinatos to accompany "Bear Dance" using bear growlers and other drums.

## Winds

Study the alto recorder fingerings below. Then **play** the melody of "Bear Dance." The sound of the alto recorder is similar to that of the cedar flute played by musicians of some Native American tribes.

### PRO TIPS

Look for the curved lines that connect two different pitches in the alto recorder part. These are *slurs*. To play a slur, articulate or tongue the first note, but not the second note. This technique results in a smooth and connected sound. Read more about slurs on page H-14 in Musical Tool Kit.

# 5

# SPIRITUAL HARMONY

"Certainly, Lord" is one of the many spirituals that are part of the musical heritage of the African American community in the United States. These rich and beautiful songs had many meanings to the people who first sang them. Some spirituals express the longing for relief from oppression and signaled the pathway to freedom. Others celebrate spirituality and the joy of living in a family and community. **Listen** for the *call* melody of "Certainly, Lord." A soloist sings the calls. Which call phrases are the same? **Sing** this melody or **play** it on a treble clef instrument.

## Arts Connection

▲ *Lift Up Thy Voice and Sing* by William H. Johnson (1901–1970)

1. Have you got good re - li - gion? ___ Have you got good re - li - gion? ___ Have you got good re - li - gion?

## Move Your Feet

Now get ready to move your feet! Here are two different ways to move. Each movement is a four-beat pattern that requires you to stay in place. Which pattern will you choose?

- **Pattern one**—Step-touch right, step-touch left.
- **Pattern two**—Move right foot forward, drag it back, left foot forward, drag it back.

## Voices

Find the melody in the arrangement on p. I-13. When is the melody also in the harmony parts? Choose whether you will sing the call (melody) or a harmony part in "Certainly, Lord." **Perform** your part with energy and spirit.

# CERTAINLY, LORD

CD 13-12

African American Spiritual

• Voices • Drums • Keyboards • Guitars • Bass • Mallets • Mariachi • Bells and Chimes • Winds • Strings

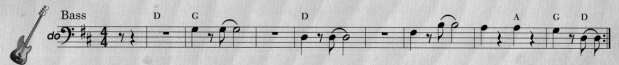

## Bass

The bass line below matches the parts and the recording of "Certainly, Lord." Practice on your own first. Then **play** the bass line to accompany the song.

## Guitars and Keyboards

**Perform** another arrangement of "Certainly, Lord" using the chord symbols shown in the music. Find the chords D, G, and A₇ (in place of A) on a guitar or keyboard by examining the photos below. Practice the chord changes until you can perform them smoothly. Look at the music and find where you will have to change chords quickly. **Create** a strumming or playing pattern, then accompany the song without the recording.

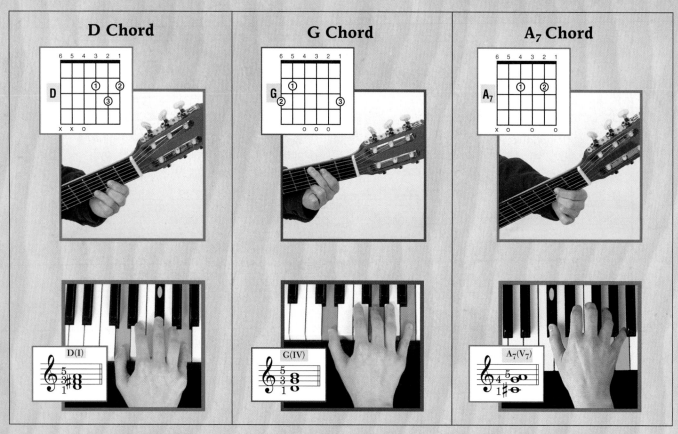

**D Chord**    **G Chord**    **A₇ Chord**

## Bass

Here is a different bass part to play with the guitar and keyboard chords. **Play** it with the guitar or keyboard part you created above.

# Move to the Music—Hands and Feet

**Read** the rhythm of the body percussion part, or hambone pattern, shown below. The pattern is performed by "patting" and "slapping" different parts of the hands on different parts of the body. This produces different timbres. For more on hamboning, see page D-2 in The Beat Goes On. Practice the hamboning pattern slowly at first. Then increase the tempo. Remember to swing the eighth notes! Then **move** to "Certainly, Lord."

Hamboning can be done with one or two hands on the side of the body.

- **Slap Left**—With an upward brushing motion, slap the side of the thigh with the palm of the hand.
- **Clap**—Continue the upward brushing motion and strike your side or your chest with the palm of your hand.
- **Slap Right**—With a downward motion, strike the thigh with the back of your hand.

Now **improvise** your own hambone pattern with the song.

# TWO CHORDS Latin Style

"*Cheki, morena*" is a street game song from Puerto Rico. You can learn the movements of the game by reading the English words. **Read** the song notation and **analyze** the chord changes shown above the music. Then **identify** the pattern. Now **sing** the song with the recording.

CD 13-14
MIDI 19

# CHEKI, MORENA
## (Shake It!)

*English Words by Alice D. Firgau*　　　　　　　　　*Folk Song from Puerto Rico*

Che - ki mo - re - na, che - ki,　　Che - ki mo - re - na, ¡Jue!
Shake it, come on now, shake it!　　Shake it, come on, now hey!

¿Que a dón - de es - ta e - se rit - mo ca - ram - ba del me - re - cum - be?
I want to hear the rhyth-m, ca -ram - ba, of the me-re - cum - be.

Un pa - si - to a - lan - te　　Y o - tro pa - ra tras
Take a little step for - ward,　　Take a little step back,

Y dan - do la vuel - ta dan - do la vuel - ta ¿Quién se que - da - ra? ¡Jue!
and turn-ing a-round and turn-ing a-round you know you've got the knack. Hey!

## Guitar and Keyboard

You can accompany "*Cheki, morena*" on guitar or keyboard. Guitar chords and a strumming pattern can be found on page F-10 in Guitars Unplugged. A keyboard part and chord diagrams can be found on page E-12 in A Handful of Keys.

## PRO TIPS

If the pitches do not sound clearly when you play the recorder, air might be escaping from the finger holes. Use the pads of your fingers to cover the holes completely.

## Winds

Add ensemble parts to your performance of *"Cheki, morena."* Study the soprano recorder fingerings below. Then **play** either version one or version two on recorder or flute. Choose the version that best suits your level of ability. Version two can be played as a duet.

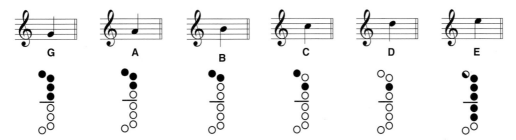

**VERSION ONE**
Soprano Recorder or Flute

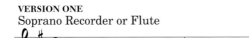

**VERSION TWO**
Soprano Recorders or Flutes

## PRO TIPS

Practice a new recorder melody by first using "chin position." Put the mouthpiece of the recorder on your chin. Practice moving the fingers and singing the names of the notes in rhythm. When the fingering is secure, play the melody with correct articulation.

## Bass

**Play** this bass part on a keyboard or another bass clef instrument. Look for the repeating patterns. Practice measures four and eight separately before playing the entire pattern. Then play it with the recording.

## Drums and Other Percussion

**Play** this ensemble with *"Cheki, morena."* The rhythm of the *claves* part is called *clave* [KLAH-veh]. **Play** with the recording. During the interludes continue to play your part or **improvise** rhythm patterns to create a contrasting section.

 **Take It to the Net** To learn more about percussion instruments from around the world go to *www.sfsuccessnet.com*.

## ON YOUR OWN

Investigate different types of instruments that are rattles or shakers. Name several instruments of each type. Choose one instrument and research its origin and how it is made. Prepare an illustration and a written description of the instrument. Share your findings with your class.

## Mallets

**Play** this accompaniment while other members of the class sing *"Cheki, morena."* Practice your part alone or with a partner, and then join the ensemble. You can also play along with the recording.

### PRO TIPS

Play the alto xylophone part by dividing the notes between two players or by playing all three notes of each chord yourself. In order to play three notes together, hold two mallets in your right hand, placing your index finger between the mallets for a solid grip. Place a third mallet in your left hand.

▲ How to hold two mallets

# 7

# AY, AY, AY Mariachi

"*Cielito lindo*" is a well-known folk song from Mexico, and it is popular throughout the Spanish-speaking world. It is also a standard *mariachi* tune. All *mariachi* musicians are expected to know it.

## Note This

This song is used frequently by experienced *mariachi* guitarists to train beginning players.

**CD 13-18**
**MIDI 20**

# Cielito lindo

*English Words by Alice Firgau*

*Folk Song from Mexico*
*Arranged by Buryl Red*

**VERSE**
Guitar: capo 3

1. De la sie - rra mo - re - na, Cie - li - to
1. From the dark, _____ dis - tant moun - tain, Cie - li - to

lin - do, vie - nen ba - jan - do, _____
lin - do, I _____ see de - scend - ing, _____

Un par de o - ji - tos ne - gros, Cie - li - to
Your dark eyes _____ flash - ing bright - ly, Cie - li - to

lin - do, de _____ con - tra - ban - do.
lin - do, love's _____ mes - sage send - ing. _____

2. Ese lunar que tienes, Cielito lindo,
   Junto a la boca,
   No se lo des a nadie, Cielito lindo,
   que a mi me toca.  Refrain

2. For your kisses, my lovely Cielito lindo,
   My heart is aching,
   And when I can't be near you, Cielito lindo,
   my heart is breaking.  Refrain

## Winds and Strings

**Play** trumpet and violin parts below to accompany *"Cielito lindo."* **Listen** to the recording and notice that the trumpet plays the melody during the refrain. Count sixteen measures of rest, then **play** only during the refrains. Your playing will support the melody in that section.

### PRO TIPS

Identify the measures where the violin and trumpet play in unison. (The trumpet part is notated one step higher than the violin because the trumpet is a B♭ instrument.) Practice this section carefully to make sure that you play it together and in tune.

## Guitars and Bass

When played together, the rhythms of the guitar and bass parts below create an "oom-pah-pah" pattern. Practice the two parts together until they sound smooth.

To prepare for accompanying *"Cielito lindo,"* identify the repeats and 1st and 2nd endings. Now play your part for a class performance.

In many places, Saturday night is a time for relaxing and having fun with family and friends. What do you do with your friends or family on Saturday nights?

"Ev'rybody Loves Saturday Night" is a song that originated in West Africa and is now familiar all around the world. **Sing** the song. Then learn the parts to perform with the recording.

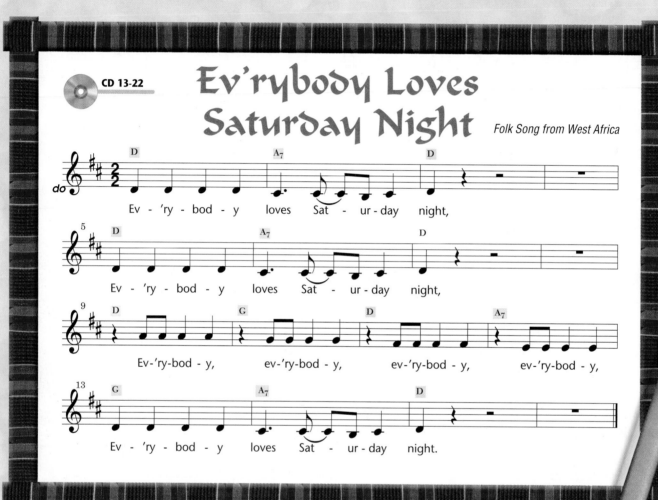

CD 13-22

## Ev'rybody Loves Saturday Night

*Folk Song from West Africa*

Ev - 'ry-bod - y loves Sat - ur-day night,

Ev - 'ry-bod - y loves Sat - ur-day night,

Ev-'ry-bod - y, ev-'ry-bod - y, ev-'ry-bod - y, ev-'ry-bod - y,

Ev - 'ry-bod - y loves Sat - ur-day night.

## Drums and Other Percussion

**Play** the rhythms on page I-25 to accompany "Ev'rybody Loves Saturday Night." They can be played with the recorded version of the song. Practice each rhythm by speaking it. For example, say *"Best night of the week"* for the rhythm of the low bell part. Develop your own phrases for the other parts. Tap the rhythm as you speak, then play it on the instrument.

The *"Kpanlogo* Ensemble" on page D-13 in The Beat Goes On also works well with this song.

# Play!

Play the low bell part throughout the entire song.

**Low Bell**

Rest for four measures and then **play** the *gankogui* part to the end of the song.

**Gankogui**

The **rattle** part begins four measures after the *agogo* starts. **Play** through to the end of the song.

**Rattle**

The **medium drum** can be played on a large conga *(tumba)*. Count eleven measures of rest, and then **play** until the end of the song.

**Medium Drum**

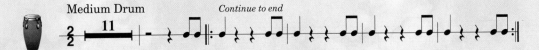

The **high drum** can be played on a *djembe* or a small conga *(quinto)*. Rest for sixteen measures. Then **play** until the end of the song.

**High Drum**

**Play** the **low drum** after twenty measures of rest or begin four measures after the high drum begins to play.

**Low Drum**

The **talking drum** comes in last. **Listen** for the entrance of the low drum and count four measures of rest. Then **play** until the end of the song.

**Talking Drum**

# Winds

**Listen** to the recording of "Ev'rybody Loves Saturday Night." During which parts of the song does the flute play? **Read** the notation of the flute part below. Find the repeat signs and the 1st and 2nd endings. What do these symbols tell you? Find the *staccato* marks. How will you play these notes?

## Bass

**Analyze** this bass part. How many pitches are in this part? Find the pitches on a bass guitar, string bass, piano, or keyboard. Then **play** the part to accompany the song.

## Keyboards

Find the chords in the music below and review how to play them. See page E-32 in A Handful of Keys. What patterns do you see? Which chord will you play the least? **Play** them to accompany "Ev'rybody Loves Saturday Night."

• Voices • Drums • Keyboards • Guitars • Bass • Mallets • Mariachi • Bells and Chimes • Winds • Strings

# Happy Holiday

"*Feliz Navidad*" is a famous Christmas song by José Feliciano. **Sing** the song with the recording. Then perform it with accompaniment parts. This song uses the C, D$_7$, and G chords. The chord changes are shown above the music. What do you notice about the order of the chords? **Play** the bass notes of the chords on a keyboard or mallet instrument and **sing** the letter names. Then sing the song while others sing the bass notes with the recording.

## Note This

ASCAP (American Society of Composers, Authors, and Publishers) has placed "*Feliz Navidad*" among the 25 all-time most-performed holiday songs of the twentieth century.

CD 13-24
MIDI 21

# Feliz Navidad
### (Merry Christmas)

*Words and Music by José Feliciano*

Fe-liz Na-vi-dad, Fe-liz Na-vi-dad, Fe-liz Na-vi-dad, Prós-pe-ro a-ño y fe-li-ci-dad. I want to wish you a Mer-ry Christ-mas, I want to wish you a Mer-ry Christ-mas, I want to wish you a Mer-ry Christ-mas from the bot-tom of my heart. a-ño y fe-li-ci-dad.

## Keyboards

Review how to play the F chord in root position and the C₇ chord in first inversion. Then **play** the part below on a keyboard. When you know the chord changes, **improvise** a new rhythm pattern that works with the song.

**PRO TIPS**

When you move your fingers from chord to chord, keep them close to the keys for smooth playing.

## Guitars

To play this guitar part, place a capo at fret 3. Then review the fingerings for the D and A₇ chords. You will find the chord frames on page F-4 in Guitars Unplugged. Then **play** along with the recording.

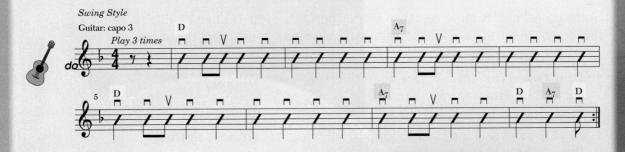

## Bass

**Play** this part on a bass instrument such as string bass, bass guitar, keyboard, or trombone. If you play it on a string bass, play *pizzicato*.

## Drums and Other Percussion

**Play** this cymbal part with the tip of a drumstick close to the center for a bell-like sound. Remember to swing the eighth notes. You can also play it at the rim with brushes to get a swishing sound. Play the part all the way through for each verse. What other instruments might you choose to play this part?

**Perform** this tambourine part during the third verse only.

## Movement

Many gospel choirs move together as they perform. Here is one possible movement pattern. Practice the pattern, then **move** as you sing the song.

- **Beat one**—step on your right foot.
- **Beat two**—bring the left foot up to the right ankle without shifting the weight, and clap your hands.
- **Beat three**—step on your left foot.
- **Beat four**—bring the right foot up to the left ankle without shifting the weight, and clap your hands.

## Performance Plan

Plan your group's performance of "He's Got the Whole World in His Hands." How many people are there in your ensemble, group, or class? Which part will each group member play or sing? Will one person be the soloist on the calls throughout the performance or will solo singers alternate on each different verse? Who will lead the group? How can you use dynamics to make your performance musically interesting? **Perform** your arrangement for the class. Then rate your own performance.

# 14

# Longshore Life

The longshoremen of the Georgia Sea Islands sang "Pay Me My Money Down" as they lifted cargo and transported it between the cargo ships and the dock. **Listen** to the song recording and read the lyrics. What do you learn about a longshoreman's life from this song?

CD 14-5

# Pay Me My Money Down

*Work Song from the Georgia Sea Islands*
*Collected and Adapted by Lydia A. Parrish*

**VERSE**

*Call*

1. I thought I heard ___ the cap - tain say,   "Pay me my mon-ey down,"__
2. As soon as the boat was clear of the bar,

*Call*

To - mor - row is our sail - ing day, _   "Pay me my mon-ey down."__
He knocked me down with the end of a spar, _

**REFRAIN**

"Pay me, __ oh, pay me, __   Pay me my mon-ey down. __

Pay me or go to jail, __   Pay me my mon-ey down."__

3. Well, I wish I was Mr. Steven's son,
   "Pay me my mon-ey down,"
   Sit on the bank and watch the work done,
   "Pay me my money down."   *Refrain*

# Voices

These vocal parts are in the recording. **Listen** to the recording and follow along with each part. Then choose a part and **sing** along.

## Guitars

For D and $A_7$ chord diagrams and a strumming pattern, see pages F-4 and F-5 in Guitars Unplugged. When transitions between chords are smooth, **create** a new strumming pattern and **play** it to accompany "Pay Me My Money Down."

## Bass

**Play** this part on any bass instrument. If you play it on a keyboard with multiple timbres, select a bass guitar sound that will be compatible with the recording.

◀ **Basketmaker**

▼ Hicks Walker

## Winds

**Listen** to the recording again and follow this flute part. Practice the part alone, then **play** with the ensemble.

## Keyboards

**Analyze** this keyboard part by comparing it to the song notation. What are the names of the chords you will play? Review the D and $A_7$ chords on page E-32 in A Handful of Keys. Practice the part alone and **play** it with a partner who will play the bass part. Then join the voices and other parts to **perform** "Pay Me My Money Down" as an ensemble.

Keyboard
**INTRODUCTION**

**VERSE** *Play 3 times*

**REFRAIN**

## Winds

This recorder part is a descant to **play** during the refrain. You can also play it on another treble instrument in C.

Recorder
**REFRAIN**

*do*

**Arts** Connection

◀ *Dawn Till Dusk* by Frances Johnson, Batik

# 15

# Mondo Rondo

A rondo is a musical form built on the idea of repetition and contrast. The **A** section of the music provides repetition. In between **A** sections, other sections provide contrast. In the "Percussion Fun Rondo," three different groups of non-pitched instruments highlight the contrasting sections.

## Drums and Other Percussion

**Analyze** the rhythms of the **A** section below. Find the measures that have syncopated rhythms. Clap and speak the rhythms and then **play** them on the instruments shown in the score. Practice with your group until all the parts fit well together.

### Percussion Fun Rondo

*Music by Konnie Saliba*

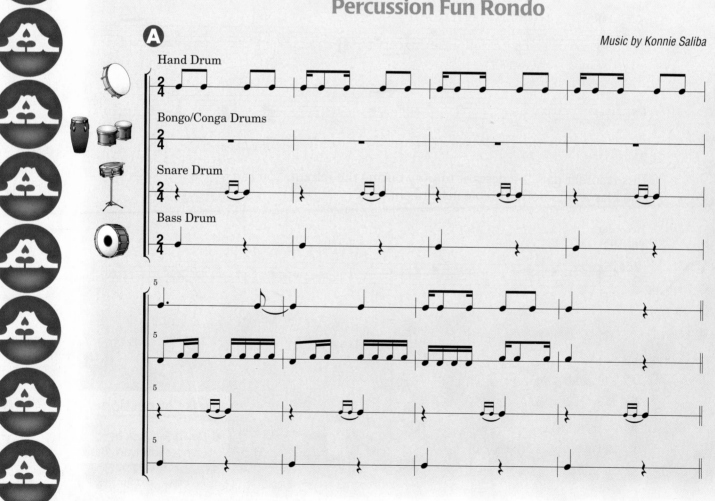

## B Is for Contrast

Test the sounds of the instruments in the score for the **B** section.
How are these timbres different from the timbres of the **A** section
instruments? Using a variety of timbres is one way to create contrast
between sections. Practice the **B** section slowly with a partner then
increase the tempo to match the tempo of section **A**. **Perform** the
**B** section with a partner.

## Dynamic Contrast

Create another contrast between the **A** and **B** sections by changing the
dynamics. For example, play the first time through loudly and play the
second time through softly. Experiment with *crescendo* and *decrescendo*.

### DYNAMICS

| | |
|---|---|
| pianissimo | *pp* |
| piano | *p* |
| mezzo piano | *mp* |
| mezzo forte | *mf* |
| forte | *f* |
| fortissimo | *ff* |
| crescendo | < |
| decrescendo | > |

### TEMPO

| | |
|---|---|
| Largo | broad, slow |
| Lento | slow |
| Andante | walking speed |
| Moderato | medium speed |
| Allegretto | lightly (less than allegro) |
| Allegro | quick |
| Vivace | vivacious, lively |
| Presto | quick, fast |
| Prestissimo | very fast |
| ritardando....rit.... | gradually slower |
| accelerando....accel.... | gradually faster |

## C Is for More Contrast

**Read** the rhythm patterns in the bongo and conga parts of the **C** section. **Identify** the patterns that are alike. Then **play** the parts. **Listen** to one another as you play so that you will stay together. If there are several tambourine players, begin the **C** section with one player and add more tambourines every two measures. How does the **C** section contrast with the **A** and **B** sections?

### PRO TIPS

Play the bass drum with the mallet held in your dominant hand. Place your other hand lightly on the head of the drum to dampen the sound. Balance the sound of the bass drum with the other instruments in sections **A** and **C** by playing softly.

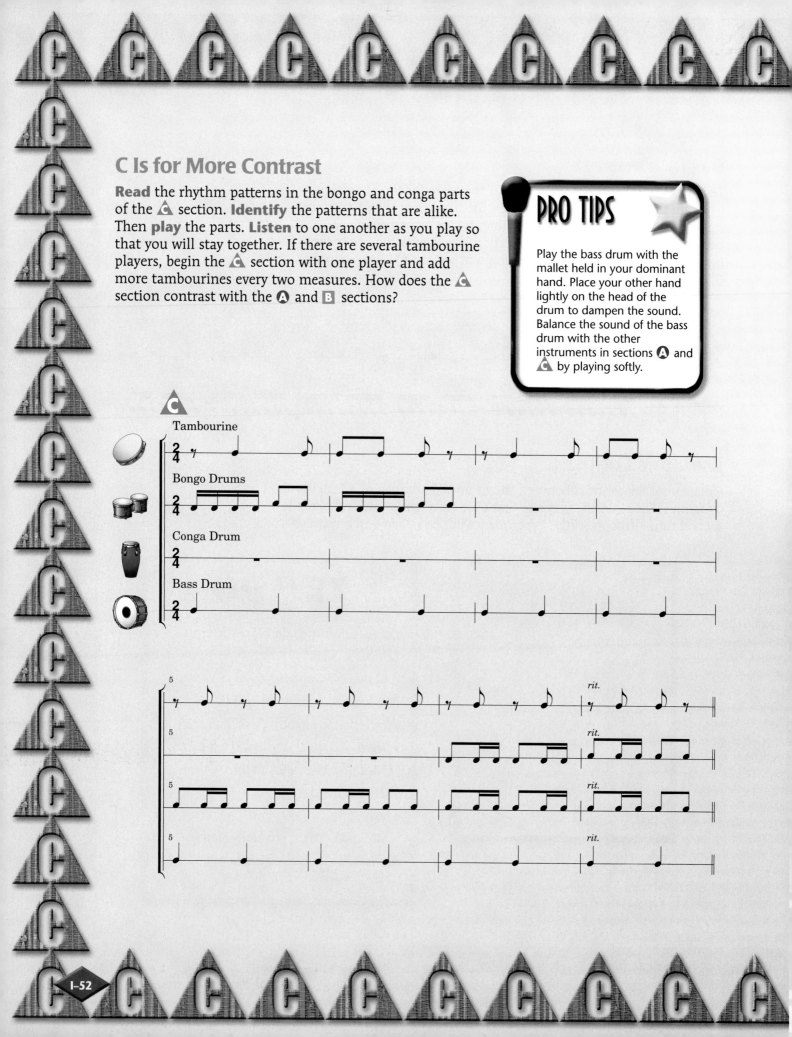

## Perform a Rondo

Now you are ready to perform the "Percussion Fun Rondo." The order of the sections in a rondo form is Ⓐ Ⓑ Ⓐ Ⓒ Ⓐ. **Perform** with no pauses between sections.

## Performance Options

Re-arrange "Percussion Fun Rondo" by playing the sections in a different order. For example, Ⓑ Ⓐ Ⓑ Ⓒ Ⓑ is a different rondo. Choose dynamic and tempo markings from p. I-51 to add more contrast to your rondo.

**ON YOUR OWN**

You can extend your performance using a Ⓓ section. Compose a Ⓓ section that is eight measures long. Think about how your music for this section will contrast with the other sections of the music.

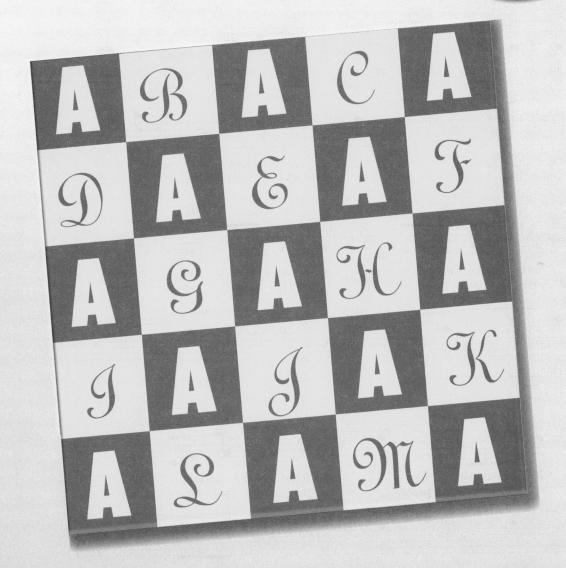

• Voices • **Drums** • Keyboards • Guitars • Bass • Mallets • Mariachi • Bells and Chimes • Winds • Strings

# Christmas Countermelodies

According to legend one Christmas Eve in Austria, an organist, Franz Gruber arrived at a church to find that mice had been gnawing at the organ bellows. The organ was broken and could not be played. So the organist and the clergyman wrote this simple song and accompanied it on the guitar. Their song, *"Stille Nacht,"* or "Silent Night," has become a Christmas favorite. **Sing** *"Stille Nacht"* in harmony. Observe the dynamic markings in the music.

**CD 14-7**

## Stille Nacht
### (Silent Night)

*Words by Joseph Mohr*

*Music by Franz Gruber*
*Arranged by Buryl Red*

16

## Guitars

**Play** the guitar to accompany the class singing of "*Stille Nacht.*" Go to page F-24 in Guitars Unplugged for a strumming pattern and follow the capo chords in the song notation.

## Winds

**Play** the flute part you hear on the recording. Observe the dynamic markings as you play.

*Music by Buryl Red*

Tap the rhythm of this countermelody for soprano recorder. **Analyze** the melody. Which measures are the same? Practice the countermelody and then **play** it with the recording.

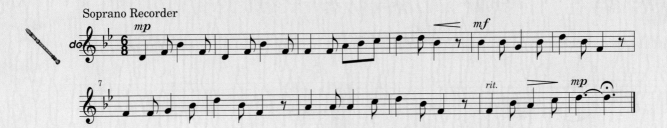

## Bells and Chimes

You can also play an accompaniment on bells or chimes. Find the note that you will play in the music below. Practice with your classmates. Then **play** your part with "*Stille Nacht.*"

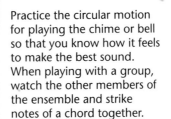

## PRO TIPS

Practice the circular motion for playing the chime or bell so that you know how it feels to make the best sound. When playing with a group, watch the other members of the ensemble and strike notes of a chord together.

*Voices • Drums • Keyboards • Guitars • Bass • Mallets • Mariachi • Bells and Chimes • Winds • Strings*

**17**

"The Star-Spangled Banner" is the national anthem of the United States of America. We sing the national anthem to honor the nation and to show pride and patriotism. Think of the times and places in which you have sung or heard the national anthem. **Sing** "The Star-Spangled Banner."

## Note This

Francis Scott Key wrote the words to "The Star-Spangled Banner." The melody is an old English song called "Anacreon in Heaven" by John Stafford Smith (1750–1836).

**CD 14-12**

# The Star-Spangled Banner

*Words by Francis Scott Key*

*Music by John Stafford Smith*

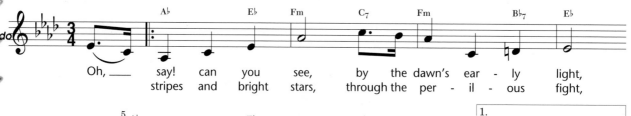

Oh, ___ say! can you see, by the dawn's ear - ly light,
stripes and bright stars, through the per - il - ous fight,

What so proud - ly we hailed at the twi - light's last gleam - ing, Whose broad
O'er the ram - parts we watched were so gal - lant - ly

stream - ing? And the rock - ets' red glare, the bombs burst - ing in air,

Gave proof through the night that our flag was still there.

I–56

Oh,    say,    does    that ___ Star - Span - gled    Ban - ner ___ yet ___ wave ___

O'er  the    land ___ of  the    free    and  the    home    of  the    brave?

## Arts Connection

*A View of the Bombardment of Fort McHenry* (circa 1814) by John Bower ▶

## Drums and Other Percussion

**Analyze** these parts for the snare drum, bass drum, and crash cymbals. Look for repeat signs and a *fermata*. What do these music symbols tell a performer to do? **Play** the part of your choice to accompany "The Star-Spangled Banner."

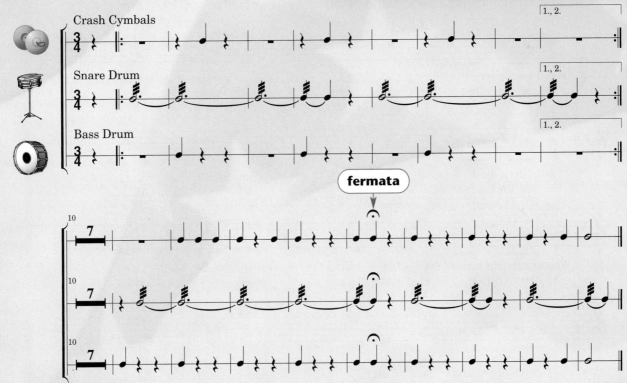

# 18

"Surfin' U.S.A." was a 1960s hit song by the Los Angeles rock group the Beach Boys. The Beach Boys wrote and performed songs about the surfing scene in southern California. Many of their songs became rock classics. **Sing** "Surfin' U.S.A."

CD 14-14
MIDI 24

# Surfin' U.S.A.

*Words by Brian Wilson*

*Music by Chuck Berry*

Guitar: capo 5

1. If ev-'ry-bod-y had an o - cean a - cross the U. S. A., ___
2. We'll all be plan-nin' out a route ___ we're gon - na take real soon. ___

Then ev-'ry-bod - y'd be surf - in' ___ like Cal - i - for - ni - a. ___
We're wax-in' down ___ our surf - boards, ___ we can't ___ wait for June. ___

You'd see them wear-in' their bag - gies, ___ huar - a - chi san-dals too. ___
We'll all be gone for the sum - mer, ___ we're on sa - fa - ri to stay. ___

A bush - y, bush - y blond hair - do. ___ Surf - in' U. S. A. ___
Tell the teach-er we're surf - in', ___ Surf - in' U. S. A. ___

You'll catch 'em surf - in' at Del Mar, ___ Ven - tu - ra Coun - ty Line, ___
At Hag - gar - ty's ___ and Swam - i's, ___ Pac - if - ic Pal - i - sades, ___

San - ta Cruz and Tress - els, ___ Aus - tra - lia's Nar - a - bine. ___
San O - no-fre and Sun - set, ___ Re - don - do Beach, L. A. ___

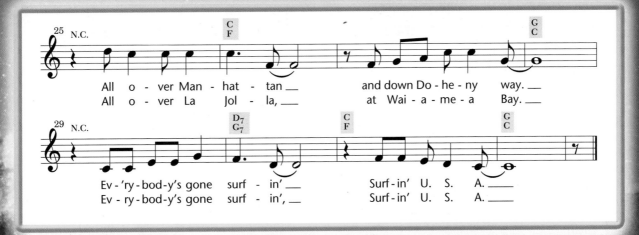

All o - ver Man - hat - tan __ and down Do - he - ny way. __
All o - ver La Jol - la, __ at Wai - a - me - a Bay. __

Ev - 'ry - bod - y's gone surf - in' __ Surf - in' U. S. A. ____
Ev - ry - bod - y's gone surf - in', __ Surf - in' U. S. A. ____

## Voices

Members of rock groups in the 1960s often sang vocal harmony parts for their songs. Sometimes vocalists toured with rock bands to sing close back-up harmony. **Sing** one of these back-up harmony parts with "Surfin' U.S.A."

Vocal Harmony

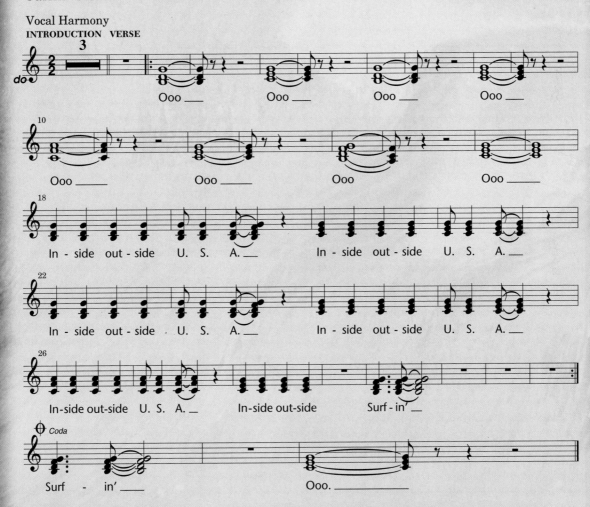

INTRODUCTION  VERSE

Ooo __ Ooo __ Ooo __ Ooo __

Ooo ____ Ooo ____ Ooo Ooo ____

In - side out - side U. S. A. __ In - side out - side U. S. A. __

In - side out - side U. S. A. __ In - side out - side U. S. A. __

In-side out-side U. S. A. __ In-side out-side Surf - in' __

Coda

Surf - in' ____ Ooo. _____

## Keyboards

Learn how to play a keyboard accompaniment for "Surfin' U.S.A." on page E-26 in A Handful of Keys.

# Drums and Other Percussion

Drummers in rock groups play drum sets that include a bass drum, hi-hat, snare drum, and tom-toms. The style of playing includes accents on the back beats, or off beats, of the measure. **Listen** to the recording of "Surfin' U.S.A." to hear the percussion parts and back beat. **Play** the percussion parts for "Surfin' U.S.A."

## Note This

The Beach Boys were inducted to the Rock and Roll Hall of Fame in 1988. The members of the group were Brian Wilson, Carl Wilson, Dennis Wilson, Mike Love, and Alan Jardine.

## Bass

The electric bass player keeps the beat and rhythm moving in a rock song. **Play** this part with "Surfin' U.S.A."

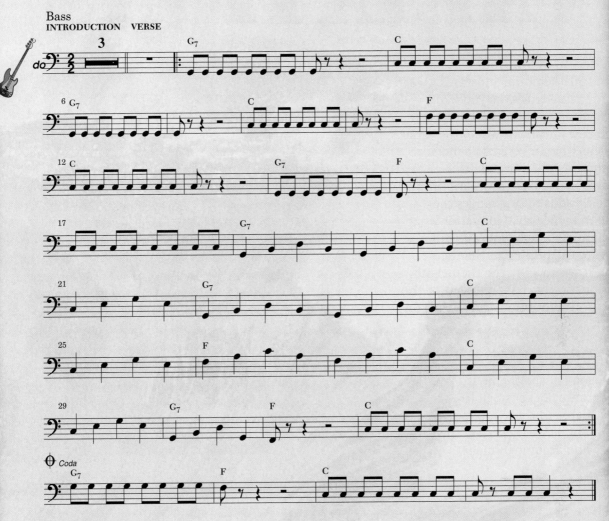

## Guitars

Look at the strumming pattern at the bottom of page F-32 in Guitars Unplugged. Then **play** the strumming pattern to accompany "Surfin' U.S.A." following the capo chords in the song notation. The guitar solos you hear on the recording are shown below. **Play** either the bottom or top notes with a partner as a duet.

# 19

# Theme and VARIATIONS

What do you like on your hamburger? ketchup? mustard? tomato? cheese? Maybe you like a combination of these. In music, a theme and variations works the same way. The "theme" is a basic melody or composition—like a plain hamburger. To make a variation, the composer adds to or changes the theme in some way. No matter what the change, though, you can still recognize the outline of the theme. As you learn to **play** the theme and variations in this lesson, **analyze** the music to find out how each variation is made.

## Theme

The melody of the theme is played by the soprano glockenspiel. **Identify** the ostinatos in the xylophone accompaniment. Then **play** the melody and accompaniment.

▲ *Marilyn Monroe* (1967) by Andy Warhol (1928–1987)

# ANDANTE

**(from Ten Little Ostinato Pieces)**

*Music by Carl Orff and Gunild Keetman*

THEME
Soprano Glockenspiel

Soprano Xylophone

Alto Xylophone

## Variation 1

For variation 1, the soprano glockenspiel players and the soprano xylophone players switch parts. Add this bass xylophone part to the accompaniment. **Perform** all of the parts together. What changed in the music? What stayed the same? How did the timbre or texture change when the bass xylophone was added?

**VARIATION 1**
Bass Xylophone

▲ *Marilyn Monroe* (1967) by Andy Warhol

## Variation 2

In the music below, the theme is played on the alto xylophone. What else has changed? Practice by tapping the rhythm of the melody and the accompaniment parts. Then **play** variation 2.

## Variation 3

For variation 3, play variation 2 and switch the bass and alto xylophone parts. **Perform** the alto glockenspiel part on an alto metallophone. **Play** variation 3 and **compare** it to what you have already played. How is variation 3 similar to variation 2? How is variation 3 similar to variation 1? How is it different?

 **Connection**

*Marilyn Monroe* (1967) by Andy Warhol. In this series of screenprints on white paper, the artist varied the "theme" of Monroe's image through the use of color and contrast, and by highlighting or outlining different features. ▶

# Variation 4

Variation 4 is in the same meter as the original theme. The melody is the same too. So what has changed? In this variation, the rhythm is augmented—the note durations have been doubled in length. **Play** variation 4.

*Marilyn Monroe (1967)*
*by Andy Warhol* ▶

# Variation 5

**Analyze** the fifth variation. The time signature is the same as the original theme, but the rhythm of the melody is diminished. How have the note durations changed from the original theme? **Play** variation 5 twice through.

*Marilyn Monroe (1967)*
*by Andy Warhol* ▶

## Transition

**Play** this part between variations 5 and 6 when you play the Theme and Variations in succession.

# Variation 6

How would the theme sound if you transposed it, or played it starting on D instead of C? What is the new scale? **Play** variation 6 to find out.

VARIATION 6
Soprano/Alto Glockenspiels

Bass Metallophone

## *Finale*—Finally!

Sometimes the last variation in a set is called the *Finale* [feen-AHL-ay]. For this *Finale,* **play** the melody of the theme (played by soprano glockenspiel on page I-62) in canon as follows.

1. Bass metallophone and bass xylophone play the ostinato parts below as four measures of introduction.

2. After the introduction all soprano and alto xylophones begin to play the melody.

3. All glockenspiels and alto metallophones begin to play the melody one measure later.

4. All soprano and alto xylophones finish playing the melody, rest for two beats, and then play quarter notes on C an octave apart.

5. All glockenspiels and alto metallophones finish playing the melody and then play quarter notes on C an octave apart.

6. Bass metallophone and bass xylophone continue to play the ostinatos until the glockenspiels finish playing the melody. Then they play quarter notes on C an octave apart.

Everyone ends at the same time on the octave C.

▼ *Marilyn Monroe (1967)* by Andy Warhol

Bass Metallophone

Bass Xylophone

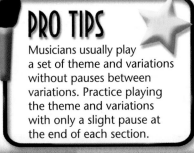

**ON YOUR OWN**

Create a new accompaniment for each variation. Use one or two nonpitched percussion instruments and compose ostinatos that complement the music. Add the percussion parts to your class performance of the theme and variations.

**PRO TIPS**

Musicians usually play a set of theme and variations without pauses between variations. Practice playing the theme and variations with only a slight pause at the end of each section.

# Made for You and Me

**20**

The lyrics of "This Land Is Your Land" take us on a journey from one landscape in America to the next in a sampler of pictures. Each of us can find our place in harmony with the land. Choose your place in the harmony parts for this popular song. One way to sing in harmony is by adding a countermelody to the song. **Sing** "This Land Is Your Land." Add the countermelody during the refrain.

CD 14-16
MIDI 25

# THIS LAND IS YOUR LAND

*Words and Music by Woody Guthrie*
*Countermelody by Ruth Tutelman*
*Arranged by Joseph Joubert and Buryl Red*

**REFRAIN**
Guitar: capo 3

*Countermelody (sing last time only)*

This land is your land, this land is

*Melody*

This land is your land, this land is my land, mine, From Maine to Mon - ta - na, des - ert to the

From Cal - i - for - nia to the New York is - land;

shore, We sing that this land is your land, this land is

From the red - wood for - est to the Gulf Stream wa - ters;

TRO–© copyright 1956 (renewed), 1958 (renewed) Ludlow Music Publishers, Inc., New York, N.Y. Used by permission.

I–66

## Voices

Here are two more harmony parts for the refrain of "This Land Is Your Land." Choose the part that matches the range of your voice. Then **sing** in harmony.

Vocal Harmony
REFRAIN

This land is your land, _____ This land is
my land, _____ From Cal-i-for-nia _____ To the New York
is-land; _____ From the red-wood for-est _____ to the Gulf Stream
wa - ters; _____ This land was made for you and me. _____

## Bass

**Analyze** this part for "This Land Is Your Land." Notice the stepwise contour of the bass line. Where will you play larger intervals or skips? What melodic and rhythmic patterns do you see? Practice on your own, then **play** this bass line to accompany "This Land Is Your Land."

Bass
REFRAIN and VERSE

## Winds

**Play** this countermelody on a flute or alto recorder. If you choose the alto recorder this harmony part will sound one octave lower than the flute. Review the alto recorder fingerings below and then **perform** with the class.

## Guitars

For a strumming pattern to play with "This Land Is Your Land," go to page F-24 in Guitars Unplugged. Then **play** it using the capo chords in the song notation on pages I-66 and I-67.

# Index of Songs

New Year's Greeting, A *(Ichi-gatsu tsuitachi)*, p. I-40
   CD 13-32

O, Chanukah *(Oy, Hanuka)*, p. I-44  CD 14-2
Oh, Freedom, p. G-30  CD 12-20
Oh, Jalisco! *(¡Ay, Jalisco no te rajes!)*, p. I-6
   CD 13-6
One Family, p. G-17  CD 12-11
Over My Head, p. G-9  CD 11-23
*Oy, Hanuka* (O, Chanukah), p. I-44  CD 14-1

*Panamam tombé*, p. D-18  CD 9-2
Pay Me My Money Down, p. I-46  CD 14-5
Proud, p. G-3  CD 11-20

Rock Around the Clock, p. B-18  CD 3-3

Shake It! *(Cheki, morena)*, p. I-16  CD 13-15
Shortnin' Bread, p. F-27  CD 11-12
*Si si si*, p. G-13  CD 12-1
Silent Night *(Stille Nacht)*, p. I-54  CD 14-8
Something Told the Wild Geese, p. G-39  CD 12-25
Star-Spangled Banner, The, p. I-56  CD 14-12
*Stille Nacht* (Silent Night), p. I-54  CD 14-7
Surfin' U.S.A., p. I-58  CD 14-14
Swing Low, Sweet Chariot, p. C-41  CD 8-3

There Come Our Mothers *(Nampaya omame)*, p. D-10
   CD 8-26
This Land Is Your Land, p. I-66  CD 14-16
Tomorrow *(Mañana)*, p. E-14  CD 9-27

Yellow Rose of Texas, The, p. I-70  CD 14-18
You Were On My Mind, p. G-23  CD 12-15